A Fireside Book

BOOKS BY IRVING CHERNEV

The Most Instructive Games of Chess Ever Played
Practical Chess Endings
Logical Chess, Move by Move
1000 Best Short Games of Chess
An Invitation to Chess (*with* KENNETH HARKNESS)
Winning Chess (*with* FRED REINFELD)
The Fireside Book of Chess (*with* FRED REINFELD)
The Bright Side of Chess
Chessboard Magic!
Winning Chess Traps
The Russians Play Chess
Chess Strategy and Tactics (*with* FRED REINFELD)

LOGICAL CHESS,

MOVE

BY

MOVE

BY **IRVING CHERNEV**

A Fireside Book Published by
SIMON AND SCHUSTER

FIRESIDE PAPERBACK EDITION
LIBRARY OF CONGRESS CATALOG CARD NUMBER: 57-12406
MANUFACTURED IN THE UNITED STATES OF AMERICA

For my wife

Contents

The Chess Master Explains His Ideas   153

Introduction

Did you ever see a chess master play twenty games at once? Have you wondered at (and perhaps envied) his confidence and ease as he stops for a few seconds at each board, gives the position on it a moment's consideration, and then casually makes a move?

Does he move quickly because he knows dozens of openings with hundreds of variations by heart? Hardly, because most of the games in such exhibitions take original turns which are not to be found in the books. Does he analyze every conceivable combination of moves at lightning speed? Or does he count on some infallible instinct to guide him through the strangest positions? If so, he would have to analyze faster than an electronic calculator or rely on being inspired a thousand times in an evening.

How does he do it? If we could follow his thought processes, if we could persuade him to tell us the meaning of each move as he makes it, we might learn the answer.

In this book we persuade him. We find out from the master the purpose of every single move he makes in the course of a game. We follow the ideas, the methods, the very thoughts of a master as he outlines them in simple detail. We learn the inner workings of his mind, and thus acquire the knowledge—yes, the instinct—for recognizing good moves and rejecting inferior ones.

To acquire this instinct it is not necessary to memorize countless variations of opening moves, nor to burden your brain with lists of formulas and principles. True, there are principles which govern proper procedure, and applying them will help you build up strong, sound, winning positions. But you will familiarize yourself with them painlessly—not by rote but by seeing their effect in the progress of a game.

Added to the pleasure of understanding every bit of play as it unfolds (and chess is the most exciting game in the world) is the fascination of watching the mental workings of a master as he reveals the wealth of ideas that occur to him in every new situation. We will learn from him the great advantages to be derived from a knowledge of *position play*. It is an understanding of position play that restrains the master from making violent moves or embarking on premature, foolish attacks; that checks the natural impulse to hunt for combinations at every turn; that counsels him in the placing of his pieces where they have the greatest potential for attack, tells him how to seize the vital central squares, to occupy the most territory, to cramp and weaken the enemy. And it is position play that assures him that definite winning opportunities will then disclose themselves, and *decisive combinations will appear on the board*. The master does not search for combinations. He creates the conditions that make it possible for them to appear!

Every single move of every game will be commented on, in simple, everyday language, and whatever analysis is needed to detail the full effects of a move or clarify a motive will be clear-cut and to the point. Frequent repetitions of the purpose of each move will impress upon you the importance of certain basic concepts. After you have been told again and again that Knights do their best work at B3, and that Rooks should control the open files, you will know that such strategy, such development of these pieces, is *generally* good. You will understand as well as any master does *what moves to look at first* when you select a good spot for a Knight or a Rook.

This does not mean that you will accustom yourself to play thoughtless, superficial chess. You will learn when and how to apply helpful principles, and when and how to defy convention. You will acquire the habit of making good moves as easily as a child absorbs a language—by hearing and speaking it, and not by studying its rules of grammar.

Each game that you play through will be an exciting adventure in chess in which courage, wit, imagination, and ingenuity reap their just reward. It is by appreciating and absorbing what they teach so pleasurably that we can best learn to play *Logical Chess, Move by Move*.

—Irving Chernev

May 1, 1957

The Notation

The moves of the following games are recorded in the English or descriptive notation. In this, King is abbreviated to K, Queen to Q, Rook to R, Knight to Kt, Bishop to B, and Pawn to P. The squares are named for the pieces standing on them at the start of the game. The King occupies King one (K1), and the Pawn directly in front, King two (K2). An advance of this Pawn two squares on the first move is recorded 1. P—K4. It is redundant to say 1. KP—K4, as only one Pawn can get to that square on this move. A similar advance by Black's King Pawn would read 1. . . . P—K4, the three extra dots signifying that the move was made by Black.

A move is described in terms of what a piece or Pawn does: the square it goes to, or the capture it makes. Thus 2. Kt—KB3 means that White at his second turn moved a Knight to the third square on the King Bishop file. It is unnecessary to mention which Knight as only the King Knight could move to that square.

Captures are indicated by an x, so that 4. B x Kt means that Bishop takes Knight was White's fourth move.

Capture *en passant* is noted thus: 8. P x P e.p.

A move or capture with check has ch following the move—for example, 3. P—Kt6ch.

Castling on the King side is indicated by O—O; on the Queen side by O—O—O.

Leaving a piece or Pawn *en prise* means exposing it to capture without being able to capture in return.

A simple test of your understanding of notation is to set up the pieces and make these three moves:

WHITE	BLACK
1. P—K4	P—K4
2. Kt—KB3	Kt—QB3
3. B—Kt5	P—QR3

This is the position:

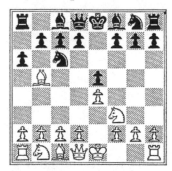

If the position on the board is like the diagram, then you know how to read notation.

5

The King-Side Attack

It is not the purpose of this book to bewilder you with magical effects. It is to show you how they are produced.

Take the popular King-side attack: it is attractive because it features combination play with its brilliant sacrifices and surprise moves. It is appealing because it aims for quick checkmate and lets you play startling moves to bring it about.

But when and how do you start a King-side attack? Must you wait for an inspiration?

The answer is simple and may be surprising, so let us look behind the scenes:

The diagram shows a castled position. The King is protected by a Knight at KB3 and the three Pawns in front of him. While these protectors stay where they are, the King is almost impervious to attack. The moment the formation is changed, the structure is loosened and weakened. *It is then vulnerable to attack.*

The position may change when a player moves P—R3 voluntarily to prevent a pin, or when he moves P—Kt3 to dislodge an enemy piece. But where this does not happen, the master (and here is the secret) *induces or compels by various threats the advance of the Rook Pawn or the Knight Pawn.* Once either Pawn makes a move it creates a weakness in the defensive structure which can be exploited. It is then that the master embarks on a King-side attack and achieves his brilliant—yes, magical—effects.

The game Scheve-Teichmann (No. 1) shows what happens when White plays P—KR3 instinctively to prevent a pin. Teichmann fixes on the Pawn which stepped out of line and makes it the object of his attack. Eventually he sacrifices a Bishop for the Rook Pawn in order to break into the position with his other pieces.

Liubarski-Soultanbeieff (No. 2) also has White moving P—KR3 in fear of a pin, and Black punishes him by a Pawn attack beginning with . . . P—KR3! (Why this move of the Rook Pawn is good, and White's is bad, is explained in the game.)

In Colle-Delvaux (No. 3) Colle forces . . . P—KR3 and then cleverly induces . . . P—KKt3. After this, a Knight sacrifice demolishes the weakened position.

Black moves . . . P—KR3 of his own free will to stave off an unlikely attack in Blackburne-Blanchard (No. 4). Blackburne sacrifices a Bishop to remove the indiscreet Rook Pawn and effects an entrance into the enemy camp.

Ruger-Gebhard (No. 5) illustrates the danger in castling prematurely, coupled with neglect of the center. When Black adds an attack on a piece with . . . P—KR3 to his other sins, he is penalized by a sacrifice which rips open a file against his King.

Zeissl-Walthoffen (No. 6) is another instance of untimely castling coupled with disregard for the importance of the center. White is compelled to play P—KKt3, weakening the white squares no longer guarded by the Pawn. Walthoffen's pieces utilize these squares to work their way into the position and get at the King.

In Spielmann-Wahle (No. 7), the player of Black advances his Knight Pawn to prevent a Knight settling too close to his King. This deprives his own King Knight of the Pawn's stout support and creates weaknesses on the squares no longer under the Pawn's surveillance. Spielmann's pieces invade, fasten themselves on the weak squares and inflict mate on the King.

Przepiorka-Prokes (No. 8) is an illustration of . . . P—KKt3 being forced, with a resultant weakening of the black squares. Przepiorka takes the precaution of destroying the Bishop which travels on the black squares (to accentuate the weakness) before launching the decisive attack.

The game between Znosko-Borovsky and Mackenzie (No. 9) shows Black trying to keep an adverse Knight out of his territory by playing . . . P—KKt3. He succeeds, but at the cost of weakening the black squares near his King. White finds them convenient for his own pieces, which take turns in occupying the critical squares.

Tarrasch-Eckart (No. 10) is an interesting example of the danger incurred in playing mechanical chess. Black is compelled to move . . . P—KB4 and then . . . P—KKt3, after which he succumbs to a Bishop sacrifice which removes all the Pawns guarding his King.

The next two games are delightful miniatures with a lot of meat in them. Flohr-Pitschak (No. 11) is a fascinating illustration of the process of chipping away at the King's guards to urge them to move. Pitschak forces the Knight Pawn to advance, then the Rook Pawn, after which he crashes the barriers with a Queen sacrifice.

Pitschak-Flohr (No. 12), in which Flohr gets his revenge, has White playing P—KR3 to evict a Bishop from his premises. It leads to the loss of the Pawn and the entrance of Flohr's Queen uncomfortably close to his King. The concentration of attacks which follows leaves him with one solitary Pawn to defend his King.

In the Dobias-Podgorny (No. 13) game, Dobias compels the advance of the Knight Pawn, then the Rook Pawn. Then he subtly undermines the weakened position and causes it to collapse.

The Tarrasch-Mieses (No. 14) game shows Tarrasch destroying the King Knight, the best defender of a castled position, and uprooting the Knight Pawn in the process. The disruption of the Pawn formation makes things easy for Tarrasch, who caps the victory with a quiet little Pawn move.

The next two games do not belong, strictly speaking, in the category of King-side attacks. I include them to show the consequences of failure to provide for the safety of the King.

Alekhine-Poindle (No. 15) has some delightfully unconventional moves by Alekhine to punish time-wasting play. Black is hindered from castling, and his King kept in the center where it is exposed to a fatal attack.

Tarrasch-Kurschner (No. 16) is a short story depicting the treatment of plausible, perfunctory chess. Tarrasch punishes his opponent's infractions of principle by driving his pieces back where they interfere with each other, prevents the King from castling and then assails him with every piece available.

GAME NO. 1

GIUOCO PIANO

WHITE   BLACK
Scheve   Teichmann
BERLIN, 1907

The chief object of all opening strategy is to get the pieces out quickly—off the back rank and into active play.

You cannot attack (let alone try to checkmate) with one or two pieces.

You must develop all of them, as each one has a job to do.

A good way to begin is to release two pieces at one stroke, and this can be done by advancing one of the center Pawns.

1. P—K4

This is an excellent opening move. White anchors a Pawn in the center of the board and opens lines for his Queen and a Bishop. His next move, if let alone, will be 2.

P—Q4. The two Pawns will then control four squares on the fifth rank, QB5, Q5, K5 and KB5, and prevent Black from placing any of his pieces on those important squares.

How shall Black reply to White's first move? He must not waste time considering meaningless moves, such as *1. . . . P—KR3* or *1. . . . P—QR3*. These and other aimless moves do nothing toward developing the pieces, nor do they interfere with White's threat to monopolize the center.

Black must fight for an equal share of the good squares. Black must dispute possession of the center.

Why all this stress on the center? Why is it so important?

Pieces placed in the center enjoy the greatest freedom of action and have the widest scope for their attacking powers. A Knight, for example, posted in the center, reaches out in eight directions and attacks eight squares. Standing at the side of the board, its range of attack is limited to four squares. It is only half a Knight!

Occupation of the center means control of the most valuable territory. It leaves less room for the enemy's pieces, and makes defense difficult, as his pieces tend to get in each other's way.

Occupation of the center, or control of it from a distance, sets up a barrier which divides the opponent's forces and prevents them from co-operating harmoniously. Resistance by an army thus disunited is usually not very effective.

1. . . .   P—K4

Very good! Black insists on a fair share of the center. He fixes a Pawn firmly there and liberates two of his pieces.

2. Kt—KB3 !

Absolutely the best move on the board!

The Knight develops with a threat—attack on a Pawn. This gains time as Black is not free to develop as he pleases. *He must save the Pawn before he does anything else,* and this cuts down his choice of reply.

The Knight develops *toward the center,* which increases the scope of his attack.

The Knight exerts pressure on two of the strategic squares in the center, K5 and Q4.

The Knight comes into play early in the game, in compliance with the precept: *Develop Knights before Bishops!*

One reason for the cogency of this principle is that the Knight takes shorter steps than the Bishop. It takes longer for him to get to the fighting area. The Bishop can sweep the length of the chessboard in one move (notice how the King Bishop can reach away over to QR6). Where the Knight takes a hop, skip and jump to get to QKt5, the Bishop makes it in one leap.

Another purpose in developing the Knights first is that we are fairly sure where they belong in the opening. We know that they are most effective on certain squares. We are not always certain of the right spot for the Bishop. We may want the

Bishop to command a long diagonal, or we may prefer to have it pin an enemy piece. So: *Bring out your Knights before developing the Bishops!*

At this point you will note that Black must defend his King Pawn before going about his business. There are several ways to protect the Pawn. He must evaluate and choose from these possibilities:

2. . . . P—KB3
2. . . . Q—B3
2. . . . Q—K2
2. . . . B—Q3
2. . . . P—Q3
2. . . . Kt—QB3

How does Black decide on the right move? Must he analyze countless combinations and try to visualize every sort of attack and defense for the next ten or fifteen moves?

Let me hasten to assure you that a master does not waste valuable time on futile speculation. Instead, he makes use of a potent secret weapon—position judgment. Applying it enables him to eliminate from consideration inferior moves, to which the average player gives much thought. He hardly glances at moves that are obviously violations of principle!

Here is what might go through his mind as he selects the right move:

2. . . . P—KB3: "Terrible! My Bishop Pawn occupies a square which should be reserved for the Knight and it also blocks the Queen's path along the diagonal. And I've moved a Pawn when I should be developing pieces."

2. . . . Q—B3: "Bad, since my Knight belongs at B3, not the Queen. Also, I'm wasting the power of my strongest piece to defend a Pawn."

2. . . . Q—K2: "This shuts the King Bishop out, while my Queen is doing a job which a lesser piece could handle."

2. . . . B—Q3: "I've developed a piece, but the Queen Pawn is obstructed, and my Queen Bishop may be buried alive."

2. . . . P—Q3: "Not bad, since it gives the Queen Bishop an outlet. But wait—it limits the range of the King Bishop, and again I've moved a Pawn when I should be putting pieces to work."

2. . . . Kt—QB3: "Eureka! This *must* be best, as I have developed a piece to its most suitable square and protected the King Pawn at the same time."

2. . . .   Kt—QB3 !

Without going into tedious analysis, Black picks out the best possible move. He follows the advice of the Frenchman who said, *"Sortez les pièces!"* He brings a piece out and saves the King Pawn *without any loss of time.*

I would caution you that this and other maxims are not to be blindly followed. In chess, as in life, rules must often be swept aside. In general though, the principles governing sound chess play do make wonderful guideposts, especially in the opening, the midgame and the ending!

3. B—B4

"The best attacking piece is the

King Bishop," says Tarrasch. So White puts this piece to work and clears the way for early castling.

The Bishop seizes a valuable diagonal in the center and attacks Black's King Bishop Pawn. This Pawn is particularly vulnerable as it is guarded by one piece only — the King. It is not unusual even early in the game to sacrifice a piece for this Pawn, so that the King in capturing it is uprooted, driven into the open and exposed to a violent attack.

3. . . .   B — B4

Is this the most suitable square for the Bishop? Let us look at the alternatives:

3. . . . B — Kt5: Inferior, as the Bishop takes no part in the struggle for control of the center and has little scope here.

3. . . . B — Q3: Poor, since the Queen Pawn is blocked, and the other Bishop may have trouble coming out.

3. . . . B — K2: Not too bad, as the Bishop looks out on two diagonals and is well placed for defense. At K2 the Bishop has made only one step forward, *but it has been developed once it has left the back rank.* The important thing to remember is that *every* piece must be put in motion.

The strongest developing move is 3. . . . B — B4. At this excellent square the Bishop commands an important diagonal, exerts pressure on the center and attacks a weak Pawn. This deployment conforms with two golden rules for procedure in the opening:

Place each piece as quickly as pos-sible on the square where it is most effective.

Move each piece only once in the opening.

4. P — B3

White's primary object is to establish two Pawns in the center. He intends to support an advance of the Queen Pawn. After 5. P — Q4, attacking Bishop and Pawn, Black must reply 5. . . . P x P. The recapture by 6. P x P leaves White with two Pawns in control of the center.

His secondary aim is to bring the Queen to Kt3, intensifying the pressure on the King Bishop Pawn.

These are its virtues, but there are drawbacks to 4. P — B3:

In the opening, pieces not Pawns should be moved.

In advancing to B3, the Pawn occupies a square which should be reserved for the Queen Knight.

4. . . .   Q — K2

Very good! Black develops a piece while parrying the threat. If White persists in playing 5. P — Q4, the continuation 5. . . . P x P 6. P x P, Q x Pch wins a Pawn. The capture *with check* gives White no time to recover the Pawn, and the extra Pawn, everything else being equal, is enough to win the game.

5. O — O

White postpones the advance of the Queen Pawn and moves his King to a safer place.

Castle early in the game, preferably on the King side.

5. . . .   P—Q3

Supports King Pawn and Bishop and strengthens the center. Now the Queen Bishop can get into the game.

6. P—Q4

With the hope that Black will exchange Pawns. This would leave White with an impressive line-up in the center, while the square QB3 is then available for his Knight. If after 6. . . . P x P 7. P x P, Q x P, White punishes the Pawn-snatching by 8. R—K1 pinning the Queen.

6. . . .   B—Kt3

But Black need not capture! Now that his King Pawn is secure, the Bishop simply retreats, still bearing down on the center from its new position.

Despite its formidable appearance, White's Pawn center is shaky. The Queen Pawn is attacked three times, and White must keep a triple guard on it while trying to complete his development. On 7. Q—Kt3, which he contemplated earlier, the Queen's protection is removed, while on 7. QKt—Q2, it is cut off. Meanwhile he is faced with the threat of 7. . . . B—Kt5 pinning and thereby rendering useless one of the Pawn's supports.

Before committing himself to a definite course of action, White sets a little trap:

7. P—QR4

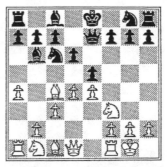

A tricky move, but an illogical one. White threatens an attack on the Bishop by 8. P—R5. If then 8. . . . B x RP 9. P—Q5 strikes at the Knight protecting the Bishop. After the reply 9. . . . Kt—Q1, White captures by 10. R x B, winning a piece. Should Black, after 8. P—R5, play 8. . . . Kt x RP, the continuation 9. R x Kt, B x R 10. Q—R4ch nets White two pieces for a Rook.

But what right has White to play combinations when his development is so backward? An attack, such as he initiates here, is premature and should not succeed.

Develop all your pieces before starting any combinations!

7. . . .   P—QR3

Prepares a retreat for the Bishop. This does not violate the precept about making unnecessary Pawn moves in the opening. Development is not meant to be routine or automatic. Threats must always be disposed of first. If more justification is needed, consider that Black's loss of time is compensated for by White's fruitless 7. P—QR4 move.

8. P—R5

There is just a wee chance that

Black will be tempted to take the Pawn.

8. . . .   B—R2

But Black does not bite!

9. P—KR3

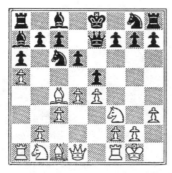

A coffee-house move! Weak players make this move instinctively (yielding to base instincts) in dire dread of having a piece pinned.

It is better to submit to the pin (a temporary inconvenience) than to prevent it by a move which loosens the position of the Pawns defending the King and weakens the structure permanently. Moving P—KR3 or P—KKt3 after castling creates an organic weakness which can never be remedied, as a Pawn once advanced cannot retreat, and the position once altered cannot be restored. The Pawn that has moved forward itself becomes a target for direct attack, while the square it guarded earlier (here it is KKt3) makes a landing field for the enemy's troops.

"You should never, unless of necessity or to gain an advantage, move the Pawns in front of the castled King," says Tarrasch, "for each Pawn move loosens the position."

Alekhine puts it even stronger: "Always try to keep the three Pawns in front of your castled King on their original squares as long as possible."

Black can now speculate on breaking up White's King side by removing his Rook Pawn, even at the cost of a piece. The recapture tears open the Knight file and exposes White's King to attack. This plan is of course not to be put into action until more pieces are brought into play.

9. . . .   Kt—B3

The Knight swings into the fray with an attack on the King Pawn.

The move is excellent and conforms with a useful tactical device:

Develop with a threat whenever possible!

Remember, that to meet the threat, the opponent must drop whatever he is doing.

10. P x P

White exchanges, and opens up lines for his pieces. Unfortunately this reacts in Black's favor, in accordance with the rule in these cases:

Open lines result to the advantage of the player whose development is superior.

10. . . .   QKt x P

Much stronger than taking with the Pawn. The Queen's Knight, beautifully centralized, radiates power in every direction (something a Pawn cannot do).

The disappearance of White's Queen Pawn has benefited Black's Bishop, hidden away at R2. Its range has been extended, so that it now controls the whole of the long diagonal leading to White's Bishop Pawn—and the King behind the Pawn!

What shall White do now? He has done nothing to relieve the plight of his King Pawn. It is still attacked by one of Black's Knights, while his Bishop is threatened by the other.

11. Kt x Kt

This looks plausible, as White gets rid of a powerfully placed piece. But in making this exchange, White's own King Knight, *the best defender of the castled position*, also comes off the board. The importance of holding on to the King Knight in such situations was pointed out by Steinitz more than seventy years ago, when he said, "Three unmoved Pawns on the King's side in conjunction with a minor piece form a strong bulwark against an attack on that wing." Tarrasch attests to the valuable properties of the King Knight with a simple emphatic statement: "A Knight at KB3 is the best defense of a castled position on the King side."

11. . . . Q x Kt

Observe that White's Knight disappeared completely from the board, but *Black's Knight has been replaced by another piece.*

This new piece, the Queen, is magnificently posted at K4. She dominates the center, bears down on the hapless King Pawn, and is poised for quick action to any part of the board.

How does White solve the problems posed by the position of the menacing Queen and the attacks on his King Pawn? He would love to dislodge the Queen by 12. P—B4, but unfortunately the move is illegal. Can he save the Pawn?

12. Kt—Q2

Desperately hoping that Black will snatch up the Pawn, when this would follow: 12. . . . Kt x P 13. Kt x Kt, Q x Kt 14. R—K1, and the pin wins the Queen.

But Black is not interested in grabbing Pawns. His positional superiority is great enough to justify his looking for a combination that will force a conclusive win. His Bishops exert terrific pressure on the long diagonals (even though one Bishop is still undeveloped!). Each of them attacks a Pawn shielding the King. Black's Queen is ready to swing over to the King side, while the Knight can leap in if more help is needed. Black controls the center, a condition which, Capablanca says, is essential for a successful attack against the King. In short, Black is entitled to a winning combination as reward for his methodical position play.

The question is: Is there a target available for the explosion of this pent-up power?

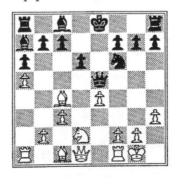

12. . . .   B x RP !

Yes, indeed! The Rook Pawn, which innocently moved to R3 to prevent a pin!

Black removes the offending Pawn—fit punishment for the crime of weakening the position and betraying his King.

13. P x B

White must capture the Bishop or be a Pawn down with nothing to show for it.

13. . . .   Q—Kt6ch !

A crashing entrance! Notice how Black exploited the two main consequences of the 9. P—KR3 move. *He captured the Rook Pawn itself and utilized as a point of invasion the square Kt6, weakened by its advance.*

14. K—R1

White may not touch the Queen, as his Bishop Pawn is pinned.

14. . . .   Q x RPch

Black destroys another defending Pawn, further exposing the King.

15. K—Kt1

White's only move. In return for the sacrificed Bishop, Black has two Pawns—and the attack.

15. . . .   Kt—Kt5

Threatens mate on the move. White must guard against the threat at his KR2 or give his King a flight-square. If he tries to give his King room by *16. R—K1*, he falls

into *16. . . . B x P* mate. So he plays:

16. Kt—B3

To guard KR2 and stop mate by the Queen.

How does Black conclude the attack? He reasons it out this way: I have captured two of the Pawns near the King. If I can remove the third Pawn it will deprive the King of the last shred of protection, and he will be helpless. This last defender, the KBP, is attacked by my Knight and Bishop, and protected by his Rook and King. I must either drive off one of the defenders or attack the Pawn a third time. Perhaps I can do both!

16. . . .   Q—Kt6ch

Again exploiting the circumstance that the Bishop Pawn is pinned, Black attacks it with a third piece, the Queen.

17. K—R1

The King must move to the corner and desert the Pawn. Only the Rook defends it now, against an attack by Queen, Knight and Bishop. The Pawn must fall, and with it the game.

17. . . .   B x P

Covers the King's flight-square, Kt1, and prevents him from returning there in answer to a check.

18. Resigns

Black's threat was *18. . . . Q—R6ch 19. Kt—R2, Q x Kt* mate. Since *18. R x B* runs into *18. . . . Kt x R* mate, there was no escape.

GAME NO. 2

GIUOCO PIANO

WHITE   BLACK
Liubarski   Soultanbeieff
LIÉGE, 1928

1. P—K4

The best move on the board! A Pawn occupies the center, and two pieces are freed for action.

One hundred and fifty years ago the great Philidor said, "The game cannot better be opened than by advancing the King's Pawn two squares." This advice is still good today.

Only one other first move, 1. P—Q4, releases two pieces at once.

1. . . .   P—K4

"Probably the best reply," says Capablanca.

Black equalizes the pressure in the center and frees his Queen and a Bishop.

2. Kt—KB3

This is superior to such developing moves as 2. Kt—QB3 or 2. B—B4, which are less energetic. The King Knight comes into play *with attack*, which cuts down the choice of reply.

Black must defend his Pawn with 2. . . . Kt—QB3 or 2. . . . P—Q3. Or he may decide to counterattack by 2. . . . Kt—KB3.

Whatever his answer, he cannot dawdle. *He must do something to meet White's threat.*

2. . . .   Kt—QB3

Undoubtedly the logical move. The Pawn is protected without loss of time, the Queen Knight developing to its most advantageous post in the opening in one move.

3. B—B4

Excellent, as the Bishop seizes an important diagonal. The Bishop strikes at KB7, *Black's weakest point.*

A Bishop is utilized to greatest effect either in controlling a long diagonal or in pinning (and rendering useless) an adverse piece.

3. . . .   B—B4

A good alternative is 3. . . . Kt—B3. Either move is in accord with the maxims of the masters, which they advocate *and put to use*:

Get your pieces out fast!

Move each piece only once in the opening.

Develop with a view to control of the center.

Move only those Pawns which facilitate the development of pieces.

Move pieces, not Pawns!

4. P—B3

White's intentions are clear: he wants to support a Pawn advance in the center. His next move, 5. P—Q4, will attack Pawn and Bishop. To save his King Pawn, Black will be forced to play 5. . . . P x P. The recapture by 6. P x P will give White a strong formation of Pawns in the center.

White's idea has some point if it can be enforced. If the plan fails, his Pawn standing at QB3 deprives the Queen Knight of its most useful square.

4. . . .   B—Kt3 !

Chess is not a game to be played mechanically. Usually, moving a piece twice in the opening is a waste of time, but *threats must be parried before continuing development*.

The Bishop retreats in order to evade the effects of White's contemplated 5. P—Q4, which attacks Pawn and Bishop.

5. P—Q4

Hoping to induce Black to exchange Pawns. Note that Black's King Pawn is attacked, *but not his Bishop*.

5. . . .   Q—K2

Instead of exchanging Pawns (as he would have been compelled to do if his Bishop were also under attack) Black defends his King Pawn while bringing another piece into play. His Queen has advanced only one square, but the move is commendable:

The act of leaving the back rank constitutes a developing move.

In addition to developing a piece and defending a Pawn, Black's last move threatens 6. . . . P x P 7. P x P, Q x Pch, winning a Pawn.

6. O—O

Besides the usual benefits derived from castling (safeguarding the King and mobilizing the Rook) White's move indirectly protects his King Pawn. If Black tries 6. . . . P x P 7. P x P, Q x P, then 8. R—K1 pins and wins the Queen.

6. . . .   Kt—B3 !

The Knight develops with a threat attack on the King Pawn.

7. P—Q5

Tempting, as it will dislodge the Queen Knight from its strong post.

The move is natural, but to be censured on several counts:

a) The Queen Pawn blocks the path of White's own Bishop, greatly limiting its action.

b) The range of Black's Bishop has been increased. Now its attack leads straight to White's King.

c) White has moved a Pawn while his Queen-side pieces are crying to be released.

In the opening, move only those Pawns that help develop the pieces.

7. . . .   Kt—QKt1

Retreat is safer than moving the Knight to the side of the board. After 7. . . . Kt—QR4, White's response is 8. B—Q3, after which he threatens to win the awkwardly placed Knight by 9. P—QKt4.

8. B—Q3

Defends the King Pawn. More consistent with opening strategy is the development of another piece. Either 8. QKt—Q2 or 8. Q—K2 protects the Pawn while bringing one more piece into play.

Do not move the same piece twice in the opening.

It is interesting to see how Black punishes these infractions of principle. On the chessboard, if nowhere else, justice does triumph.

8. . . .   P—Q3

No exception can be taken to this

Pawn move: it strengthens the center, opens a path for the Queen Bishop and relieves the Queen of the burden of watching over the King Pawn.

9. P—KR3

To prevent Black from pinning his Knight by 9. . . . B—Kt5, but as Publius Syrus observed some time ago, "There are some remedies worse than the disease."

In disturbing the position of the Pawns shielding his King, White weakens *organically* the structure of the King-side castled position *and sets up the unfortunate Rook Pawn itself as a convenient target for direct attack.*

All chess theorists affirm the validity of this concept of leaving the King-side Pawns unmoved, from Staunton, who said more than a hundred years ago, "It is seldom prudent in an inexperienced player to advance the Pawns on the side on which his King has castled," to Reuben Fine, who says today, "The most essential consideration is that the King must not be subject to attack. He is safest when the three Pawns are on their original squares."

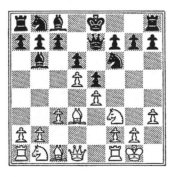

How does Black take advantage of White's last move? What is the best way to expose its imperfections?

9. . . .   P—KR3 !

By playing a move similar to the one I have severly censured!

What is the justification for Black's advance of the Rook Pawn?

Black has not weakened his defensive position, since his King did not castle on the King side. *His advance of the Rook Pawn is a gesture of attack*, not a timid attempt to ward off a pin. The Rook Pawn will constitute a base for the Knight Pawn, which will march up to Kt4 and then Kt5. From there it will strike in two directions, at White's Knight and his Rook Pawn. White will be compelled either to capture this Pawn or let it capture his Rook Pawn. No matter which exchange occurs, it results in an opening up of the Knight file, along which Black can align his pieces for an attack on the King.

10. Q—K2

A developing move, but it may be too late.

10. . . .   P—Kt4 !

A bayonet thrust! The next step is Kt5, where the Pawn will break up White's position.

11. Kt—R2

To prevent the intended advance. If the Pawn moves on, it will be attacked three times and defended only twice.

Has Black's plan miscarried?

11. . . .   P—Kt5 !

Not at all! If necessary, Black will sacrifice a Pawn for the sake of ripping away the defensive screen around the King.

12. P x P

Practically forced, as Black was threatening 12. . . . P x P, as well as 12. . . . P—Kt6.

White has managed to close the file, for the time being.

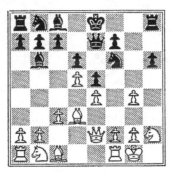

12. . . .   R—Kt1

Now it is Black who attacks the Knight Pawn three times, while only two pieces defend it!

Obviously, White may not give his Pawn more support by 13. P—B3, as it's against the law. It exposes his King to check.

13. B x P

Desperately snatching at a loose Pawn. In view of his retarded development and the plight of his King, such a capture is risky policy. If any hope remains it lies in some such move as 13. B—K3. Not only does this bring another piece into play, but in opposing one force with another of equal strength, it neutral-

izes the pressure of Black's Bishop.

The text move disregards the admonition:

Do not grab Pawns at the expense of development or position.

13. . . .   Kt x KtP

Gaining time by threatening the Bishop—among other things.

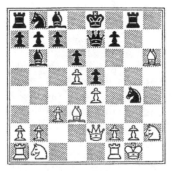

Can White save the game?

If he tries 14. Kt x Kt, Black forces the win by 14. . . . B x Kt (attacking the Queen) 15. Q—B2, B—B6 (threatening 16. . . . R x Pch 17. K—R1, Q—R5 mate) 16. P—KKt3, Q—R5 !, and mate will come at R8.

In this line of play, Black skillfully exploits the helplessness of White's pinned Pawns.

14. B—K3

The Bishop flees and attempts to repel one of the assailants.

14. . . .   Kt x Kt

This capture greatly limits White's choice of reply. The Knight has taken a piece and now threatens the Rook.

15. K x Kt

On the alternative 15. B x B, Black wins by 15. . . . RP x B 16. K x Kt, Q—R5ch 17. K—Kt1, R x Pch ! (the fastest) 18. K x R, B—R6ch !, and White must either walk into mate by 19. K—Kt1, Q—Kt4ch 20. K—R2, Q—Kt7 mate, or into a discovered check by 19. K—R2, B x R dis. ch 20. K—Kt1, B x Q, when the loss of material is ruinous.

15. . . . Q—R5ch

Black has two major pieces operating with full force on the two open files near the King. The attack plays itself.

16. K—Kt1

White's only move.

16. . . . Q—R6

Threatens mate on the move.

17. Resigns

There is no defense that will postpone the mate for long:
If 17. P—KKt3, R—R1 18. P—B3, B x Bch 19. Q x B (or 19. R—B2, Q—R8 mate) Q x P mate. Or if 18. P—B3 (guarding the Knight Pawn with his Queen) B x Bch 19. R—B2, Q x KtP is mate.
Strange that White, who feared the pin so much, should perish by the pin!

GAME NO. 3

QUEEN'S PAWN GAME
(Colle System)

WHITE	BLACK
Colle	Delvaux

GAND-TERNEUZEN, 1929

1. P—Q4

Modern players consider this to be the strongest opening move. It is equal in value to 1 P—K4 in that two pieces are freed for action, while a Pawn seizes a center square. The Queen Pawn, though, stands protected in the center whereas the King Pawn would be vulnerable to an early attack.

1. . . . P—Q4

This move or 1. . . . Kt—KB3 is practically compulsory. White must not be allowed to play 2. P—K4 and dominate the vital center squares with his Pawns.

2. Kt—KB3

So great an authority as Lasker, World's Champion for twenty-seven years, says of this move, "In my practice I have usually found it strongest to post the Knights at B3, where they have a magnificent sway."

2. . . . Kt—KB3

Black follows suit in trumps, developing his King Knight to its most useful square.

3. P—K3

Generally, it is dubious strategy to release one Bishop while shutting in the other. In this game, White is adopting a system which calls for a storing up of dynamic energy behind the lines, which is released at the right time by an explosion at the key square K4.
To this end, White develops so that his pieces exert their maximum pressure at K4. His Bishop will therefore occupy Q3, and his Queen

Knight Q2. If more concentration of force is needed, his Queen will supply it by developing at K2, or his King Rook by moving to K1. Then with all this potential energy ready to let loose, the King Pawn advances to K4, to rip the position apart and open fire on the King side.

Development in the Colle system is on positional lines, but the objective is a King-side attack!

3. . . .   P—K3

This deserves censure because it is a routine developing move which seems to take no thought of crossing White's plans. Clearly, it was better strategy either to attack White's Pawn center by 3. . . . P—B4 or to counter by 3. . . . B—B4. Not only is this latter a simple, sound developing move, but it prepares to oppose White's Bishop, which is headed for Q3, with an equal force. The exchange of Bishops, which follows sooner or later, will deprive White of a most valuable weapon in King-side attacks.

4. B—Q3

Notice the difference! White's Bishop commands a beautiful (and undisputed) diagonal, while Black's Bishop, covering squares of the same color, is hemmed in by the King Pawn.

4. . . .   P—B4 !

Very good! Black strikes at the Pawn formation in the center and gives his Queen access to the Queen side.

This freeing move of the Bishop is of the greatest importance in Queen Pawn openings.

5. P—B3

"Move only one or two Pawns in the opening!" say all the authorities, but no principle must be followed uncompromisingly.

In the event of a Pawn exchange, White can recapture with the Bishop Pawn and maintain a Pawn at Q4. Why not with the King Pawn? The King Pawn's future has previously been determined. It must stay at K3 and be ready to push on to K4 when the right moment comes, to spearhead a King-side attack.

5. . . .   Kt—B3

Another good move. The Knight comes into play toward the center, increasing the pressure on the Queen Pawn.

6. QKt—Q2

A queer-looking sortie. Not only does this Knight block the paths of the Queen and a Bishop but the piece itself seems to be doing little good. Yet, an expert would make this move without a moment's hesitation! For one thing, the Knight adds its weight to the pressure on the strategic square K4, the springboard of the coming attack. For another, *it is mobilized once it gets off the back rank.* Finally, it can hop out of the way of the Queen and the Bishop when it is expedient for it to do so.

6. . . .   B—K2

Black brings another piece into

play (remember that the Bishop is doing a job once it leaves the last rank) and prepares to get his King into safety by castling.

7. O—O

The King flees to a less exposed sector, while the Rook comes out of hiding.

7. . . .   P—B5

This is the sort of move instinctively made by a beginner. Its purpose is to chase off an annoying piece from its favorable post. The move is weak because it releases the pressure on White's center. Tension must be maintained if Black is to have something to say about affairs in this vital area.

Counterplay in the center is the best means of opposing a King-side attack. And to secure counterplay, the Pawn position must be kept fluid.

8. B—B2

Naturally the Bishop retreats, but stays on the diagonal leading to the square K4, where the break will come.

8. . . .   P—QKt4

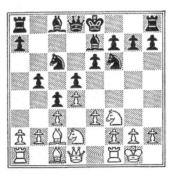

Primarily to make room at Kt2 for his Queen Bishop, but also with an eye to making trouble with an advance of his Queen-side Pawns.

9. P—K4 !

The key move in this opening! It will open up lines for an attack by White's pent-up pieces.

9. . . .   P x P

Not an attractive choice for Black, but he cannot have the threat of 10. P—K5 (displacing his Knight and severely cramping his movements) perpetually hanging over his head.

10. Kt x KP

With this recapture, White's pieces that were crouched in the background spring onto the field.

White has the initiative and a commanding position in which to exercise it. If no immediate attacking opportunities present themselves, he can quietly put on more pressure by Q—K2, KR—K1, B—B4 (or Kt5) and QR—Q1, and wait for Black's game to crack.

10. . . .   O—O

It might have been wiser to postpone castling (which ordinarily is highly recommended) as White is poised for an attack in that direction. This is another case where the value of a precept is conditioned by circumstances.

Black would do better to try for counterplay by 10. . . . Q—B2, followed by 11. . . . B—Kt2 and 12. . . . R—Q1.

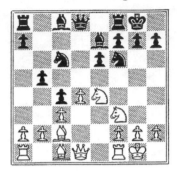

11. Q—K2

A developing move which contains a threat of winning a piece. The idea is 12. Kt x Ktch, B x Kt 13. Q—K4, and the threat of mate on the King side wins the exposed Knight on the Queen side.

11. . . .   B—Kt2

Black guards his Knight while developing another piece.

12. Kt(B3)—Kt5!

Threatens 13. Kt x Ktch, B x Kt 14. Kt x RP, and White has won a Pawn.

Why an exclamation mark for a one-move threat to win a miserable Pawn? Why glorify this move when Black can not only save the Pawn but also cause White to lose time? Black simply moves the Pawn one square, rescues the Pawn, and forces White's Knight to retreat.

The answer to the first question is that the advantage of an extra Pawn is enough to win, everything else being equal. Winning a Pawn at the cost of ruining one's position is of course meaningless.

The answer to the second question is that White's purpose with his brilliant Knight move *is to compel one of the Pawns defending the King to step forward.*

The secret of conducting a Kingside attack successfully is to create a breach in the cordon of Pawns surrounding the King; to induce or force one of the Pawns to move. The change in the line-up of Pawns fixes the defense with *a permanent weakness.*

12. . . .   P—KR3

"Touch the Pawns before your King with only infinite delicacy," says Santasiere. But, alas, it's too late! Black must disturb the Pawn position.

Had he tried 12. . . . Kt x Kt, the recapture by 13. Q x Kt threatens mate, and compels 13. . . . P—Kt3 —and the Pawns are disarranged!

13. Kt x Ktch

Destroys the King Knight, the best defender of a castled position.

13. . . .   B x Kt

The alternative 13. . . . P x Kt loses quickly. White could win either by gobbling up Pawns with 14. Kt x KP, P x Kt 15. Q—Kt4ch, K—R1 (15. . . . K—B2 16. Q—Kt6 mate) 16. Q—Kt6, P—B4 17. Q x RPch, K—Kt1 18. Q x Pch, and the Bishop Pawn falls next, or with 14. Kt—R3 (threatening 15. B x P) K—Kt2 15. Q—Kt4ch, K—R1 16. B x P, R—KKt1 17. Q—R5, and the discovered check will be fatal.

14. Q—K4

Threatens instant mate.

14. . . .   P—Kt3

Making room for the King's escape by *14. . . . R—K1* does not look inviting, as after *15. Q—R7ch, K—B1 16. Kt—K4*, White's attack looks dangerous. It is preferable, though, to Black's actual move, which prevents the Queen's coming any closer, but alters the Pawn configuration. This change in the arrangement saddles Black with a weakness that is *organic*, one that can turn out to be fatal.

All this is encouraging to White, but how does he proceed? How does he exploit the weaknesses in Black's position? And above all, what does he do about his Knight which is still under attack? Shall it retreat shamefacedly?

Before moving the Knight back to B3 mechanically and unthinkingly, White looks carefully at the situation. The opportunity to strike a decisive blow may be here at this very moment, but one hasty "obvious move" may give his opponent just enough breathing time to reorganize his defenses.

This is the position, and here is how White reasons out his attack:

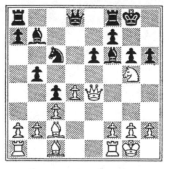

The key point must be Black's King Knight Pawn, which guards his King from invasion. If anything happens to this Pawn—if it is captured—the defense crumbles, and I can break into the fortress. How do I go about removing it from the board?

The Knight Pawn is protected by the Bishop Pawn. Suppose I destroy its support by sacrificing my Knight for the Bishop Pawn? After *15. Kt x BP, K x Kt* (or *15. . . . R x Kt*) *16. Q x KtPch*, and I have two Pawns for my Knight, with a third one in sight, as the Rook Pawn must fall. Material is then approximately even, but his position is completely broken up, and clinching the win should be easy.

This might be the general plan, but before putting it in motion, White analyzes the combination for possible flaws and comes up with this: If *15. Kt x BP, R x Kt* (bringing another piece to the defense) *16. Q x KtPch, R—Kt2 17. Q x P, Kt x P!*, and suddenly Black is the aggressor! He threatens mate in two by *18. . . . Kt—K7ch 19. K—R1, B x P mate*, as well as outright ruin by *18. . . . R x Pch*, followed by a deadly discovered check.

Clearly this line of play is too dangerous. Is there another way to break through, without letting Black's Rook come into the game? Can I get rid of the Bishop Pawn without disturbing the Rook? It is important that I remove this Pawn, as it supports the Knight Pawn and the King Pawn. Wait a minute! *There is a clue in the last sentence.* The Bishop Pawn, guarding two other Pawns, is serving two masters. Obviously it is overworked! I must add to its burden by luring it away from its present important post! Therefore:

15. Kt x KP !

The Knight captures a Pawn and attacks Queen and Rook.

15. . . . P x Kt

Black must accept the sacrifice or lose Rook and Pawn for the Knight.

16. Q x KtPch

Stronger than taking the King Pawn, after which Black has four ways to get out of check. Each of these replies might lose, but it is more practical to attack the enemy with blows that leave him little choice of reply.

16. . . . B—Kt2

The only move, as 16. . . . K—R1 walks right into mate.

17. Q—R7ch

White has other attractive continuations in 17. B x P or 17. Q x KPch, but this forces the King out into the open where White's other pieces can get at him.

17. . . . K—B2

The only move.

18. B—Kt6ch

Stronger than 18. B x P, to which Black retorts 18. . . . Q—B3, followed by 19. . . . R—R1. The text move keeps him on the run.

18. . . . K—B3

Certainly not 18. . . . K—K2

when 19. Q x Bch lets White pick up a couple of Bishops.

19. B—R5

White is still angling for 20. Q—Kt6ch, K—K2 21. Q x Bch, and both Bishops come off the board.

19. . . . Kt—K2

The only way to prevent the Queen's check.

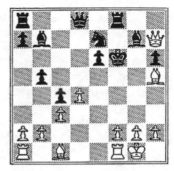

20. B x P

White is not playing to pick up stray Pawns, but the capture brings another piece to the attack. The Pawn that is added to the collection is incidental to the general scheme of things.

20. . . . R—KKt1

To parry the threat of 21. Q x Bch, K—B4 22. Q—K5 mate.

On 20. . . . B x B, White intended 21. Q x Bch, K—B4 22. QR—K1, and the threat of mate either by the Rook or the Knight Pawn is decisive.

21. P—KR4

New threat: 22. B—Kt5 mate.

21. . . . B x B

Loses on the spot, but there was no defense: if *21. . . . P—K4 22. B x Bch, R x B 23. P x Pch*, and the King must abandon the Rook.

22. Q—B7 mate

KING'S GAMBIT DECLINED

WHITE	BLACK
Blackburne	Blanchard

LONDON, 1891

1. P—K4

Values were constant in many fields of endeavor, at the time this game was played:

Stories began, "Once upon a time,"

Tic-tac-toe players put a cross in the center square,

Checker masters started with 11—15,

Chess masters opened with *1. P—K4.*

Despite the researches of the scientists, these remain good beginnings.

1. . . . P—K4

Black opens lines for two of his pieces and establishes equilibrium in the center.

2. P—KB4

An offer of a Pawn to induce Black to surrender the center.

Accepting the gift enables White to continue with *3. P—Q4*, and dominate the center with his Pawns. In addition, the opening of the Bishop file will offer White the op-portunity of directing his attack at the vulnerable point KB7. This is a tender spot whether Black's King stays at home or castles.

2. . . . B—B4

Probably the safest way to decline the gambit:

a) The Bishop bears down on the center and controls an excellent diagonal.

b) The Bishop supplements the Pawn's attack on Q5 and prevents White from moving his Pawn to Q4.

c) The Bishop's presence at B4, overlooking KKt8, forbids White from castling in a hurry.

3. Kt—QB3

White avoids *3. P x P*, as the re-ply (coming like a shot, probably) *Q—R5ch 4. P—Kt3* (even worse is *4. K—K2, Q x KP mate), Q x KPch* wins a Rook for Black.

White's actual move is not as energetic as *3. Kt—KB3*, but Black-burne was trying to lure his oppo-nent into playing *3. . . . B x Kt 4. R x B, Q—R5ch 5. P—Kt3, Q x RP*, when *6. R—Kt2* followed by *7. P x P* gives White a fine game.

3. . . . Kt—QB3

A simple retort to the dubious in-vitation.

Black continues mustering his forces out on the field of action. In the fight for control of the center, his Knight does its share by exerting pressure on the squares K4 and Q5.

4. Kt—B3

Did White miss a chance to get

an advantage in space by 4. P x P,
Kt x P 5. P—Q4? No, because 4.
P x P is met by 4. . . . P—Q3,
Black offering a Pawn for the sake
of securing a free, easy development.

The text move puts an end to the
possibility of being bothered by a
Queen check and revives the threat
of winning the King Pawn.

$$4. . . .\qquad P x P$$

This is a poor move on at least
four counts:

a) In moving a Pawn instead of
a piece, Black loses sight of the chief
objective in all opening strategy:
Move the pieces! Get them off the
back rank and on the job!

b) He surrenders his hold on the
center and the privileges it confers.

c) He wastes time capturing a
Pawn which he cannot retain.

d) He permits White to seize
the center next move, which forces a
retreat by his Bishop and a consequent loss of time.

Tarrasch considered a move such
as the one made by Black a worse
offense than an outright blunder,
like leaving a piece *en prise*.

Instead of this, Black might
better have played 4. . . . P—Q3,

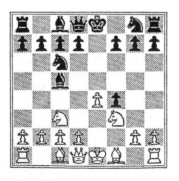

which holds everything and lets the
Queen Bishop see daylight.

$$5. P—Q4 !$$

Of course! No player should take
more than half a second to see the
power of this Pawn push! The Pawn
seizes control of a good bit of the
center (occupying Q4 and attacking
two other important squares), dis-
lodges the Bishop from its strong
position, and uncovers an attack by
his own Bishop.

$$5. . . . B—Kt5$$

The retreat to K2 instead, where
the Bishop is invaluable for defense,
was sounder strategy.

$$6. B x P$$

White gains a tempo with this
capture, as he recovers the Pawn he
lost and develops a piece at the same
time.

$$6. . . .\qquad P—Q4$$

An attack on White's King Pawn,
to dispute possession of the center.
Meanwhile, Black gives his Queen-
side pieces more air.

$$7. P—K5$$

All moves by Pawns have positive
and negative values. (Tarrasch used
to say, "Every Pawn move loosens
the position.")

One drawback for White in the
advance of his King Pawn is that the
occupation of K5 by a Pawn deprives his pieces of a useful square.
The Knight especially operates to
great advantage when posted at K5.

In compensation, the Pawn exercises a general cramping effect on

Black's entire position and imposes particular restraint on the King Knight, which cannot develop naturally at KB3.

7. . . .   B x Ktch

Black is intrigued by the prospect of saddling Blackburne with a doubled Pawn. But why capture a piece which is pinned and can do no harm? Why relax the pressure at all?

A more commendable procedure was to bring up the reserves, starting with 7. . . . B—KB4.

8. P x B

In return for the handicap of the doubled Pawns (little enough, since an advance of P—B4 forces an exchange and undoubles the Pawns) White enjoys advantages in his two Bishops and in the open Knight file which his Rook will put to good use.

8. . . .   B—K3

A superficial move. The Bishop could develop to greater effect at B4. There it would hinder White from freely posting his Bishop at Q3, except at the cost of permitting an exchange of Bishops.

Developing the pieces to squares where they are most effective assures an advantage; preventing the opponent from doing likewise, increases it.

It is important to fight for control of the vital squares.

9. B—Q3

Clearly an excellent deployment: the Bishop reaches out in two directions, ready to take a hand on either side of the board.

9. . . .   P—KR3

Apparently to prevent 10. Kt—Kt5 or 10. B—KKt5.

White, who is interested only in completing his development, has not the slightest intention of making either of these moves.

The move P—KR3 should be played only if the Rook Pawn is to form a base for an attack by Pawns —if it supports an advance by the Knight Pawn. Defensively, the move does more harm than good, as it loosens the Pawn structure and weakens its resistance to attack. It is especially dangerous if the King has castled on that side of the board, as the Pawn itself, standing out from the ranks, provides a convenient target. Also (as if the foregoing were not enough) it does nothing to further the cause of development. It wastes time which should be devoted to the liberation of pieces which are still shut in.

10. O—O

At one stroke White secures the safety of his King and brings his Rook out to head an open file. It is true that the file is cluttered up by a Knight and Bishop, which interfere with the Rook's influence. But they are pieces, not Pawns. Pieces can move quickly out of the way.

10. . . .   KKt—K2

Not the happiest spot for the Knight, but how else can it get into the game? Poor as this development is, it is by far preferable to letting the Knight stay uselessly at home.

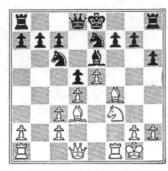

11. R–Kt1 !

The master makes this move in a flash! The run-of-the-mill player never even looks at it!

What is the Rook's future on this file? It attacks a Pawn, but the Pawn is easily protected. Why not try for a King-side attack, instead of this futile demonstration?

The answer lies in this: the master's instinct (or perhaps his knowledge or experience) tells him that he must seize any files that are open —control them at once with his Rooks or his Queen. "Make the moves," it says, "that conform with the requirements of the position, and you will be suitably rewarded. Play the moves necessary to establish a superior position! Develop your pieces so that they enjoy maximum mobility, and control most of the territory. Direct your efforts to weakening the position of the enemy, cramping the movements of his pieces, and reducing the capacity of his resistance before you make the first move of a combination. When the time is ripe, the attack will play itself. The decisive combination will stare you in the face."

11. . . .   P–QKt3

This too is a move that distinguishes the master from the amateur!

How easy it is to advance the Pawn, safeguard it from attack, and let the Rook bite on granite! Obvious as this defense is, no top-ranking player would rush to adopt it! He would try to avoid disturbing the Pawn formation and consider instead such alternatives as 11. . . . R–QKt1 or 11. . . . Q–B1.

After the actual move, the white squares on Black's Queen side have been weakened. More to the point, the advance of the Pawn deprives the Queen's Knight of solid support —an interesting circumstance which White will exploit in his forthcoming attack on the King, *away over at the other side of the board.*

12. Q–Q2

The Queen leaves the first rank to enable the Rooks to get in touch with each other. They may wish to increase the pressure on an open file by doubling on it, or otherwise work in concert.

The full meaning of White's Queen move might easily be overlooked by an opponent who makes plausible but superficial replies.

Chess must not be played mechanically, even in the simplest, most placid positions.

12. . . .   O–O

Walks right into the teeth of the storm!

Before making a move that suggests itself so readily, Black might have asked himself, "How can I exploit White's one weakness, the doubled Pawns on the Queen Bishop file?"

He might then have hit upon 12. . . . Kt—R4, with the object of swinging the Knight over to B5. There it blockades the doubled Pawn, interferes with the free movement of White's pieces, and in general sticks like a bone in the throat. White could capture the Knight, but then he parts with one of his valuable Bishops, and his Pawn position (as a result of the exchange) is inferior to Black's. Finally, Black could then anchor one of his pieces to great effect on Q4, a square from which it could never be evicted by any Pawns.

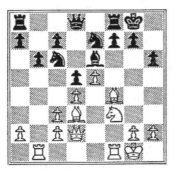

13. B x P

Blackburne must have snatched this Pawn up at lightning (186,324 miles per second) speed!

At the price of a Bishop, he gets two Pawns immediately as material return, demolishes the barricade of Pawns near the King—and more, as we shall see.

13. . . .   P x B

Black must capture the Bishop, or be a Pawn down without any positional compensation.

14. Q x P

Let us see what White's return is for the piece he sacrificed:

a) He has two Pawns in tangible assets.

b) His Queen is powerfully placed in enemy territory—threatening mate on the move, in fact!

c) He has ripped away the screen of Pawns that sheltered Black's King.

d) He has a strong attack in prospect, starting with 15. Kt—Kt5.

e) If more help is needed, he can call up the reserves (after 15. Kt—Kt5) by 16. R—B3, followed by 17. R—KKt3.

14. . . .   Kt—Kt3

Was there any other defense?

If 14. . . . Kt—B4 (to interfere with the action of the Bishop), then 15. B x Kt, B x B 16. Q x Kt picks up the unprotected Knight on the Queen side, a consequence of Black's instinctive advance of his Queen Knight Pawn at his eleventh move.

If 14. . . . B—B4 15. B x B, Kt x B 16. Q x Kt, and again White scoops up the unfortunate Knight.

If 14. . . . P—B4, Black's Bishop is left *en prise*. White would capture it following Tartakover's advice: "Take it first and philosophize afterward!"

15. Kt—Kt5

Again threatening mate at R7. This is speedier than the brutal alternative 15. B x Kt, P x B 16. Q x Pch, followed by 17. Q x B, which wins material, and eventually the game.

Blackburne heeds the injunction

laid down by Baron von Heydebrand und der Lasa, who flourished a century ago: "The simplest and the shortest way of winning is the best way."

15. . . .   R—K1

Offers the King a flight square.

16. R x BP

Again there is a pleasant choice of winning methods:
16. B x Kt, and if 16. . . . P x B
17. Q—R7 is mate.
16. . . . Kt—R7, followed by 17. Kt—B6ch and quick mate.
The move actually made nails down the King and renews the threat of mate on the move.

16. . . .   B x R

Forced, if Black wants to play on.

17. Q—R7ch

Nudges the King into a fatal situation.

17. . . .   K—B1

The only move.

18. Q x B mate

The danger in playing plausible but perfunctory chess is finely illustrated in this game. Blackburne, who conducted this and seven other games blindfolded at one time, relied on order and method to achieve victory. It proved easily superior to the move-to-move groping of his seeing opponent.

GAME NO. 5

GIUOCO PIANO

WHITE	BLACK
Ruger	Gebhard

DRESDEN, 1915

1. P—K4

The most important thing to do in the opening is to develop the pieces as fast as possible in order to occupy and control the center.

White's first move fixes a Pawn in the center, and as the first step in getting his pieces off the back rank, opens avenues for his Queen and Bishop.

1. . . .   P—K4

Black equalizes the pressure in the center and releases two pieces for action. He must be content with this, as he cannot hope at this early stage to wrest the initiative by force.

2. Kt—KB3

It is good strategy to make developing moves which embody threats, as it cuts down the choice of reply. Against the passive 2. Kt—QB3, which develops a piece but attacks nothing, Black can choose from among such good responses as 2. . . . Kt—KB3, 2. . . . Kt—QB3 or 2. . . . B—B4. Likewise, if White's second move is the quiet 2. B—B4, Black has three good options in 2. . . . Kt—KB3, 2. . . . B—B4 and 2. . . . P—QB3 (with a view to an early . . . P—Q4).

2. . . .   Kt—QB3

Black saves his King Pawn and

develops a piece. The Knight comes into play efficiently: its action is directed toward influencing the center. It defends the square K4 and attacks Q5.

3. B—B4

The Bishop comes out, taking up a post where it commands the diagonal leading to Black's King. It attacks a Pawn which is peculiarly vulnerable as it is defended only by the King.

This does not mean that White will capture the Pawn in the next few moves, *but the threat is always there*. Many a short brilliancy owes its life to similar captures in which the Bishop is sacrificed simply to get the King out into the open where White's other pieces can get at him.

3. . . . B—B4

Black follows suit, bringing his Bishop out to the most suitable square.

In the opening, the Bishop is best placed for attack when it controls a diagonal in the center or when it pins a hostile Knight and puts it out of play. Defensively, the Bishop does a fine job at K2, where it radiates power in several directions, making an intrusion by an adverse piece difficult.

4. P—B3

Supports an advance of the Queen Pawn with a view to controlling the center. White postpones castling as his King is in no danger.

4. . . . Kt—B3

A powerful counter to the threat:

Black develops a piece which attacks a Pawn.

5. P—Q4

White meets this by attacking a piece.

5. . . . P x P

Practically forced, as 5. . . . B—Q3 guarding the King Pawn is clumsy, since it blocks the Queen Pawn, while 5. . . . B—Kt3 permits 6. P x P, KKt x P 7. B x Pch, K x B 8. Q—Q5ch, and White regains his piece, remaining a Pawn ahead. White could also play 7. Q—Q5, attacking the Knight while threatening mate, instead of 7. B x Pch.

6. P x P

White's array of Pawns looks impressive, but can the center be maintained?

6. . . . B—Kt5ch

Far superior to the timid 6. . . . B—Kt3, after which Black is crushed somewhat like this: 7. P—Q5, Kt—QKt1 8. P—K5, Kt—Kt1 (both Knights return home ingloriously) 9. O—O, Kt—K2 10. P—Q6, Kt—Kt3 11. Kt—Kt5, O—O (Black's King is protected by three Pawns and the Knight; in four moves the Knight and one Pawn disappear, while the remaining two Pawns are pinned and helpless) 12. Q—R5 (threatens 13. Q x P mate) P—KR3 13. Q x Kt (again threatening mate—the Queen is of course taboo), P x Kt 14. B x KtP, Q—K1 15. B—B6, and White, exploiting a double pin, forces mate next move.

This is the final situation:

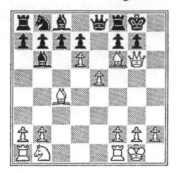

After the actual move, White must get his King out of check, and if possible save the threatened Pawn.

7. Kt–B3

White prefers this, which offers a Pawn, to 7. B–Q2, B x Bch 8. QKt x B, and the King Pawn is protected.

7. . . .   O–O

"Chess is not for timid souls," wrote Steinitz in a letter to Bachmann. Castling early in the game is *generally* sound strategy. In this case it is inappropriate, as White's center is formidable and must be destroyed. Black must play 7. . . . Kt x KP, accepting the offer of a Pawn, and take his chances of surviving whatever attack might follow. It cannot be worse than this passive castling which results in both his Knights being evicted from their fine posts. Pillsbury gave as his rule, which he said was "absolute and vital: Castle because you will or because you must; but not because you can."

8. P–Q5

Ordinarily, such moves are suspect, as Q5 should be occupied by a piece. But here the Pawn does serv-

ice in dislodging the Knight and in preventing Black forever from freeing his game by . . . P–Q4.

8. . . .   Kt–K2

As good as there is. The shift to QR4 is countered by 9. B–Q3, and the Knight is stranded at the side of the board.

9. P–K5

Now a shot at the other Knight!

9. . . .   Kt–K5

Retreating to K1 does not look attractive, so Black plays to exchange Knights.

10. Q–B2

Protects his own Knight, which was twice attacked, and threatens the enemy's.

10. . . .   Kt x Kt

Practically forced, as defending the Knight by 10. . . . P–KB4 allows 11. P–Q6 dis. ch, and the other Knight falls.

11. P x Kt

The recapture gains a tempo: Black's Bishop must lose a move retreating, while White's advantages increase. Now he enjoys the benefits of an open Knight file for his Queen Rook and an extra diagonal for his Queen Bishop.

11. . . .   B—B4

Naturally, this offers better chances than moving to R4, the only other flight square.

A comparison of the two positions shows that White's is decidedly superior. He has more pieces in the field, and they have far more mobility than Black's. He has better prospects too of bringing more pieces into the battle.

The recommended recipe now is to occupy Black with threats—keep him on the run and give him no time to put up an effective resistance.

12. Kt—Kt5 !

Ostensibly to scare Black by the threat of mate; actually the purpose is to induce a weakening advance of one of the King's retinue of Pawns.

If one of these Pawns does move, Black is done for! For example, if 12. . . . P—B4 13. P—Q6 dis. ch wins a piece, or if 12. . . . P—Kt3 13. Kt—K4 forces 13. . . . B—Kt3, when 14. B—R6 drives the Rook to

K1, and 15. Kt—B6ch wins the exchange.

12. . . .   Kt—Kt3

The only defense! The King-side Pawns are intact, but Black has been compelled to place his pieces where White wants them. Under such circumstances the chances of his putting up a good fight are not too bright.

White must avoid Black's error in castling as a matter of routine development. Such a quiet course gives Black time to play 13. . . . P—Q3 or 13. . . . P—KR3, beating the Knight back. White must not give his opponent a moment to catch his breath. He must attack, attack, attack!

13. P—KR4

Threatening to move on to R5, dispossess the Knight, and then mate with the Queen.

13. . . .   P—KR3

What else is there? Black tries to drive off the menacing Knight. He cannot do this by 13. . . . P—KB3 as 14. P—Q6 dis. ch, K—R1 15. Kt—B7ch wins the exchange.

14. P—Q6!

A powerful stroke! Black's Bishop is cut off from the defense, while a line is opened for White's Bishop. White now threatens 15. Q x Kt, as the pinned Pawn could not touch the Queen.

14. . . .　　P x Kt

Black might as well take whatever material he can.

15. P x P!

The Knight will not run away (the penalty being 16. Q—R7 mate). Meanwhile, the Rook has a lovely open file, and the Queen still threatens to capture the Knight.

15. . . .　　R—K1

The King needs more room!

16. Q x Kt

Regains the piece without relaxing the pressure. White threatens mate in one, and two mates in two.

16. . . .　　R x Pch

Black consoles himself by equalizing the inventory of tangible assets and gives one despairing check before he yields.

17. K—B1

Simplest, as the mate threats are still on tap. There was little likelihood that White would blunder into 17. K—Q2, Q x Pch 18. Q x Q, R x Q, and all the good work has gone for naught.

17. . . .　　Resigns

Black can avoid mate on the move by 17. . . . Q—K1 (incidentally threatening mate himself!), only to fall into 18. Q—R7ch, K—B1 19. Q—R8 mate.

GAME NO. 6

RUY LOPEZ

WHITE	BLACK
Zeissl	Walthoffen

VIENNA, 1899

1. P—K4

"Always deploy," says Franklin K. Young, "so that the right oblique may be readily established in case the objective plane remains open or becomes permanently located on the center or on the King's wing, or that the crochet aligned may readily be established if the objective plane becomes permanently located otherwise than at the extremity of the strategic front."

If this is somewhat obscure (and I see no reason to believe otherwise) the conclusion it reaches is stated in limpid prose by the same writer:

"The best initial move for White is 1. P—K4."

1. . . .　　P—K4

Black's best chance to equalize is to get a fair share of the most important squares—those in the center. With 1. . . . P—K4 he stakes out his claim, meanwhile freeing two of his pieces.

2. Kt—KB3

You may play this confidently, secure in the knowledge that no master alive can make a better move. The Knight develops in one move to its most suitable square in the opening.

It exerts pressure on two of the four squares in the vital central area.

It comes in toward the center so that it enjoys maximum mobility.

It helps clear the King side, enabling early castling of the King on that side.

It is posted ideally for the defense of the King after he castles.

It comes into play with a gain of time—an attack on a Pawn!

In short, it's a very good move!

2. . . .   Kt—QB3

A commendable reply: Black develops a piece, protecting his Pawn at the same time.

3. B—Kt5

Probably the strongest move on the board. The Bishop puts a restraining hand on the Pawn's defender. There is no immediate threat of winning the Pawn as after 4. B x Kt, QP x B 5. Kt x P, the reply 5. . . . Q—Q5 regains the Pawn. But there is pressure on the Knight, and this pressure becomes intensified when Black, sooner or later, advances his Queen Pawn and the Knight is then pinned.

3. . . .   P—B4

A bold attempt to seize the initiative. The idea is to lure White into surrendering the center by taking the Bishop Pawn.

4. P—Q4

An aggressive player would like White's counterattack on the King Pawn. A solid, positional player would simply defend his King Pawn by 4. Kt—B3, quietly developing a piece, while one who is truly conservative might be content with 4. P—Q3 supporting the King Pawn, so that in the event of an exchange he would retain a Pawn in the center.

4. . . .   BP x P

Black's capture is intended mainly to evict the Knight from its strong post.

5. Kt x P

Apparently a strong move. White gets his Pawn back and prevents 5. . . . P—Q3 or 5. . . . P—Q4. After either of these moves, the continuation 6. Kt x Kt, P x Kt 7. B x Pch wins the exchange.

White also has a powerful threat in 8. B x Kt, QP x B 9. Q—R5ch, K—K2 10. Q—B7ch, K—Q3 11. Kt—B4 mate.

This is all very tempting, as the possibility of mating so early in the game is attractive to the young player, but such ambition should be suppressed. Premature mating attacks are usually repulsed with loss of time or material to the aggressor.

A safer continuation is 5. B x Kt, QP x B 6. Kt x P.

5. . . .   Kt x Kt

Removes the best defender of White's King-side position and puts an end to any combinative notions White might have entertained.

6. P x Kt

White has nothing to show for the too-energetic 4. P—Q4 move.

The development of the Queen Knight instead was preferable.

6. . . .   P—B3 !

A Pawn move when pieces should be brought into play? Yes, if the move is justified by the particular position. Black has four good arguments for the Pawn push:

a) He must drive off the Bishop before he can advance his Queen Pawn (otherwise the King is in check).

b) The time lost in moving a Pawn is compensated for by the fact that the Bishop must also lose a move in retreating.

c) He opens a fine diagonal for his Queen.

d) The attack on the Bishop will result in winning a Pawn, and "A Pawn is worth a little trouble," according to Steinitz.

7. B—QB4

Ordinarily, this is an excellent place for the Bishop, but K2 is more consistent with the requirements of the position. White has lost the services of the King Knight, and the Bishop might help the defense of the King side.

7. . . .   Q—R4ch

Double attack on King and Pawn.

8. Kt—B3

The best way to get out of check. White places the Queen Knight where it belongs in the opening.

8. . . .   Q x KP

Black has won a Pawn, which is a good start toward winning the game.

His aim now is to get an attack rolling in the direction of White's denuded King side.

9. O—O

Plausible—and bad! It was more discreet to conceal his intentions, develop the Queen-side pieces, and castle later, perhaps on the Queen side.

9. . . .   P—Q4 !

Of course! Black seizes the center, chases off the adverse Bishop, and enables his own to make an appearance. All this in one move!

10. B—Kt3

Here too the defensive maneuver 10. B—K2, where the Bishop overlooks two diagonals, is preferable.

10. . . .   Kt—B3

Organizing a King-side attack by a simple process—developing his pieces!

11. B—K3

Partly to prevent Black from moving 11. . . . B—QB4, partly to dislodge the centralized Queen by 12. B—Q4 or 12. Q—Q4.

11. . . .   B—Q3 !

A fine move which has more significance to it than the mere development of a piece combined with a mating threat. The ulterior object is to create a *permanent irremediable weakness* in White's King-side position by forcing one of the defending Pawns to make a move.

12. P—Kt3

The only possible defense. If instead *12. P—B4*, P x P e.p. *13.* Q x BP, Q x Pch *14. K—B2*, B—KKt5, and Black wins.

After the actual move, Black launches an attack. He does not sacrifice a piece uselessly for the Knight Pawn, nor does he try to break into the position by the Pawn assault *13. . . . P—KR4*, R5 and R6.

12. . . .   B—KKt5 !

He bases the attack on the theme of *penetration*. White's KB3 and KR3 have been weakened by the move *12. P—Kt3*, as these squares are no longer guarded by the Pawn. These squares are now "holes," as Steinitz first named them. Enemy pieces that settle themselves on these squares stand firm, as *no Pawns can ever drive them away*.

The Bishop attacks the Queen, with the object of insinuating itself into B6 without loss of time.

13. Q—Q2

As good as there is. If White interposes the Knight at K2 instead, then *13. . . . Q—R4*, attacking the Knight once more, forces *14. R—K1*, whereupon *14. . . . Q—R6* plants a piece in one hole. Black's following move is *15. . . . B—B6*, occupying the other hole, and the stage is set for the mate at Kt7.

13. . . .   B—B6

The second step in the process of penetration.

14. B—KB4

Hoping for something like *14. . . . Q—K2 15. B x B*, Q x B *16. Q—B4*, when an exchange or two might ease his difficulties.

After White's fourteenth move, Black has a forced mate in five moves, which he might flamboyantly announce:

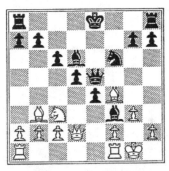

14. . . .   Q—B4 !

Deserts the Bishop, but Black is interested only in getting the Queen to R6, with a death grip on the white squares.

15. Kt—Q1 !

The only possible chance. The Knight is to be brought to K3 to guard the square KKt2, where mate impends.

15. . . .   Q—R6

Threatening instant mate.

16. Kt—K3

Defends the critical square.

16. . . .　　　Kt—Kt5

New threat: mate at R7. Notice the clever use of the weakened white squares as Black's pieces infiltrate the enemy position.

17. KR—B1

Room for the King!

17. . . .　　　Q x RPch

And mate comes next move.

GAME NO. 7

FRENCH DEFENSE

WHITE　　　　　　BLACK
Spielmann　　　Wahle
VIENNA, 1926

1. P—K4

This move accomplishes a great deal:

A Pawn is fixed in the center of the board.

The Pawn gets a grip on Q5 and KB5, and keeps Black's pieces from settling on those squares.

White's Queen and Bishop immediately have breathing space.

1. . . .　　　P—K3

With several objects in view:

One, to prevent White from dictating the opening. After the conventional reply 1. . . . P—K4, White can play the powerful Ruy Lopez line, the Giuoco Piano, the Vienna Game, the Max Lange attack, or even a dangerous gambit of some sort.

Another is that Black's cramped position often induces a premature attack, which can be disastrous to White.

A third is that the Pawn at K3 supports an advance by 2. . . . P—Q4, an attack on the King Pawn which might wrest the initiative.

The French Defense is not to be underestimated. It conceals a great deal of dynamic energy behind a modest façade.

2. P—Q4

If it's worth while to establish one Pawn in the center, then keeping two Pawns there should double the benefits.

2. . . .　　　P—Q4

Black gives his Queen more scope and challenges the center.

3. Kt—QB3

Clearly an excellent response, as the Knight develops to its proper square, protects the King Pawn, and bears down on Q5.

3. . . .　　　Kt—KB3

Black in turn brings his King Knight to its strongest position with a gain of time—further attack on the Pawn.

4. P x P

Many players prefer to add to the pressure by 4. B—KKt5 (which develops a piece and renders one of the enemy's impotent) to this move, which relaxes the tension.

Spielmann, who likes wide-open positions, clears away a couple of

Pawns to give his pieces more room for their activities.

Which move is better? Which should you play? The answer is: play the move that you like, the one that best suits your style and temperament. If you are a careful, cautious player who knows the full value of a Pawn—that each one is a potential Queen, and that the loss of a Pawn may be the loss of the game—stick to 4. B—KKt5 and the openings of positional chess, the Ruy Lopez, the Queen Pawn openings, the Réti and the English. On the other hand, if you prefer daring, adventurous chess, and a Pawn is simply a barrier to the sweeping onrush of an attack by your pieces, play openings which allow scope for your imagination, the Evans, Danish, King's and other gambits.

The best openings to play are the ones you are most at home in.

4. . . .　　P x P

Better than taking with the Knight. Black keeps a Pawn in the center and frees his Queen Bishop.

5. B—KKt5

Pins the Knight and threatens to break up the game by 6. B x Kt, P x B (6. . . . Q x B loses the Queen Pawn) and Black is left with a weak doubled Pawn.

5. . . .　　B—K2

The simplest way of unpinning the Knight. Moving the Bishop only one square may not seem much of a move, but it complies with the first law of rapid development:

Get your pieces off the back rank!

6. B—Q3

This Bishop's stand is aggressive, especially against King-side castling.

6. . . .　　Kt—B3

While this Knight's debut is even more menacing, as it threatens to take the Queen Pawn.

7. KKt—K2 !

After the customary development 7. Kt—B3, Black pins the Knight by 7. . . . B—KKt5 and again threatens the Queen Pawn. White could save the Pawn, say by 8. B—K2, but would lose the initiative.

After the text move, if Black pins the Knight, 8. P—B3 repels the Bishop and causes it to lose time retreating.

7. . . .　　Kt—QKt5

Intending to get rid of a dangerous piece and also to assure himself of a little advantage in keeping both his Bishops.

8. Kt—Kt3

Now we see another reason for developing the Knight to K2. White wants to anchor a piece at KB5, a dominating position for a Knight or a Bishop. A piece need do no more than just stand there and look menacing to rattle the opponent.

8. . . .　　Kt x Bch

Mission accomplished. Black has a slight technical superiority in retaining two long-range Bishops against White's Knight and Bishop, but . . .

9. Q x Kt

. . . at a loss of time. Black has made three moves with the Knight to exchange it for a Bishop which moved only once. More than that, his Knight came off the board completely, while the Bishop left a piece in its place. The result is that White has four active pieces in the field against two of Black's. White is also prepared to castle on either side and mobilize both Rooks quickly. Whatever advantage exists is therefore White's.

9. . . .   P—KKt3

The Pawn move prevents White from placing his Knight at KB5, but it creates an organic weakness in Black's position, *one that is irremediable*. The squares KB3 and KR3, no longer guarded by the Pawn, are weak *and remain so permanently*.

Notice that the Pawn was induced but not forced to move forward. The mere threat of an inroad by the Knight was enough to influence Black to make a natural preventive move. It is the sort of move nine out of ten players make automatically in similar situations, which is why it is important to know how to exploit its defects. For no move is weak unless proper advantage is taken of it.

This is the position, with White to move:

10. O—O

No violence, please, until the reserves have been brought up. Blackburne used to say, "Never start an attack until your Queen's Rook is developed."

White secures the safety of his King and gets one Rook out of hiding.

10. . . .   P—B3

Strengthens the Pawn center and opens another avenue for his Queen.

11. QR—K1

White seizes the only open file (since Rooks belong on open files or on files likely to be opened) and pins the Bishop.

It is worth noting that a pinned piece not only is unable to move but is also powerless to capture. *It does not protect any other pieces, since it is completely paralyzed.* Hence it follows that not only is the Bishop unable to move and in danger of its life (as it may be attacked again and again) but the Knight that depends on it for protection is no longer secure. Briefly, Black is now threatened with loss of a piece by *12. B x Kt.*

11. . . .   O—O

The King takes refuge in flight, incidentally unpinning the Bishop and preserving his Knight.

Spielmann's strategy to this point and the decisive combination which follows would have pleased Lasker, who once said, "In the beginning of the game ignore the search for combinations, abstain from violent moves. Aim for small advantages, accumulate them, and only after having attained these ends search for the combination—and then with all the power of will and intellect, because then the combination must exist, however deeply hidden."

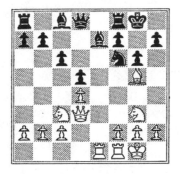

A glance shows that White has achieved the requisite positional superiority. If there is a combination to be evolved, it must be now, before Black has time to reorganize his pieces for defense. Now, while he has five pieces actively in play against two of Black's. Now, while he has an open file—enough! enough! The combination *must* be there!

Here is White's reasoning:

Black's advance of the Knight Pawn has deprived the Knight of a stable support. It is still guarded by two pieces, but *if the Bishop were not there* it would be defended only once. In fact, *if the Bishop were not there*, the Knight would be pinned and subject to an enduring attack. *The Bishop appears in both equations.* Obviously the Bishop is the culprit, and it must be destroyed! And at once, before Black has time for 12. . . . B—K3 !

12. R x B !!

"When we know about the inspiring ideas, how simple the sacrifices appear!" says Znosko-Borovsky.

12. . . .   Q x R

Black must recapture, leaving the Knight pinned and a fine target for further attack.

13. Q—B3

Putting pressure on the pin, and threatening to take the Knight.

13. . . .   K—Kt2

The King comes to the rescue. Against the alternative defense 13. . . . B—B4, Spielmann had this pretty continuation: 14. Kt x B, P x Kt 15. Q—Kt3 (threatening mate on the move by 16. B x Kt) K—Kt2 (or 15. . . . K—R1 16. Q —R4, K—Kt2 17. Q—R6ch, K— Kt1 18. B x Kt, and White wins) 16. B x Kt dble. ch, K x B 17. Q— R4ch, K—K3 18. R—K1ch K—Q2 19. Q x Qch, and all Black's pieces come off.

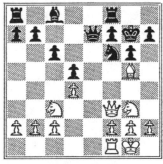

14. Kt(B3)—K4 !

White must keep hammering at the pinned Knight, no matter how many brilliant moves he has to find!

Again, White's immediate threat is simple: 15. B x Ktch, winning instantaneously.

14. . . .   P x Kt

Black must take this Knight or lose his own.

15. Kt x P

Three pieces now attack the helpless Knight. "Chess is not for the kindhearted," says the French proverb.

White now threatens 16. B x Ktch followed by 17. B x Q.

15. . . .   Q—K3

On 15. . . . Q x Kt, White has the pleasant choice of winning the Queen by 16. B x Ktch (removing the protector of the Queen), followed by 17. Q x Q, or forcing mate by 16. Q x Ktch, K—Kt1 17. B—R6, followed by 18. Q—Kt7 mate.

In the last line of play, notice how White screws pieces firmly into the two holes in Black's position, KB3 and KR3, the squares no longer guarded by the Knight Pawn after its advance.

With his last move, Black saves the Queen. He is still ahead in material but has a lost game, as White's pieces will insinuate themselves along the black squares to get at the King.

16. B x Ktch

Regains a piece and limits Black to two moves.

16. . . .   K—Kt1

If 16. . . . K—R3 17. Q—B4ch and mate next move.

17. Q—B4

Threatening a final invasion at R6 followed by a mate at Kt7—triumph on the black squares.

Black, powerless to prevent mate, resigned the game.

GAME NO. 8

QUEEN'S PAWN GAME
(*Colle System*)

WHITE	BLACK
Przepiorka	Prokes

BUDAPEST, 1929

1. P—Q4

One reason for the popularity of Queen Pawn openings is that from the very first move they present problems for the defender. There is no method by which Black can seize the initiative or even equalize in a hurry.

Despite its inherently positional nature, the Queen's Pawn appeals tremendously to attacking players and has always been a favorite weapon of such aggressive spirits as Alekhine, Keres, Pillsbury, Bogolyubov, Spielmann and Colle.

1. . . .   Kt—KB3

Brings a piece into play where it has an influence on the center. The Knight move prevents White from continuing with 2. P—K4.

A master moves his Knight to KB3 as instinctively as he breathes.

2. Kt—KB3

The Knight develops toward the

center, where he has the greatest freedom of action and the widest scope for his activities.

The Knight possesses the peculiar property of being able to attack any other piece (except another Knight) without being under attack in return. This attribute makes it a most fascinating piece to maneuver about the board. Combinations involving play with the Knights often have a balletlike aspect about them.

2. . . . P—K3

Black can avoid the general attack of the Colle by playing 2. . . . P—Q4, ready to reply to 3. P—K3 with 3. . . . B—B4. Then on 4. B—Q3, B x B exchanges Bishops and Black rids himself of White's most dangerous attacking piece (in this form of the opening).

With the actual move, Black releases his King Bishop and does not commit himself to any specific line of defense.

3. P—K3

Indicating his design: obviously White is preparing the typical Colle formation of Bishop at Q3 and Queen Knight at Q2, to control the key square K4, a jumping-off point for the pieces in this attack.

3. . . . P—Q4

Black plants a Pawn firmly in the center.

4. B—Q3

White begins the concentration of pressure on K4, essential in the Colle. Generally speaking, it is a good plan to mobilize the pieces on the King side first, to enable early castling on that side.

4. . . . P—B4

This move is almost indispensable in Queen Pawn openings. It is important not to play . . . Kt—QB3 first, as the Bishop Pawn must not be obstructed.

Black's move strikes at the center and establishes a state of tension in that area.

5. P—B3

Strengthens the Queen Pawn. In the event of 5. . . . P x P, White can recapture with the Bishop Pawn and maintain a Pawn in the center. It is necessary not to disturb the King Pawn, which must remain at K3 waiting for further instructions.

It may seem that White's last move denies the Queen Knight his best square, but in this form of attack the Knight belongs at Q2.

5. . . . QKt—Q2

This is probably superior to placing the Knight at B3. At Q2, the Knights are in touch with each other, so that if the King Knight is exchanged the other can get to KB3, an ideal square for attack or defense. At Q2, the Knight keeps clear of the Bishop file. The more open the file is, the more useful will it be for the Queen or Rook that occupies it. Finally, should White play 6. P x P, the Knight recaptures and comes strongly into the game.

In Queen Pawn openings, Black's Queen Knight often does a better job at Q2 than at QB3.

6. QKt—Q2

Intensifying the pressure on K4. To the uninitiated, White's development has an awkward look. The pieces seem to be in each other's way, but as will be seen they can spring into action smoothly and easily.

6. . . .   B—Q3

This is more energetic than 6. . . . B—K2, where the Bishop is limited to defensive duties.

7. O—O

White secures the safety of his King before starting any decisive action. It is dangerous to open up the position and leave the King in the center, exposed to a possible counterattack.

White's castling is aggressive in character as the King Rook plays an important role in the coming attack.

7. . . .   O—O

Black's castling is a defensive measure. But why give the King's permanent address when White has revealed that he is preparing an assault on the King side? Better strategy would be to keep the opponent in the dark—delay castling for a while and continue developing the pieces (which surely can do no harm). Black might bring his Queen to B2, with a view to an early . . . P—K4, and then fianchetto his Queen Bishop (. . . P—QKt3, followed by . . . B—Kt2).

8. R—K1

Still more pressure on K4! The Rook gets a grip on the King file. It is closed now but it will be opened after White plays P—K4 and Pawns are exchanged.

8. . . .   Q—B2

An ideal location for the Queen. From B2 the Queen bears down on the center, especially K4, and exerts great pressure on the Queen Bishop file.

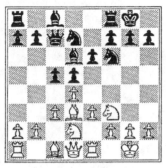

9. P—K4 !

The key move in the Colle! With this move White intends to blast the position wide open and release all the stored-up energy of his pieces in a searing attack.

The immediate threat is 10. P—K5, a simple, brutal attack on two pieces.

9. . . .   BP x P

As compensation for being on the defensive, Black controls the open Bishop file—temporarily.

10. BP x P

Better than taking with the Knight, which lets Black place pieces on his K4 and QB4.

White meanwhile renews the

threat of winning a piece by *11.
P—K5.*

10. . . .   P x P

Parries the threat and saddles
White with an isolated Queen's
Pawn. Such a Pawn is especially vulnerable to attack as it cannot be
protected by another Pawn, the
nearest one being a couple of files
away.

11. Kt x P

Certainly not *11. B x P,* as
11. . . . Kt x B would be the response, and White loses the services
of his valuable King Bishop. "As
Rousseau could not compose without his cat beside him, so I without
my King's Bishop cannot play chess,"
says Tarrasch. "In its absence the
game to me is lifeless and cold. The
vitalizing factor is missing, and I can
devise no plan of attack."

11. . . .   P—QKt3

Intending to mobilize his Queen
Bishop. Somewhat more to the point
was *11. . . . B—B5,* restraining one
of White's menacing Bishops.

12. B—KKt5

The Bishop attacks, and vacates
the square QB1. The Queen Rook
will swing over there, drive the
Queen off and assume complete control of a beautiful open file.

12. . . .   Kt x Kt

Apparently Black was afraid to
continue *12. . . . B—Kt2* as the
continuation *13. Kt x Ktch, Kt x Kt
14. B x Kt, P x B* breaks up his King-
side Pawn position.

13. R x Kt !

Superior to the natural *13. B x
Kt,* when Black might reply *13. . . .
B—Kt2,* forcing *14. B—Q3* (to
avoid exchanging Bishops). Then he
could play *14. . . . B x Kt 15.
Q x B, B x Pch,* consoling himself
with a Pawn for his troubles.

13. . . .   B—Kt2

There is hardly anything better
than this, which offers the Bishop a
long diagonal. If for example
13. . . . Kt—B3, 14. R—R4 is
hard to meet. The threat of winning
a Pawn by *15. B x Kt, P x B 16.
B x Pch* could not be parried by
14. . . . P—KR3 as *15. B x Kt,
P x B 16. R x P* still wins a Pawn.

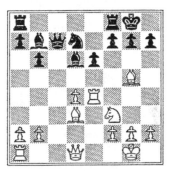

14. R—B1 !

A fine in-between move! The
Rook is developed effectively on the
open file, while the Queen is ban-
ished to the first rank. There she interferes with the Queen Rook, preventing its development for a long
time—forever, as it turns out!

14. . . .   Q—Kt1

There is nothing else: the continuation *14. . . . B x R 15. R x Q,*

B x Kt 16. Q x B, B x R 17. Q—QB6 wins a piece for White.

15. R—R4 !

The point! White's threat of 16. B x Pch forces one of the Pawns in front of the King to move forward. White gets an advantage, no matter which Pawn advances, as:

Every Pawn move loosens the defending structure.

Every undefended square (occasioned by such an advance) creates a weakness in the position.

15. . . .   P—Kt3

If Black tries defending the Rook Pawn by 15. . . . Kt—B3, 16. B x Kt, P x B 17. B x Pch wins the Pawn just the same. Or if Black advances the Rook Pawn, then 16. B x P, P x B 17. R x P is an obvious sacrificial combination which shatters the cordon of Pawns and exposes the King to a mating attack.

White has accomplished what he set out to do. He has forced an advance of the King Knight Pawn. But how does he exploit the resulting weakness? Is there an attack against the Pawn? Apparently there isn't, as in order to strike at it with the Rook Pawn, he must move the Rook out of the way, and then play P—KR4 and P—R5, a process which takes time and achieves little.

What other line is there? Sacrificing a piece for the Knight Pawn? Obviously, this is useless, as White still does not break through.

But the Pawn did advance, and *there is a weakness somewhere.* We know this fact to be true, and *in this fact there must be the clue to the winning combination.*

The Pawn's advance weakened the squares KR3 and KB3, as they are no longer guarded by the Pawn. This means that White must try to get control of these squares, either seize and occupy them with his pieces, or use them as a means of penetrating into the enemy camp.

But wait! Doesn't Black's Knight still guard his KB3 square? Indeed it does, and this knowledge provides us with the information we need. The Knight is the guardian of the black squares, and the Knight must be destroyed!

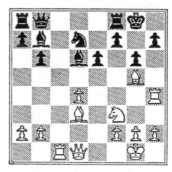

16. B—Kt5 !

Attacks the Knight, which strangely enough has no place to escape to!

16. . . .   Q—K1

What other ways are there to protect the Knight?

If 16. . . . B—B1 17. B—QB6 wins the exchange.

If 16. . . . B x Kt 17. Q x B, Q—K1 18. Q—QB6 wins a piece.

After the actual move, the Knight is pinned and a good target for further attack.

17. Kt—K5

In chess you may hit a man when he's down.

17. . . .   B—B1

No better is 17. . . . B x Kt 18. P x B (uncovering the Queen's attack on the Knight), B—B1 (or . . . B—Q4) 19. R—B7 and the miserable creature must perish.

18. R x B !

Taking the props out from under the Knight! The technique is simple: if you cannot aggravate the pressure on a piece, see if you can dispose of one of its defenders.

18. . . .   Q x R

Certainly not 18. . . . R x R, when 19. B x R wins two pieces for a Rook, and then corners the Queen!

19. B x Kt

White has two pieces for the Rook—and the attack!

19. . . .   Q—B2

Not 19. . . . Q—Kt2 or 19. . . . Q—Kt1, as 20. B—B6 wins the exchange. The alternative was 19. . . . Q—R3, but Black hopes for some counter-play on the Bishop file.

20. Kt—Kt4 !

The first step toward exploiting the weak black squares brings with it a threat of mate by 21. Kt—B6ch, K—R1 (or 21. . . . K—Kt2) 22. R x P mate.

20. . . .   P—KR4

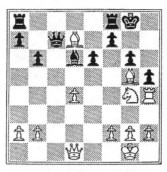

The King needs lots of room. The freeing attempt by 20. . . . P—B4 loses by 21. B x Pch, K—R1 (21. . . . K—Kt2 22. B—R6ch wins the exchange) 22. Kt—B6, and resistance is hopeless.

21. Kt—B6ch

The Knight comes in on one of the critical black squares to strike the first blow.

21. . . .   K—Kt2

If 21. . . . K—R1 22. R x Pch forces quick mate.

22. Kt x Pch

Sacrificing the Knight to sweep away the Pawns shielding the King.

22. . . .   P x Kt

Black must take the Knight, as after 22. . . . K—Kt1 (or R2) 23. Kt—B6ch, K—Kt2 24. R—R7 is mate.

23. Q x P

The Queen's first move! With it, White threatens two mates on the move, on the Rook file.

23. . . .   R—R1

The only move to stop mate—temporarily.

24. B—R6ch

Appropriately enough, White administers the *coup de grâce* on the second critical black square.

24. . . . Resigns

Mate follows in two moves.

GAME NO. 9

RUY LOPEZ

WHITE	BLACK
Znosko-Borovsky	Mackenzie

WESTON-SUPER-MARE, 1924

1. P—K4

This first move occupies the center with a Pawn and frees four squares for the Queen and five for the King Bishop. One of the reasons many players prefer 1. P—K4 to any other opening move is that it gets the King-side pieces rolling quickly, enabling early castling on that side.

1. . . . P—K4

In the old days this was almost compulsory. It indicated that you were willing to stand toe to toe and slug it out. Only a coward would avoid 1. . . . P—K4, and a possible gambit by White.

Objectively considered, the text is Black's strongest response. It challenges possession of the center and prevents White's monopolizing it by continuing with 2. P—Q4.

2. Kt—KB3

What happens if White persists and plays 2. P—Q4? The reply 2. . . . P x P leads to 3. Q x P, Kt —QB3 4. Q—K3, Kt—B3, and Black has two pieces in play to one of White's. This amounts to taking the initiative away from White early in the game.

The text move is far more effective than random development of the Knight, say at KR3, where it is out of touch with affairs in the center, or at K2, where it blocks all traffic.

2. . . . Kt—QB3

The logical way to meet the attack on the Pawn; a minor piece develops toward the center and defends the Pawn.

The general plan of mobilization is to establish a Pawn in the center, develop the minor pieces (the Knights before Bishops, wherever feasible), then castle to get the Rooks toward the center files, and finally bring the Queen out—but not too far from home. Premature development of the Queen is dangerous, as it is subject to annoying attacks by Pawns and minor pieces.

3. B—Kt5

The most natural move on the board: White strikes at the defender of the Pawn he attacks. It is true he cannot win the Pawn at once, as after 4. B x Kt, QP x B 5. Kt x P, Q—Q5 regains the Pawn. But the pressure on Black is constant, and the threat is always in the air.

The Ruy Lopez is probably the strongest of all King-side openings. White has more to say in the center, since he will be able to play P—Q4 without much trouble, while Black will find it difficult to do likewise. White's pieces have more room to move around in, while Black's game is considerably cramped in many variations of play.

3. . . .   P—QR3

This can become like the story "The House that Jack Built": the Pawn attacks the Bishop that attacks the Knight that defends the Pawn that the Knight attacks.

The purpose of Black's move is to dislodge the Bishop from its favorable position. The loss of time involved in moving a Pawn is compensated for by the fact that the threatened Bishop must also lose a move in retreating.

4. B—R4

This is in the spirit of the opening as it maintains pressure on the Knight. The alternative withdrawal to B4 is inferior, as White could have reached that position in three moves instead of four.

4. . . .   Kt—B3

Develops a piece, attacks a Pawn and prepares for early King-side castling. More could hardly be expected of one move.

5. O—O

White brings his King to safety and swings the Rook over toward the center files.

5. . . .   B—K2

A favorite continuation with many players is 5. . . . Kt x P. Not with the idea of winning a Pawn, as White regains it easily, but in order to obtain a free, open game. The danger in this line is that it leaves Black's position in the center somewhat insecure.

The text leads to a close position, difficult to break through, but requires patience on Black's part. The Bishop's development at K2 is satisfactory even though it has moved only one square away from home. The important thing is that it has left the back rank and facilitated castling.

6. R—K1

Brings the Rook toward the center. In lieu of an open file, the Rook prepares to take command of a file likely to be opened. In guarding his own King Pawn, White renews the threat of 7. B x Kt, QP x B 8. Kt x P, winning a Pawn.

The Rook's move is preferable to developing the Queen Knight to B3. White may want to provide a retreat for his Bishop by P—B3, guarding it against an exchange.

6. . . .   P—QKt4

Meets the threat by forcing the Bishop back.

7. B—Kt3

Obviously the only move.

7. . . .   P—Q3

Protects the King Pawn, releases the Queen Bishop and prepares for 8. . . . Kt—QR4 to remove the troublesome adverse Bishop.

At first glance it seems illogical to give one Bishop freedom while hemming in the other, but since the

King Bishop does a good job at K2, it remains for the Queen Bishop to go out into the world.

8. P—B3

With two objects:

To provide refuge for the Bishop against an attempt to remove it by 8. . . . Kt—QR4.

To support an advance of the Queen Pawn, establishing a strong Pawn center.

8. . . .   Kt—QR4

Not so much to strike at the Bishop as to make way for 9. . . . P—B4 to dispute control of the center squares. In this line of the Lopez, Black's best counter-chances lie in action on the Queen side.

9. B—B2

Naturally, White wants to keep both Bishops. He loses a tempo, but it is offset by Black's posting of a Knight at the side of the board.

9. . . .   P—B4

Intensifies his pressure on Q5 and provides an egress (as the old books used to say) for the Queen.

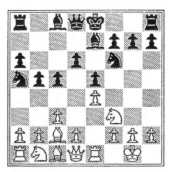

10. P—Q4

One of the chief objectives in King Pawn openings is to advance *the Queen Pawn* to the center as soon as circumstances permit, just as in Queen Pawn openings it is desirable to get *the King Pawn* to K4 when there is an opportunity to do so.

White again threatens to win the King Pawn by the double attack on it.

10. . . .   Q—B2

Black gives his Pawn further support and develops his Queen at the same time. It would not do to exchange by 10. . . . KP x P 11. P x P, P x P 12. Kt x P as it surrenders the center and leaves Black with an isolated center Pawn, and "An isolated Pawn," says Tartakover, "casts gloom over the entire chessboard." White would benefit too in that his Knight, standing firmly in the center of the board, could not be dislodged by unfriendly Pawns.

11. P—KR3

To prevent a pin which might embarrass the Knight and the piece it shields, the Queen. Both pieces are needed for the protection of the Queen Pawn and the maintenance of the Pawn formation in the center. An exchange of the Knight (after the pin), and the recapture by the Queen, removes at one stroke two supports of the Queen Pawn.

Is White violating principle in moving one of the Pawns near his King? Maybe, but one must know when to slight conventions as well as observe them. In this particular situation it is important to prevent an attack on the Knight, its exchange, and the break-up of White's Pawns in the center. The move of the Rook Pawn is weakening, but a lesser evil than would result from permitting the pin. But wait a moment! Is it a weakening move if Black is unable to benefit by it? Is it detrimental to the position if Black cannot exploit it by a King-side attack?

The answer is no! A move is weak only if the opponent can turn its imperfections to his advantage. The entire position is strong or weak *only in relation to the position of the opponent*. In this case, the move of the Rook Pawn is expedient as it conforms to the requirements of the particular position involved.

11. . . .   Kt—B3

The Knight returns and adds weight to the pressure on the Queen Pawn.

Black threatens a series of exchanges by 12. . . . KP x P 13. P x P, P x P 14. Kt x P, Kt x Kt 15. Q x Kt, Q x B, resulting in the gain of a Pawn. He hopes to tempt White into playing 12. P—Q5 to meet this threat. This looks good, as it would evict the Knight from a good post, but it has the drawback (for White) of releasing the tension in the center, as well as making Q5 unavailable for the use of his pieces.

12. B—K3

White is in no hurry. He brings aid to the Queen Pawn by developing another piece.

12. . . .   O—O

Removes the King to safer quar-

ters and impresses the Rook into active service.

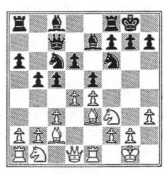

13. QKt—Q2

This Knight has been developed where he has little mobility and seems to have no future to speak of, but *it is the first step that counts*. Little as this is, its consequence is worth emphasizing:

The Knight's move clears the first rank and enables the major pieces (the Queen and the Rooks) to get in touch with each other.

Get your pieces off the back rank and into active play!

13. . . .   B—Q2

Black does likewise: his Bishop vacates the back row to let the Rooks come to the center files.

The Rooks are powerful pieces and must not be shut in.

14. R—QB1

In the early stages of the game, the Rooks may not do much but they must be ready for action when it comes. This they best do by placing themselves at the head of open files. If none are available, then they should work on partly open files. If none of those exist, the Rooks should still be brought toward the center, as those files are most likely to be opened. But in any case, *get the Rooks out of the corners!*

14. . . .   Kt—K1

Planning to advance the Bishop Pawn. This Pawn will dispute the center with White's King Pawn while opening the Bishop file for the Rook.

15. Kt—B1 !

The Knight retreats to gain momentum to leap to Kt3 and then KB5, a beautiful outpost.

15. . . .   P—Kt3

Not only to keep the Knight out but also to support 16. . . . P—B4, a thrust at the center.

The advance of the Knight Pawn weakens the squares KB3 and KR3, as they are no longer guarded by the Pawn. This may strike the average player as an interesting but perhaps insignificant point. But recognizing a weakness and knowing how to take advantage of it marks the master player. Good players do not win games by waiting for you to make monumental mistakes. They don't expect you to leave pieces *en prise.*

16. B—R6

White immediately anchors a piece on one of the vulnerable squares.

16. . . .   Kt—Kt2

The only move to prevent loss of the exchange by 17. B x R.

17. Kt—K3

The Knight comes back into the game by a slightly different route than was planned earlier. Not only does it add to the pressure on B5, but it also threatens to settle down powerfully on Q5.

17. . . .   QR—K1

Black could not stop the Knight coming in by 17. . . . B—K3 as 18. P—Q5 in reply wins a piece.

He abandons the contemplated break by 17. . . . P—B4, as it opens the position, and open lines favor the player whose development is superior and who is better equipped to use these lines to his advantage in an attack.

With his actual move, Black tries to keep a tightly knit defensive position, one that is difficult to break through.

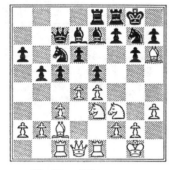

18. Kt—Q5 !

A very fine move whose object is more profound than the obvious one of fixing a piece on a strong central square.

18. . . .   Q—Kt2

The Queen must flee from the Knight's attack.

19. Kt x Bch !

This is the point! The Knight gives up his good position for a worthy cause. It is important, in order to capitalize on the weakness of the black square KB3, to remove the guardian of this square, the Bishop who travels on black squares. With this Bishop out of the way the weakness is accentuated and White can then consider some means of invading, and then fastening a piece on the critical square.

19. . . .   R x Kt

This is forced, as 19. . . . Kt x Kt 20. P x KP, P x P 21. Kt x P costs a Pawn.

20. P x BP

The purpose of this exchange is to open a nice long file for the Queen.

20. . . .   P x P

Black must recapture or lose a Pawn.

21. Q—Q6

Beautiful exploitation of the open Queen file! The attack on the Bishop Pawn gains a tempo toward the Queen's entry at KB6.

21. . . .   P—B5

Black must lose a move in saving this Pawn.

22. Q—B6 !

With this move, which incidentally threatens instant mate, White fastens another piece in the holes in Black's position occasioned by the advance of his King Knight Pawn. The play for a win is what the books call "a matter of technique," and the process of realizing on the advantage is an interesting one.

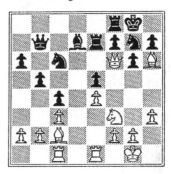

22. . . .   Kt—KR4

Stops the mate and attempts to drive the Queen away.

23. Q—R4

It would be a mistake to play 23. Q—Kt5, as Black instead of moving his threatened King Rook would first retort 23. . . . P—B3, banishing the Queen completely from his premises.

23. . . .   Kt—Kt2

The Knight blocks the Bishop's attack on the Rook and is prepared to refute 24. Q—B6 by 24. . . . Kt—KR4, repeating the device of menacing the Queen.

How does White continue, to force a win?

24. B—K3 !

By rearranging his pieces and bringing up the reserves!

This first move in the new formation gains time by the threat of 25. B—B5 winning the exchange.

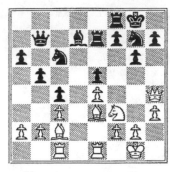

24. . . .   Kt—K3

The only way to prevent 25. B—B5, after which White completely dominates the black squares.

25. Q—B6

Once more into the breach! Black cannot save the game by repeating moves: if 25. . . . Kt—Kt2 26. B—B5, R—K3 (26. . . . Kt—KR4 27. Q—R4, and White wins the exchange) 27. Q—R4, KR—K1 28. Kt—Kt5, and the threat of mate will corral the Rook at K3.

25. . . .   Q—B2

Black must hang on to the valuable King Pawn.

26. B—R6

Once again White has his ideal position, with pieces firmly planted in the holes near the King. It will be hard for Black to chase them off as he does not have the earlier resource of . . . Kt—KR4.

26. . . .   R—B1

The Rook must flee the Bishop's attack. Interposing the Knight instead is of course a blunder as mate follows instantaneously.

27. QR—Q1

Before proceeding to the final attack, White gets a stronger grip on the position by seizing the open Queen file. The next step (since Black must wait helplessly) is 28. R—Q5, attacking the King Pawn a third time and threatening to double Rooks on the file. This ought to be enough to beat down resistance if no more quickly decisive means occurs to White.

Note that White has not embarked on dubious long-range combinations. His plan, in most cases aimed at increasing his positional superiority, is made *for a few moves only*. Don't believe all those stories you hear of chess masters analyzing intricate combinations with dozens of variations for thirty moves ahead. They don't do this because they don't have to! It is far easier and more to the point to look only a few moves ahead and try to maintain at least an equal game at every stage. It is more consistent with a common-sense approach to win by accumulating little advantages—to strengthen one's own position gradually while undermining that of the opponent—than to seek to overwhelm him with bewildering combinations and venturesome sacrificial attacks. It is more pertinent to apply order and method to our thinking than to indulge in fruitless speculative fancies.

27. . . .   R(K2)—K1

Black's idea is to reduce the pressure by offering an exchange of Queens. White will either have to accept, or withdraw his Queen.

28. Kt—R2 !

A very fine move! The Knight, which seemed well posted at KB3, is rerouted to augment the pressure on the black squares.

28. . . .   Q—Q1

Continuing the action to evict White's Queen from his camp.

29. Kt—Kt4 !

Supports the Queen and is ready in the event of an exchange of Queens to keep a tight grip on the black squares. If Black plays 29. . . . Q x Q, 30. Kt x Qch, K—R1 31. R x B wins a piece for White.

29. . . .   Q—K2

This does not help, but there is no way to save the game: if 29. . . . R—K2 30. B—K3 (threatens 31. Kt—R6ch, K—B1 32. Q—R8 mate), R—K1 31. Kt—R6ch, K—B1 32. Q x BP mate.

30. Q x Q

The simplest. If no mate is in sight, the modern master dispenses with the fireworks. Dawdling is for dilettantes, so he simplifies and cuts down any chance of resistance. After 30. . . . R x Q 31. Kt—B6ch, K—R1 32. R x B winning a piece, gives Black no opportunity to complicate the ending.

30. . . . Resigns

G A M E   N O.   1 0

FRENCH DEFENSE

WHITE	BLACK
Tarrasch	Eckart

NUREMBERG, 1889

1. P—K4

This opening move makes an outlet for two pieces, the Queen and King Bishop. It does more than that. It frees a square for the King and gives an extra one to the King Knight. It is true that the Knight is best developed at KB3, but there are times when it is expedient to bring it to K2—perhaps to reach KB5 by way of Kt3. It is just as well to add to the Knight's freedom of movement, if no time is lost thereby. As to the King, there's no harm in letting him have a bit more breathing space too. Many a King has been smothered by a lack of consideration, or by carelessness.

Consider this case history, from a minor tournament held at Dundee in 1893:

WHITE	BLACK
McGrouther	McCann
1. P—K4	P—QB4
2. Kt—KB3	Kt—QB3
3. P—Q4	P x P
4. Kt x P	P—K4
5. Kt—B5	KKt—K2
6. Kt—Q6 mate	

And if this seems farfetched, here is another specimen, which took place at Munich, again in a minor tournament:

WHITE	BLACK
Arnold	Boehm
1. P—K4	P—QB3
2. P—Q4	P—Q4
3. Kt—QB3	P x P
4. Kt x P	Kt—Q2
5. Q—K2	KKt—B3
6. Kt—Q6 mate	

1. . . .   P—K3

Though not so aggressive as 1. . . . P—K4, this move does release two pieces and has the advantage of restricting White's choice of attack. White cannot play some favorite opening to which he has devoted time and study, nor can he offer his Bishop Pawn to involve Black in a dangerous King's Gambit.

The French defense conceals a great deal of potential dynamic energy and is a fine weapon against an overenthusiastic attacking player. Black's position is not easily assaulted despite its cramped appearance.

2. P—Q4

As strong as it is natural. Of this Pawn formation, Staunton, more than a hundred years ago, said, "It is generally advantageous for your Pawns to occupy the middle of the board, because when there they greatly retard the movements of the opposing forces. The King Pawn and the Queen Pawn at their fourth squares are well posted, but it is not easy to maintain them in that position, and if you are driven to advance one of them, the power of both is much diminished."

2. . . .   P—Q4

Black attacks the King Pawn while giving his Queen more mobility.

It is important to dispute control of the center.

3. Kt—Q2

White has two reasons for developing the Knight at Q2:

He wants to avoid the Knight's being pinned, as might occur after 3. Kt—QB3.

He is prepared, in the event of an attack on his Queen Pawn by 3. . . . P—QB4, to reply 4. P—QB3, supporting the center. Should Pawns be exchanged, he recaptures with the Bishop Pawn and maintains a Pawn in the center.

It is true that his Queen's Bishop is blocked, but this condition is only temporary. *Pieces can get out of each other's way.*

3. . . .   Kt—KB3

Here is one of those rare cases where this natural move is out of place. We have been told that King Knights belong at B3, and so they do, *but only if they can stay there.* It is no earthly use to develop a piece to a good square, if it can immediately be dislodged from there.

Black's Knight move is routine, automatic, mechanical—and therefore thoughtless. A move to be good must conform with the requirements of the position on the board. Chess is not a matter of memorizing a set order of shifting the pieces about.

Black's proper procedure was to fight for control of the center by 3. . . . P—QB4, incidentally permitting his Queen the use of another diagonal and access to the Queen side.

4. P—K5

Why does White disregard Staunton's advice about keeping two Pawns on the fourth rank? He knows that the Pawn may be weaker at K5, but he weighs strengths and weaknesses. At K5 the Pawn drives the Knight away from its most useful post and sends it off to another square where it interferes with the free movements of the other pieces.

Clearly, the value of this or any other move is arrived at by estimating the benefits it confers against any disadvantages that might accrue.

4. . . .   KKt—Q2

Just about the only move left. On 4. . . . Kt—K5, 5. B—Q3 in reply threatens to capture, and win a Pawn. Black would have the sorry choice between 5. . . . Kt x Kt 6. B x Kt, leaving two pieces in play for White against none for Black, or 5. . . . P—KB4 6. Q—R5ch, P—Kt3, and Black, with so many of his Pawns fixed on white squares, is riddled with organic, permanent weaknesses on the black squares.

5. B—Q3

White gets his King-side pieces rolling to facilitate early castling on that side.

5. . . .   P—QB4

Very good, as Black must not delay in trying to free his constricted position. The Pawn move strikes at the center and opens another path for Black's Queen.

6. P—QB3

Ready to reply to 6. . . . P x P with 7. P x P, and preserve the Pawn chain which so cramps the enemy.

6. . . .   Kt—QB3

The Knight develops with tempo, as the Queen Pawn is now twice attacked.

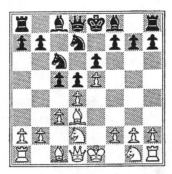

7. KKt—K2 !

One of those rare times when the Knight belongs here instead of at KB3. It is true that KB3 should be occupied by a Knight, and White will arrange to have one there. His plan is to swing the Queen Knight to KB3, meanwhile freeing his Queen Bishop.

7. . . .   Q—Kt3

Black puts more pressure on the Queen Pawn, threatening to win it by 8. . . . P x P 9. P x P, Kt x QP 10. Kt x Kt, Q x Kt.

8. Kt—B3 !

A clever Knight shift protects the Pawn and clears the decks for the Queen Bishop's appearance.

Some astute reader will be sure to discover that Black's play to this point, including 3. . . . Kt—KB3, which I inveighed against, was adopted by no less a player than Capablanca in his game with Alekhine at Avro in 1938. Aside from the circumstance that Capablanca, as a consequence of inferior opening play, was tied up so badly that he could not stir and that he resigned with nearly all his pieces still on the board, it is not wise for the average player to experiment with moves whose ill effects the greatest masters seldom overcome.

8. . . .   B—K2

Another plausible move, but far too passive. For good or ill, he should try to destroy the Pawn chain which hems his pieces in, by 8. . . . P—B3 or by 8. . . . P x P 9. P x P, B—Kt5ch.

The latter procedure would have Nimzovich's sanction, as he says, "Freeing operations in the region of a Pawn chain can never be set on foot soon enough," and recommends an attack on the base of the chain as a strategical necessity.

9. O—O

The King must be spirited off to a safer spot before any violent action is undertaken.

9. . . .   O—O

Black is still playing mechanical chess, unconscious of possible danger. With this move he misses the last chance of striking at the Pawn chain by 9. . . . P—B3.

10. Kt—B4 !

Definitely putting an end to any possibility of disturbing the line-up of Pawns, as 10. . . . P—B3 is refuted by 11. Kt x KP, while 10. . . . P x P 11. P x P, Kt x QP 12. Kt x Kt,

Q x Kt 13. B x Pch, uncovering an attack on the Queen, is unthinkable.

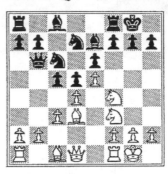

10. . . .   Kt—Q1

Black recognizes at last that his pieces remain impotent until he rids the board of White's annoying King Pawn. He therefore protects his own King Pawn so that he can enforce 11. . . . P—B3 and break up the Pawn formation.

11. Q—B2

Obviously a threat on Black's King Rook Pawn. The profound purpose of the move is to compel one of the Pawns near the King to move forward.

The advance of any Pawn around the King loosens the defensive structure and results in a permanent weakening which can be exploited, while the Pawn that made the forward step itself often becomes a target for direct attack.

11. . . .   P—B4

What choice is there? If Black plays 11. . . . P—KR3 or 11. . . . P—Kt3, he can never afterward move . . . P—B3 without making the square KKt3 vulnerable to invasion by White's pieces or the focal point of a sacrificial attack that would demolish his King side.

12. P x P e.p.

This relaxes the bind on Black, but it opens up lines for an attack. Open lines favor the player whose development is superior and whose pieces enjoy greater mobility.

12. . . .   Kt x P

Not only to get the Knight back into the game but also to defend his Rook Pawn, which again was threatened.

13. Kt—Kt5

Once more menacing the Pawn, this time including a threat of 14. B x Pch, K—R1 (or 14. . . . Kt x B 15. Q x Kt mate) 15. Kt—Kt6 checkmate.

13. . . .   P—Kt3

Forced, as 13. . . . P—KR3 saves the Pawn but allows the mate.

With the advance of the Knight Pawn, a target comes into view at which White can direct an attack. He can visualize a decisive blow, one which will wreck Black's entire defensive structure!

14. B x P !

A sacrifice which must be accepted, as otherwise Black is a Pawn down with nothing to show for it but a shattered position. If he tries 14. . . . P—R3, then 15. B—R7ch, K—Kt2 (or 15. . . . K—B2 16. Q—Kt6 mate) 16. Q—Kt6ch, K—R1 17. Q x P, and the threat of mate by the Knight as well as the menace of discovered check is too much to withstand.

14. . . .   P x B

One lone Pawn remains of the three which surrounded the King, and that one is not long for this world.

15. Q x Pch

With this dramatic entrance on the scene, the Queen, attended by her two Knights, will quickly force submission.

15. . . .   K—R1

The only move.

16. Q—R6ch

Clearing the square Kt6 for the Knight.

16. . . .   K—Kt1

Interposing the Knight instead allows mate on the move.

17. Kt—Kt6

And the threats of mate by 18. Q—R8 or 18. Kt x B cannot both be parried.

QUEEN'S PAWN GAME

(*Colle System*)

WHITE	BLACK
Flohr	Pitschak

BILIN, 1930

1. P—Q4

In chess you cannot win by serving an ace. There is no trick move in the opening that will catch even a fair-to-middling player off-balance.

What you can do is apply order and method in your conduct of this phase, so as to get a favorable if not a superior position. All you need do is follow a few simple rules for sound development:

Begin with 1. P—K4 or 1. P—Q4, either of which moves releases two pieces.

Anchor at least one Pawn in the center and give it solid support. Pawns in the center keep enemy pieces from settling themselves on the best squares.

Wherever feasible, bring out your Knights before the Bishops. Broadly speaking, the Knights do their best work at KB3 and QB3, where their power is tremendous for defense as well as offense.

Of two developing moves, select the more aggressive one. Develop with a threat if you can.

Move each piece only once in the opening. Place it at once on a square where it has some bearing on the center and where it has the greatest scope for attack.

Move only one Pawn or two in the early stages of the game. *Play with the pieces.*

Develop the pieces with a view to controlling the center, either by occupying it or bearing down on it from a distance, as fianchettoed Bishops do.

Develop the Queen, but close to home to avoid her being harassed by Pawns and minor pieces.

Do not chase after Pawns at the expense of development.

Secure the safety of the King by early castling, preferably on the King side.

Capablanca summed it up when he said, "The main thing is to develop the pieces quickly: get them into play as fast as you can."

Now back to Flohr and Pitschak: White's first move fixes a Pawn in the center and liberates two pieces.

1. . . . Kt—KB3

Black brings his King Knight out to its most favorable post and hinders White from continuing with 2. P—K4.

2. Kt—KB3

Napier recalls that in the first of several lessons he took from Steinitz, The World Champion said, "No doubt you move your Knight out on each side before the Bishop? And do you know why?" Napier says he was stuck for an intelligent answer. Steinitz went on to explain: "One good reason is that you know where the Knight belongs before you know that much of your Bishop; certainty is a far better friend than doubt."

2. . . . P—K3

Black postpones the straightforward reply 2. . . . P—Q4, which lets him in for the regular lines of the Queen's Gambit. Meanwhile he opens a line for the King Bishop.

3. QKt—Q2

A typical Knight maneuver in the Colle attack: the Knight puts pressure on the critical square K4 without blocking the Bishop file.

3. . . . P—B4

Black strikes a blow at the Queen Pawn in an attempt to secure control of the center. This flank thrust is almost compulsory in Queen Pawn openings as Black must try to disturb White's center formation.

The immediate threat is 4. . . . P x P, so that the recapture by 5. Kt x P leaves no White Pawn in the center.

4. P—K3

Shores up the Queen Pawn and provides an outlet for the King Bishop.

4. . . . P—QKt3

Black too props up his advanced Pawn and prepares to fianchetto the Queen Bishop.

5. B—Q3

Customary practice in this system of attack: the Bishop adds his strength to the pressure exerted on K4 in preparation for an advance by the King Pawn, which will open up lines of attack for the pieces in the background. The Bishop also aims at Black's King Rook Pawn, a fine

target after the King castles on that side.

5. . . . B—Kt2

This solves one of Black's chief problems in Queen Pawn openings — an effective disposition of the Queen's Bishop. By means of this fianchetto arrangement the Bishop commands the longest diagonal on the board and participates in the fight for domination of White's K4, the strategic square in the Colle system of attack.

6. O—O

As part of the process of development, White shields his King from danger and brings his Rook closer to the center files.

6. . . . B—K2

Despite its modest appearance, there is a great deal of latent energy in the placement of this Bishop at K2. It is close enough to home to help defend the King, yet easily maneuverable to a more aggressive post if occasion requires.

7. P—B4

More in the spirit of the Colle formation is the quiet 7. P—B3, to supply a support for the Queen Pawn. The King Pawn is then free to advance, and if Black at any time plays . . . P x P, White recaptures with the Bishop Pawn and maintains a strong Pawn in the center.

The idea of the text move apparently is to prevent Black's pieces from using his Q4 square as a pivot for their movements about the board.

7. . . .   O—O

Black goes quietly about the business of mustering out all the troops. At one stroke his Rook appears on the scene while the King is whisked away.

8. P—QKt3

Clearly in order to develop the Bishop at Kt2. This fianchettoing of the Bishop is not conventional procedure in the Colle, but Flohr may have wanted to test some ideas of his own.

8. . . .   P—Q4

Black seizes the opportunity to dispute possession of the center. He also puts an end to White's contemplated advance of the King Pawn, as he bears down on the critical square (White's K4) with Knight, Pawn and Bishop, while White has only two pieces trained on it.

It is true that the Queen Bishop's diagonal is blocked, but this condition is only temporary.

9. Q—B2

Considerably better was the simple development of the Queen Bishop at Kt2, for which he prepared with his previous move.

The purpose of 9. Q—B2 is to secure control of K4 and to prevent Black from establishing an outpost on that square by 9. . . . Kt—K5. The trouble with the move is that it permits Black to seize the initiative and thereafter direct the course of events.

9. . . .   Kt—B3 !

A powerful move which combines development, aggressive intent and prophylaxis!

Development, in that the Knight is placed at once on its most suitable square.

Aggression, in the Knight's threat to swing over to Kt5, attack Queen and Bishop and force an exchange which rids the board of the dangerous King Bishop.

Prophylaxis, in the prevention of 10. P—K4, the continuation after which would be 10. . . . Kt—QKt5 11. Q—B3, Kt x B 12. Q x Kt, P x KP, and Black wins a piece.

10. P—QR3

White must preserve his valuable King Bishop.

Unfortunately, the time lost in being forced to make a Pawn move is costly, as we shall see.

10. . . .   P x QP

Black exchanges to clarify the position in the center and to open the Bishop file for the convenience of his Queen Rook.

11. BP x P

The alternative capture by 11. KP x P was not pleasant as the reply

11. ... P x P forces 12. Q x P (otherwise White's Queen Pawn is lost) when 12. ... R—QB1 exercises uncomfortable pressure on White's center. Another possibility instead of the text move is 11. Kt x P, Kt x Kt 12. P x Kt, P x P 13. Q x P (to save the Queen Pawn), R—B1 14. Q—R4, B—B3 15. Q x P (or 15. Q—B4, B x KtP and Black wins easily), R—R1, and Black wins the Queen.

11. ...   Q x P

Black nets a Pawn with this and (as if it were not enough) takes over the attack.

The Queen is in no danger, as White's pieces are not well enough developed to cause her any annoyance.

12. P x P

White opens the position to get some counterplay. He hopes to utilize the King file for his Rook and the square K4 as a pivot for his pieces.

The attractive 12. P—K4, instead, does not accomplish much, as after 12. ... Q—KR4 the vital square K4 is occupied by a Pawn, making it unavailable for the maneuvering of pieces, while Black benefits in having a passed Pawn on the Queen file.

12. ...   Kt x P

An attack on the Queen which gains time as White must lose a move with his Queen.

13. Q—Kt1

Obviously 13. Kt x Kt would not do, as Black's Queen pounces down with instantaneous mate, while 13. Q—Kt2, Kt x Ktch 14. Kt x Kt, Q x B costs a piece. On 13. Q—B3, Black plays 13. ... KR—Q1 followed by 14. ... QR—B1, and again the Queen must flee.

White's actual move is probably the least of the evils.

13. ...   KR—Q1

Intensifying the pressure on the Queen file, particularly on the Bishop, whose life is threatened by 14. ... Kt x Ktch 15. Kt x Kt, Q x B 16. Q x Q, R x Q.

14. Kt—K1

White protects his Bishop as well as the vulnerable King Knight Pawn.

Against 14. B—B2, Black can choose from these themes:

Simplification (being a Pawn ahead), by 14. ... Kt x B.

Augmenting of pressure, by 14. ... QR—B1, banishing the Bishop to the first rank.

Combination, by 14. ... Kt—K7ch 15. K—R1, B—R3 (threatening to win the exchange by 16. ... Kt—B6) 16. R—K1, Kt—Kt5 17. Kt—K4, Q x Kt ! 18. B x Q, Kt x BP mate.

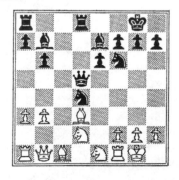

14. . . .   Q—KR4 !

There is no visible menace in this Queen move. Black threatens to threaten! He intends to storm White's citadel of Pawns with his Queen supported by a minor piece, say by 15. . . . B—Q3 or 15. . . . Kt—Kt5. This would compel one of the Pawns to leave its base and create weaknesses which Black could exploit. The advanced Pawn itself might be susceptible to attack, or avenues might be opened leading to the King.

This chipping away at the foundation is an interesting process for rendering an apparently strongly fortified position vulnerable to assault.

15. B—Kt2

White has no dependable defense (especially against nebulous threats) so continues to develop his pieces. The more he has in play, the better his chances of surviving the coming storm.

15. . . .   B—Q3

With a simple but unmistakable threat: mate on the move!

How does White defend?

If 16. Kt(K1)—B3, Kt x Ktch 17. Kt x Kt, B x Kt 18. P x B, Q x RP mate.

If 16. P—B4, B—B4 (threatening 17. . . . Kt—K7 dble. ch 18. K—R1, Kt—Kt6 mate) 17. K—R1, Kt—Kt5 18. P—KR3, Q x Pch, and mate next move.

If 16. P—R3, Q—K4 (again aiming at the R7 mate) 17. P—Kt3, Q—Q4 (now trying for 18. . . .

Q—R8 mate) 18. P—B3, Q—KKt4, and White's game falls to pieces.

16. P—Kt3

By a process of elimination, the only defense, if one still exists.

16. . . .   Kt—Kt5

White's Knight Pawn has had to step forward. Now the threat of 17. . . . Q x P mate forces the Rook Pawn's advance.

17. P—KR4

White has no other move than this, which keeps the Queen out—or does it?

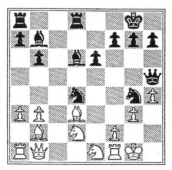

17. . . .   Q x P !

This is brilliant! Not because of the fact that the Queen is offered, but because it makes an appropriate climax to the systematic exploitation of Pawn weaknesses cleverly brought into being.

Black adds the threat of mate at R8 to the one he had of mating at R7.

18. Resigns

White does not care to take the Queen as the reply 18. . . . B—R7 mate would come quick as a flash.

ENGLISH OPENING

WHITE	BLACK
Pitschak	Flohr

LIEBWERDA, 1934

1. P—QB4

Despite the fact that only one piece is freed by this move, against two that are released by 1. P—K4 or 1 P—Q4, the English is one of the strongest opening weapons in White's arsenal. It appeals to those who like originality right from the start, as it allows maneuvering about of the pieces without coming to grips too early with the enemy. In many forms of this debut, White does not even try to occupy the center. He lets Black mass pieces and Pawns there, and then attacks them from the sides. He might fianchetto his Bishops, for example, and strike at the center from a distance, in order to undermine it.

Should White decide to temper his originality with caution, he can transpose from the English to some form of Queen's Pawn opening and still retain a fine game.

1. . . . P—K4

Black develops in the good old-fashioned way: he plants a Pawn in the center and frees two pieces for action.

2. Kt—QB3

White brings a piece out in preference to advancing a center Pawn. In fact, on 2. P—Q4, P x P 3. Q x P, Kt—QB3, the Queen must retreat and lose a move. Or if 2. P—K4, he remains with a backward Queen's Pawn, while the King Bishop cannot get to QB4.

2. . . . Kt—KB3

Black watches the order of his moves. The Knight's move is not merely routine development of a piece. Its purpose is to offset the pressure of White's Knight and Pawn on his (White's) Q5 square.

3. P—KKt3

Clearly with the intention of making room for the Bishop at Kt2, where it will operate on a long diagonal and also contribute to the pressure on Q5.

3. . . . P—Q4 !

Black frees his game by opening new paths for the Queen-side pieces. Simultaneously with this, he puts the question to White's Bishop Pawn.

4. P x P

White is happy to exchange a flank Pawn for a center Pawn. At the same time, his Queen Bishop file, now clear of Pawns, offers good prospects for his Queen Rook when it gets to QB1.

4. . . . Kt x P

Such recaptures are practically compulsory. A delay might give White time to protect and hold on to the extra Pawn.

5. B—Kt2

Develops a piece with gain of tempo—an attack on the Knight.

In the old days, Black would probably meet this by 5. . . . B—K3, protecting the Knight while developing another piece. Today's players regard with suspicion even the most natural moves, in their search for truth (and new ways to win).

5. . . .   Kt—Kt3 !

The Bishop can wait! It may be needed for more than a mere supporting role.

Too, from his odd vantage point, the Knight exerts a great deal of influence on the central square Q4. There is another bit of subtlety in the Knight's move, one that the modern master frequently utilizes. The Knight takes advantage of the Bishop's fianchetto development and bears down heavily on QB5, *a square weakened by the Bishop's absence.*

It will not be giving away the plot to tell you that the Knight, as it later turns out, is beautifully poised to deliver the knockout blow!

6. Kt—B3

Again one of White's pieces develops with a threat—this time against the King Pawn.

6. . . .   Kt—B3

Black defends in the simplest, most natural way by posting the Queen Knight on its most effective station.

Despite the fact that Black has less pieces in play than White, his game is not inferior. He does have a Pawn in the center, and his Bishops, undeveloped as yet, have great potentialities, as their cruising range is more extensive than White's.

7. O—O

White does not commit himself, but spirits away the King and mobilizes one of his Rooks.

7. . . .   B—K2

As in the previous game, the Bishop's unobtrusive position at K2 is deceptive: it is prepared to keep out invaders and is on the alert as well to switch to the attack.

8. P—Q3

Makes room for the Queen Bishop to take a hand in the game.

8. . . .   O—O

Removes the King from the danger area and gets the Rook up on deck.

9. B—K3

With the Bishop at this square, White may be able to get in 10. P—Q4 and rid himself of Black's cramping center Pawn.

9. . . .   B—KKt5 !

An excellent deployment, as the Bishop has a powerful restraining effect on White's King side, as well as on the contemplated advance of his Queen's Pawn.

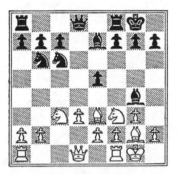

If White does try 10. P—Q4, the response 10. . . . Kt—B5 is hard to meet. If White replies by 11. Kt x P, then after 11. . . . Kt(B3) x Kt 12. P x Kt, Kt x B 13. P x Kt, he is left with a rickety column of Pawns on the King file. Or if White plays 11. Q—B1 (to save his Knight Pawn and to recapture at K3 with the Queen) then 11. . . . Kt x B 12. Q x Kt, P x P 13. Q—K4, B x Kt, followed by 14. . . . P x Kt wins a piece for Black.

White's best line is probably 10. Kt—QR4, in order to swing the Knight over to QB5, a square which White must try to control in Queen Pawn and allied openings. Or he might continue developing by 10. R—B1 and then consider the Knight maneuver.

10. P—KR3

A move which is impelled by a desire to make the annoying Bishop declare his intentions—either take the Knight or vacate the premises! Unfortunately, moves such as this, dictated more by instinct than reason, have an injurious effect on the castled position, as the structure is loosened. Once the Pawns near the King make a move, they themselves become more susceptible to attack, in spite of the cluster of pieces ranged around them for protection.

10. . . .   B—R4

The Bishop retreats one square but maintains the pressure. Despite the Bishop's restricted mobility, its continued bearing down is more troublesome to White's position (and his frame of mind) than would be its return to K3, where it enjoys more freedom but does nothing to disturb the opponent.

11. R—B1

Evidently in order to control the Bishop file and perhaps work up an attack on the Queen side.

A good alternative is 11. Q—Kt3, followed when feasible by QR—Q1 and P—Q4, to open the Queen file for his Rooks and get some counterplay in the center. *Action in the center is the best specific against a Kingside attack.*

11. . . .   Q—Q2

All the pieces must do their bit! The Queen moves only one step forward and dominates a long diagonal!

Development of the Queen serves another purpose in that the first rank is cleared for the Rooks. They can now switch over toward the center and get control of the most important files.

12. Kt—QR4

White's idea is to create a diversion by taking command of QB5 with his Knight and keep Black occupied with threats on the Queen side.

Against routine defensive moves, say 12. K—R2, Black gets an attack rolling by 12. . . . P—B4 and 13. . . . P—B5, and the Pawn will demolish White's King-side Pawn formation.

12. . . .   B x Kt

Presenting White with an unhappy choice of recapture: if he takes with the Pawn, his Queen Pawn becomes isolated and weak; if he takes with the Bishop, he loses a Pawn immediately.

13. B x B

White gives up the Rook Pawn, trusting that he will regain a Pawn quickly by his next exchange of pieces.

13. . . .   Q x RP

After this capture, Black's attacking prospects are very bright. Without bothering to analyze the petty details, he can visualize winning lines of play beginning with 14. . . . P—B4 followed either by 15. . . . P—B5, to destroy White's Knight Pawn (the key to the defensive structure), or by 15. . . . R—B3, and then swinging the Rook over to KKt3 or KR3.

14. B(B3) x Kt

Better than this, which regains the Pawn, is 14. B—Kt2, banishing the Queen from the neighborhood of his King.

14. . . .   P x B

Forced, but an agreeable obligation. Black is quite pleased to see the last of this long-range Bishop.

15. R x P

Material is now equal, but White's King is in danger, with the enemy Queen breathing on his neck.

15. . . .   Kt—Q4 !

A tremendous move! One threat of this beautifully centralized Knight is 16. . . . Kt x B 17. P x Kt, Q x Pch 18. K—R1, Q—R6ch 19. K—Kt1, B—Kt4, and White's game is in ruins, while another threat is 16. . . . Kt—B3, followed by 17. . . . Kt—Kt5 and 18. . . . Q—R7 mate.

16. Q—K1

An awkward move that is absolutely necessary to save the Knight Pawn from 16. . . . Kt x B 17. P x Kt, Q x Pch. Should this Pawn fall, his King could not withstand the attack.

White may have intended to play 16. B—B5, whereupon after 16. . . . Kt—B3 he might have put up a fight with 17. R x Kt, B x R 18. B x R, but at the last moment saw this refutation: 16. B—B5, B x B

17. Kt x B, Kt—B3, and in order to stop 18. . . . Kt—Kt5 and 19. . . . Q—R7 mate, he must give up his Rook for the Knight, a course which means eventual loss.

16. . . .   P—B4 !

Not at once 16. . . . Kt—B3 as 17. P—B3 keeps the Knight out (note how essential it is to have the Knight's Pawn protected).

With his last move Black prepares to play 17. . . . P—B5. If then 18. P x P, R x P 19. B x R, Kt x B, and Black mates at Kt7. If White does not take the Pawn but plays 18. B—B5, Black wins cleverly by 18. . . . P—B6 (threatening 19. . . . Q—Kt7 mate) 19. P x P, Kt—B5 (again aiming at the mate) 20. P x Kt, R—B4, and White cannot stop 21. . . . R—R4, followed by mate.

17. B—B5

With a faint chance of holding out after 17. . . . B x B 18. Kt x B, Kt—B3 19. P—B3, or if 17. . . . Kt—B3 by 18. R x Kt.

If White tries to rid himself of Black's troublesome Knight by 17. Kt—B3, Black pursues the attack by 17. . . . Kt—B3 18. P—B3, Kt—R4 (concentrating on the vital Knight Pawn) 19. B—B2, B—R5 (still hammering at the Pawn) 20. P x B, Kt—B5, and forces mate at Kt7.

17. . . .   P—B5 !

Not only to strike at the Knight Pawn but to clear a path for the Rook's passage to B4 and R4 to assist the Queen in a mating operation.

18. B x B

White exchanges to reduce the number of pieces besetting his King. He hopes for the simple recapture by 18. . . . Kt x B, and the Knight, no longer centralized, is less of a menace.

If instead 18. P—KKt4 to keep the Rook out, Black has three or four easy wins on tap:

a) 18. . . . P—B6 19. P x P, Kt—B5, followed by mate at Kt7.

b) 18. . . . Q x Pch 19. K—R2, R—B4, and mate by the Rook.

c) 18. . . . Q x Pch 19. K—R2, P—B6 20. R—Kt1, Q—R5 mate.

18. . . .   P x P

With a simple, brutal threat of 19. . . . Q—R7 mate.

19. P x P

The only reply.

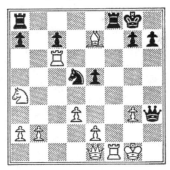

19. . . .   Kt—K6 !

Threatens   20. . . . Q—Kt7 mate.

20. Resigns

There is no defense: if 20. R—B2, Q x Pch 21. K—R1, R x R wins easily, or if 20. R x Rch, R x R 21.

Q—B2, R x Q 22. K x R, Q—Kt7ch
23. K x Kt, Q x R, and the rest is elementary.

Flohr avenges his loss to Pitschak in the previous game by adopting the technique with which he was defeated. He weakens the Pawns around the castled King and then rips up the defenses with a devastating attack.

GAME NO. 13

FRENCH DEFENSE

WHITE	BLACK
Dobias	Podgorny

PRAGUE, 1952

1. P—K4

This is one of the best ways to begin what is a race and a struggle: a race to get the pieces out rapidly and onto squares where they can operate most efficiently; a struggle to gain control of the center.

At one stroke the King Pawn takes up an important square in the center and attacks two others, while the Queen and Bishop control nine more squares.

1. . . .　　P—K3

A quietly aggressive move which prepares to dispute White's center by 2. . . . P—Q4.

This defense has the merit of avoiding the many strong openings White can play after the customary 1. . . . P—K4 reply.

2. P—Q4

Of a similar move, Philidor in his *Chess Analyzed* (1791) says, "This

Pawn is played two Moves for two very important Reafons: the firft is, to hinder your Adverfary's King's Bifhop to play upon your King's Bifhop's Pawn; and the fecond, to put the Strength of your Pawns in the Middle of the Exchequer, which is of great Confequence to attain the making of a Queen."

We may ftill follow the advice if not the fpelling.

2. . . .　　P—Q4

An attack on the King Pawn which immediately challenges the center.

3. Kt—QB3

Of the various courses open to White (advancing the King Pawn, exchanging Pawns, sacrificing his center Pawn or protecting it) he takes that which enables him to develop a piece and maintain the pressure.

3. . . .　　P x P

Temporarily allowing White greater freedom of action, but Black hopes to play . . . P—QB4 later and destroy the troublesome Queen Pawn.

4. Kt x P

The recapture leaves White with a slight edge in his centralized Knight and Pawn position.

4. . . .　　QKt—Q2

Preparing a support for the King Knight's development at KB3. If White then exchanges Knights, he can recapture with the Queen Knight.

If he played instead 4. . . . Kt—KB3, then comes 5. Kt x Ktch, and Black must either break up his King-side Pawns by 5. . . . P x Kt or capture with the Queen and risk its being bothered by the minor pieces. A sample of what could happen (after 4. . . . Kt—KB3 5. Kt x Ktch, Q x Kt) is this little trap: 6. Kt—B3, B—Q2 (to seize the center diagonal) 7. B—Q3, B—B3, 8. B—KKt5, B x Kt 9. Q—Q2 !, Q x P 10. B—Kt5ch, and White wins the Queen.

5. Kt—KB3

The best possible way to put the King Knight to work—by developing it at KB3 where it has enormous influence on the center, and where it stands peerless in defense of the castled King.

5. . . .   B—K2

A noncommittal developing move (it does bring a piece off the back rank and helps the King castle quickly) but not so good as the conventional 5. . . . KKt—B3.

If Black tries instead the fianchetto formation for his Queen Bishop (tempting in view of White's exposed Knight), there is a pretty trap he can stumble into: 5. . . . P—QKt3 6. B—QKt5, B—Kt2 7. Kt—K5 !, B x Kt (or 7. . . . B—B1 8. B—Kt5, KKt—B3 9. Kt—B6, winning the Queen) 8. B x Ktch, K—K2 9. B—B6 !, and Black must lose some material.

6. B—Q3

This is probably sharper than 6. B—QB4, but either move places the Bishop in a good spot and clears the first rank for King-side castling.

6. . . .   KKt—B3

Black too prepares to get his King into safety by developing (at long last) his King Knight.

7. Q—K2

White develops a piece and supports his central Knight strongly with Queen and Bishop.

This is more restraining on Black's cramped position than 7. Kt x Ktch, B x Kt, when Black can initiate an attack on White's center with . . . P—B4.

7. . . .   O—O

The King seeks security in the corner. There was no easy, freeing maneuver in 7. . . . Kt x Kt 8. B x Kt, Kt—B3 as 9. B x KtP, B x B 10. Q—Kt5ch, followed by 11. Q x B wins a Pawn for White.

8. O—O

While the castling of this King is less to escape danger than to let the King Rook take an active part in the game.

White's position is so promising as to offer him a good attacking line in 8. B—KKt5, Kt x Kt 9. Q x Kt, P—KKt3 (certainly not 9. . . . Kt—B3 to prevent mate, as 10. B x Kt wins on the spot) 10. P—KR4, and White can castle on the Queen side and storm the enemy bastions with his King-side Pawns.

8. . . .   Kt x Kt

Black exchanges to get some elbowroom.

9. Q x Kt !

Takes command of the board with a threat of mate! Offhand it looks risky to make this capture and leave the Queen exposed to harassment by the minor pieces, but Black is in no position (in either sense of the word) to make trouble. He has all he can do to stay alive!

9. . . .   Kt—B3

Naturally, Black does not wish to advance one of the King-side Pawns, say 9. . . . P—KKt3, unless compelled to. But what's wrong with the move he plays, 9. . . . Kt—B3? Does it not bring the Knight to its best square, guard against mate, beat off the Queen, and free his own Queen side?

Indeed it does do all these things, and under the circumstances it is probably Black's best move. It is strange withal that a move made under duress does not have the tonic effect on one's game of a move made of one's own volition.

10. Q—R4

After this, Black's Knight, which to be sure stands on a good square,

must remain on that square to guard against mate.

10. . . .   P—QKt3

The Queen's Bishop, barred by Black's very first move from coming out to the King side, seeks other means to take part in the battle. Development at QKt2 looks attractive, as from there it commands the long central diagonal.

11. B—KKt5 !

Excellent strategy! White attacks the most important defensive piece, the Knight which guards against mate. The specific threat is 12. B x Kt, B x B 13. Q x P mate.

A simple threat and easy to meet. All Black has to do is move 11. . . . P—KKt3 or 11. . . . P—KR3. What then is White aiming at?

The hidden purpose is *to force Black to move one of the King-side Pawns*, to avoid being mated. A move of any of these Pawns creates a looseness in the defensive structure which can never be repaired. It weakens the position organically as it makes a breach which can never be closed. The Pawn that advances can never go back to its former position in the line of defensive Pawns.

11. . . .   **P—Kt3**

On the alternative *11. . . . P—KR3*, White can choose from two powerful continuations:

12. B x Kt, B x B 13. Q—K4, and the threat of mate wins the Queen Rook, an innocent bystander.

12. B x P, P x B 13. Q x P, B—Kt2 14. QR—K1 (threatening *15. R—K5* and *16. R—Kt5* mate), *B—Q3 15. R—K5!, B x R 16. P x B*, and wins: the Knight dare not move, and if it stays, there comes *17. P x Kt*, followed by checkmate.

12. P—B4

A very good move! To begin with, it prevents Black from playing *12. . . . Kt—Q4*, to remove by exchange White's attacking pieces. Offensively, it prepares an advance of the Queen Pawn, which will break up the Pawn structure at Black's K3. Once this is done, White's Rook will have a point of entry on the King file.

12. . . .   B—Kt2

Black has no effective counter-attack. The best he can do is keep on developing pieces on the most favorable squares to make a hard fight of it.

13. P—Q5

Threatening, after the preparatory *14. QR—Q1*, to take the King Pawn so that the recapture by *15. . . . P x P* deprives Black's King Knight Pawn of one of its props.

13. . . .   **P x P**

This seems to win a Pawn, as

should White recapture by *14. P x P* the reply *14. . . . Kt x P* not only holds on to the Pawn but compels an exchange of Bishops which takes the edge off White's attack.

14. KR—K1 !

An unexpected *Zwischenzug* (an in-between move) which threatens immediate victory by *15. R x B, Q x R 16. B x Kt, Q—Q3 17. Kt—Kt5, P—KR4 18. Q x P !, P x Q 19. B—R7 mate!*

14. . . .   P—KR3

Black offers a Pawn to deflect one of the pieces bearing down so heavily on his King Knight and Bishop.

There was no relief in *14. . . . K—Kt2*, further to defend the Knight, as White responds with the brutal *15. B—R6ch*, winning the exchange.

15. Q x P

But not *15. B x RP*, which permits *15. . . . Kt—K5*, driving off White's Queen.

White now plans *16. B x P, P x B 17. Q x Pch, K—R1 18. Kt—Q4* (threatening to win by *19. Kt—K6* or *19. Kt—B5* or *19. R—K3*, followed by 20. R—R3ch), Q—K1 19. Q—R6ch, K—Kt1 20. Kt—B5, R—B2 21. B x Kt, winning easily.

15. . . .   Kt—Kt5

White has a neat win against the defense by 15. . . . Kt—K5. He plays 16. B x B, Q x B 17. P x P (threatening to capture the pinned Knight next), B x P 18. B x Kt, B x B 19. R x B !, Q x R 20. Kt—Kt5, and Black must lose the Queen or be mated.

The text move is of course an attempt to chase the Queen away.

16. Q—R4

Supports the Bishop, attacks the Knight and threatens to win by 17. B x B. What else can one move do?

16. . . .   B x B

Returning the Knight to B3 leads to catastrophe, viz: 16. . . . Kt—B3 17. R x B, Q x R 18. B x Kt, and White attacks the Queen while threatening 19. Q—R8 mate.

17. Kt x B

Once again the theme song—mate at R7.

17. . . .   Kt—B3

And Black must dance to the tune, by bringing the Knight back to B3.

Here too Black posts the Knight on a good square, but not of his own free will.

18. Q—R6

This restricts Black more than would maneuvering the Rook over

to KR3 by way of K3. For example, if 18. R—K3, R—K1 19. R—R3, K—B1, and the King escapes immediate disaster.

After White's actual move, if Black tries 18. . . . R—K1 he falls into 19. B x P, R x Rch 20. R x R, P x B 21. Q x Pch, K—R1 22. Kt—B7 mate.

18. . . .   P—Q5

To prevent 19. R—K3, and to give the Bishop more play on the long diagonal.

How does White continue the attack? Can he bring up the reserves without losing too much time? Or can he weaken the defensive formation and make it vulnerable to immediate assault?

Is there a hint in the last question? Yes, indeed!

Black's chief defense lies in his Knight, which guards against the mate at R7, and the King Bishop Pawn supporting the all-important Knight. If White could strike at these two defenders—threaten them, remove them, get them out of the way somehow. . . .

There is a move, the kind that looks absurd at first glance!

Hint #2: A master player looks at every move he would *like* to make, *especially the impossible ones.*

19. R—K6 !!

Threatens to capture the Knight, and then mate with the Queen.

19. . . .   R—K1

Had   Black   played   19. . . .

P x R, this would have followed: 20.
Q x Pch, K—R1 21. Q—R6ch, K—
Kt1 22. B—R7ch, K—R1 23. B—B5
dis. ch, K—Kt1 24. B x Pch, R—B2
25. B x R mate.

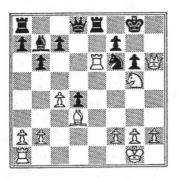

It is interesting to note how the
startling 19. R—K6 move not only
threatens to take the Knight but also
exploits the fact that the Bishop
Pawn dares not capture the Rook
and abandon the defense of the
Knight Pawn.

Black's last move is intended to
clear the square KB1 for the King, if
White should take the Knight and
then check at R7 with his Queen.

20. B x P

Breaks through the Pawn barrier!
White's threat is simple: 21. B x P
mate.

20. . . .   Resigns

If 20. . . . P x R 21. B—B7
mate.

If 20. . . . P x B 21. Q x Pch,
K—R1 22. Kt—B7 mate.

If 20. . . . Q—Q2 21. B—R7ch,
Kt x B (or 21. . . . K—R1 22. Q x
Kt mate) 22. Q x Ktch, K—B1 23.
Q—R8 mate.

FRENCH DEFENSE

WHITE   BLACK
Tarrasch   Mieses

BERLIN, 1916

1. P—K4

This is an excellent start toward
developing the pieces, since lines are
immediately opened for the Queen
and a Bishop. The King Pawn itself
helps in the battle for the center by
occupying a key square and attacking two others, Q5 and KB5.

1. . . .   P—K3

In spite of its modest appearance,
this move is more aggressive than
the straightforward 1. . . . P—K4.
Black's idea is to follow up with 2.
. . . P—Q4, attacking White's center. He is then prepared to reply to
3. P x P by recapturing with the
King Pawn, thus maintaining a
Pawn in the center.

2. P—Q4

Naturally! White planks down
another Pawn in the center, now
making K5 and QB5 forbidden territory for Black's pieces. Meanwhile,
his own Queen and Queen Bishop
have more freedom of movement.

2. . . .   P—Q4

Puts the question to the King
Pawn!

White has a choice of various replies:

a) 3. P x P, in order to simplify.

b) 3. P—K5, to cramp Black
with the Pawn chain.

c) 3. Kt—QB3 (or 3. Kt—Q2 or 3. B—Q3), to protect the Pawn and develop a piece at the same time.

The first method was favored by Morphy, who liked open positions that gave his pieces wide scope for attack. Nowadays, it is rarely adopted, as after the exchange of Pawns, the positions are equal and symmetrical and an attack is difficult to whip up, unless you are a Morphy.

The cramping move 3. P—K5 has a great many advocates, but the argument against this system is that White's Pawn chain is rigid and susceptible to undermining tactics. Black initiates a strong counterattack on the base of the Pawn chain by 3. . . . P—QB4, followed by . . . Kt—QB3 and . . . Q—Kt3, and White finds himself defending a center no longer flexible.

There remains the third way, which is simple and consistent with common sense in chess—to support the King Pawn and bring a piece out on the scene.

3. Kt—QB3

Typically Tarrasch: he selects the method which furthers his development and maintains tension in the center. He therefore brings a Knight out, protects the King Pawn and increases the pressure on Q5.

3. . . .   P x P

Tarrasch disapproves of this exchange of Pawns, as Black surrenders the center without any compensation. If results are a criterion for the merit of an opinion, his was sustained in this match. Mieses played

3. . . . P x P seven times with Black, with the consequence that two games were drawn and five were won by Tarrasch.

4. Kt x P

Now White has a beautifully centralized Knight, pressure on K5 and QB5, and a superior Pawn position (a Pawn at Q4 to one at K3) which assures him greater freedom of action.

4. . . .   Kt—Q2

Intending to support the King Knight when it reaches KB3. If Black plays 4. . . . Kt—KB3 at once, White can inflict a troublesome pin by 5. B—KKt5, or exchange Knights at once. Black's recapture either brings his Queen too early into the game, or if 5. . . . P x Kt, allows his King side to be broken up.

5. Kt—KB3

This is where the King Knight is most useful, so why not place it there at once?

Even the greatest masters do not play startling, bizarre or "brilliant" moves in the opening in an effort to be different, or to impress others with their ability to find extraordinary moves in commonplace positions. They are content to develop the pieces quickly, placing them on squares where they will operate to greatest effect and then wait for Nature to take its course. When the time is ripe for combination play, the odds are it will turn in favor of the fellow whose development is superior.

5. . . .   KKt—B3

A sound developing move. Not only does the King Knight stand on the square most suitable for its powers, but it challenges the sovereignty of White's Knight and disputes its hold on the center.

6. B—Q3

Rather than retreat, White supports the Knight by developing another piece. In the event of an exchange, White remains with a piece in the center.

6. . . .   B—K2

The Bishop is well placed at K2, and the decks are cleared for early King-side castling.

An interesting alternative is 6. . . . Kt x Kt 7. B x Kt, Kt—B3 8. B—Q3, and the time lost by the Bishop's retreat compensates Black for the tempo he lost when he played 3. . . . P x P.

7. O—O

The King hides behind a Pawn barricade while the Rook moves in toward the half-open King file.

7. . . .   Kt x Kt

Black exchanges to free his crowded position and let the Queenside pieces get some air.

8. B x Kt

The recapture gives White a monopoly on the important squares and faces Black with the problem of attaining equality.

8. . . .   Kt—B3

This is always a fine square for the Knight, and in this case the Knight gets there with a gain of time by its attack on the unprotected Bishop.

9. B—Q3

This mobile Bishop is too valuable for White to allow its exchange. Any such transaction benefits Black as a reduction in the number of pieces on the board eases the pressure on him.

9. . . .   P—QKt3

Understandably, Black wants his Queen Bishop on the job and intends developing it at Kt2. There is danger though in attempting this before the King has castled. Not only is there the risk of a check on the diagonal which might compel the King to move and forfeit his right to castle, but there is the possibility of White planting a Knight on QB6, a square weakened by the advance of Black's Knight Pawn.

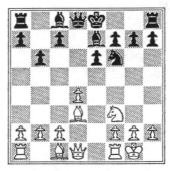

10. Kt—K5 !

A wonderful outpost station for the Knight, which will put a restraining hand on Black's ambition to expand.

10. . . .   O—O

Black realizes that 10. . . . B—
Kt2 is refuted by 11. B—Kt5ch to
which he must respond with
11. . . . K—B1 and lose the castling privilege, or 11. . . . P—B3,
giving up a Pawn.

Naturally, it would be silly to
snatch a Pawn by 10. . . . Q x P
and fall into 11. B—Kt5ch, losing
the Queen by a discovered attack.

11. Kt—B6

Immediately pouncing on the
weakened square, with a view to removing Black's King Bishop. But
why give up the Knight, which I
said a moment ago was occupying a
wonderful outpost station, for a
Bishop which seems to have little
potential?

There are at least three good
reasons:

The exchange deprives Black of
one of his Bishops, and the mere
possession of both Bishops is a formidable attacking weapon, no matter how placid the position.

The reduction in force increases
the dynamic power of White's pair
of Bishops, which have more space
to work in. The emptier the board,
the better they can sweep the area,
one operating on white and the
other on black diagonals.

The third reason is rather subtle:
Black's King-side position is stoutly
defended by the Knight, and the
Knight in turn by the Bishop and
Queen. In order to get at the
Knight, which must eventually be
destroyed for a King-side attack to
succeed, White first removes one of

its firm supports, the Bishop. The
substitution of Black's Queen for
the Bishop will make a pin on the
Knight a potent one – one which can
not easily be shaken off.

11. . . .   Q—Q3

As good as any other move the
Queen can make.

12. Q—B3 !

A very important *Zwischenzug*
(an in-between move). It is stronger
than the immediate 12. Kt x Bch
and causes Black to modify his
plans. Let us analyze both moves:

If White plays 12. Kt x Bch, then
after 12. . . . Q x Kt 13. Q—B3
attacks the Rook. The Rook evades
the Queen by escaping to Kt1, and
Black's next move, 14. . . . B—Kt2,
drives the Queen off the long diagonal, leaving Black's Bishop in control of it.

After the actual move 12. Q—B3,
Black is threatened with 13.
Kt x Bch, Q x Kt 14. Q x R—loss of
a Rook. This time the Rook cannot
run from the Queen, as the flight
square Kt1 is covered by White's
Knight, and the response 12. . . .
B—Kt2 (to interpose the Bishop,
meanwhile developing it on the long
diagonal) fails after 13 Kt x Bch,
Q x Kt 14. Q x B, and White wins a
piece.

12. . . .   B—Q2

The upshot of all this is that in
order to save the Rook's life the
Bishop must be content to move to
Q2, where it has little scope.

13. Kt x Bch

Strategically, this represents a triumph for White. Not only does he remain with the advantage of the two Bishops against Black's Knight and Bishop, but he has compelled Black's Queen Bishop to take up an unfavorable post, while he retains control of the long center diagonal.

13. . . .   Q x Kt

Black completes the exchange with the impression that his position is solid enough, though defensive in character.

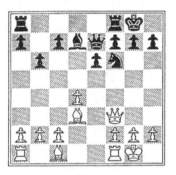

14. B—KKt5 !

A powerful pin which puts paralyzing pressure on the Knight. Before going any further, let's review the bidding:

By means of doing nothing more remarkable than making simple developing moves, White has a tactical advantage in his pair of Bishops, a better all-around position, more pieces in play, and an enduring initiative.

More pieces in play? Yes, his Queen and both Bishops are *actively* posted, while Black's Knight is unable to move, his Queen must hover about the Knight (or lose a Pawn

after B x Kt) and his Bishop has little mobility, shut off as it is from the King side by Black's own King Pawn. The Pawn position in the center also favors White, in that his Queen Pawn at the fourth square has more to say about affairs than the adverse Pawn at K3.

White now plans to create a breach in the line-up of Pawns screening Black's King, by next playing the surprising but logical 15. Q—K4. Black could not reply 15. . . . Kt x Q to this, as after 16. B x Q (attacking two pieces), KR—K1 17. B x Kt gives him no time to take the Bishop as his Queen Rook is under attack. The idea underlying 15. Q—K4 is not to induce Black to snatch the Queen, but by the threat of 16. B x Kt, Q x B 17. Q x P mate to compel him to advance 15. . . . P—Kt3. The effect of this Pawn move would be to loosen the defensive structure shielding the King, remove a prop from under the pinned Knight, and offer White points of entry on the weakened black squares KR3 and KB3, no longer guarded by the Knight Pawn. One possibility, for example, is this: 15. Q—K4, P—Kt3 16. Q—R4 (attacking the Knight), K—Kt2 17. B—R6ch, and White wins the exchange.

14. . . .   QR—B1

Black shifts the Rook from the line of fire, so that on 15. Q—K4, Kt x Q 16. B x Q, KR—K1 retains equality in material.

Constructively, Black intends to follow up with 15. . . . P—B4, coming to grips with White's center

Pawn and opening the Bishop file
for his Rook.

15. KR–K1

A useful developing, restraining
and preparatory move:

It brings the Rook out to a half-
open file.

It prevents any attempt by Black
to free himself by prying open the
King file.

It makes provision for utilizing
the Rook in a King-side attack,
somewhat like this: 16. Q–R3
(again threatening to win by 17.
B x Kt), P–KR3 17. B x P, P x B
18. Q x RP, and the Rook comes in
decisively by way of K5 and KKt5 to
inflict the mate.

15. . . .   KR–K1

Vacating a square for the King.
Black abandons the projected
15. . . . P–B4. Against this, Tar-
rasch intended (according to his
own comments) 16. Q–R3 (threat-
ening 17. B x Kt), P–KR3 17.
B x P, P–B5 18. B x KtP, K x B 19.
Q–Kt3ch, K–R1 20. Q–R4ch,
K–Kt2 21. Q–Kt5ch, K–R1 22.
Q–R6ch (pretty zigzagging by the
Queen!), K–Kt1 23. R–K5, and
quick mate follows. Or if after 17.
B x P, P x B 18. Q x RP, P x P (to
meet 19. R–K5 with 19. . . .
R–B4) 19. P–QKt4! (to keep
Black's Rook out) and then 20.
R–K5, with an easy win.

16. Q–R3 !

The winning move—although it
appears that White has been playing
a long string of winning moves!

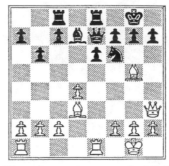

The pressure is now redoubled on
the Rook Pawn, which White
threatens to win either by 17. B x Kt
followed by 18. Q x RPch or simply
by taking it at once with the
Bishop, since Black's pinned Knight
dares not recapture, and his King
may not touch the Bishop.

How does Black defend himself
against White's threats?

If 16. . . . P–KR3 17. B x P,
P x B 18. Q x RP, Q–B1 (otherwise 19. R–K5 will lead to mate)
19. Q x Kt, and White, two Pawns
up, wins easily.

If 16. . . . P–Kt3 (saving the
Rook Pawn but depriving the Knight
of an excellent support) White wins
by 17. Q–R4, K–Kt2 18. R–K4 !,
followed by 19. R–B4, and the
Rook too hits out at the helpless
Knight.

If 16. . . . P–K4 (uncovering
an attack on the Queen) 17. B x Kt,
B x Q (or 17. . . . Q x B 18. Q x B,
and White wins a piece) 18. B x Q
and White is a piece ahead.

Finally, if 16. . . . P–B4 17.
B x Pch, K–B1 18. B–K4 (threatening the devastating check at R8),
K–Kt1, and Black a Pawn down is
still on the defensive.

All these variations are pleasant—

especially if you are on the winning side!

16. . . .   Q—Q3

Hoping that 17 B x Kt, P x B 18. Q x RPch, winning a Pawn, will appease White.

17. B x Kt

Removes the only defender in the neighborhood of Black's King, and . . .

17. . . .   P x B

. . . uproots the Knight Pawn, exposing the King.

18. Q—R6 !

Holds the King fast! The idea is to keep him from escaping by way of KB1 while facing him with deadly threats. The *modus operandi* after the text move is 19. B x Pch !, K—R1 20. B—Kt6 dis. ch, K—Kt1 21. Q—R7ch, K—B1 22. Q x P mate.

If you can play this sort of move (18. Q—R6) as White did, you are a cut above the average player. Most young players (in a chess sense) have a tendency to try checking the King to death only to find after something like 18. Q x RPch, K—B1 19. Q—R8ch, K—K2, that the King has escaped and the attack is exhausted. What is worse is that White's Queen and Queen Pawn are threatened, and that saving both by 20. Q—R4 lets Black respond with 20. . . . R—KR1, and suddenly White is thrown on the defensive!

18. . . .   P—KB4

Intercepts the Bishop's line of attack.

19. R—K3

Obviously threatening check at Kt3, followed by mate, to prevent which Black would have to give up his Queen.

Notice how the occupation of the partly open King file by the Rook is justified by the convenient use of K3 as a transfer point, enabling the Rook to switch over to the open files on the King side.

19. . . .   Q x QP

Guarding his Kt2 square, so that after 20. R—Kt3ch, K—R1, White has no check there with his Queen.

If instead 19. . . . P—KB3 (to try escaping with the King) 20. R—Kt3ch, K—B2 21. Q—Kt7 is mate. Or if 19. . . . K—R1 20. R—R3 forces 20. . . . K—Kt1 when 21. R—Kt3ch is fatal.

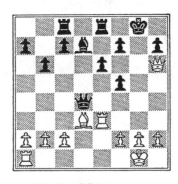

20. P—QB3 !

A beautiful *coup de repos!*

Black is helpless: his Queen dares not leave the diagonal leading to his KKt2, and if 20. . . . Q—Kt2 21. R—Kt3 pins the Queen, while

20. . . . Q—R1 succumbs to 21.
R—Kt3ch, and the poor King's only
flight square is occupied by his
Queen!

20. . . .   Resigns

This game was awarded a brilliancy prize.

GAME NO. 15

RUY LOPEZ

WHITE   BLACK
Alekhine   Poindle
(Simultaneous)
VIENNA, 1936

1. P—K4

With his first move, White gets a
foothold in the center and begins
the development of his King-side
pieces.

1. . . .   P—K4

Black must also establish a Pawn
in the center, while preventing 2.
P—Q4 from being freely played.

What if White does move 2.
P—Q4? After 2. . . . P x P   3.
Q x P, Kt—QB3 4. Q—K3, Kt—B3
5. Kt—QB3, B—Kt5, Black has
three pieces in play with an easy development. It is true that White has
a Pawn in the center, but it will
need constant care, and his Queen
meanwhile has lost valuable time.
In short, after 1. . . . P—K4,
White may respond 2. P—Q4 but
not to advantage.

2. Kt—KB3

The Knight is posted without
delay on its most effective square in

the opening. The move is ideal, as
the Knight develops with a threat.
This limits the opponent's choice of
replies, since he must do something
to meet the threat before going
about his business.

2. . . .   Kt—QB3

The best way to protect the
Pawn. The Knight's development is
natural, and no time is lost meeting
the threat.

3. B—Kt5

The strongest move on the board,
this characterizes the Ruy Lopez,
the most powerful of King-side
openings. As Reuben Fine puts it,
"One reason why the Ruy Lopez is
so strong is that the most natural
sequence of moves leads to an ideal
position for White."

3. . . .   Kt—B3

Black brings his King Knight out
toward the center with an attack on
the King Pawn.

Lasker favored the Knight's development at this point, but modern
theory inclines to interpolating
3. . . . P—QR3 first, to make the
Bishop declare its intentions, and in
any case to dislodge it from its fine
position.

4. O—O

Very much to the point: the
King is whisked away into safety
while the King Rook is activated.

4. . . .   Kt x P

Should Black capture this Pawn?
Lasker's view was: "When you are

conscious not to have violated the rules laid down, you should accept the sacrifice of an important Pawn, as the King Pawn, Queen Pawn or one of the Bishop Pawns. If you do not, as a rule, the Pawn which you have rejected will become very troublesome to you."

5. P—Q4

This is stronger than 5. R—K1. Black's King Pawn is doubly attacked, while lines are opened up for White's Queen and Queen Bishop.

5. . . .   Kt—Q3

Puts the question to the Bishop, which apparently must capture the Knight or retreat.

A simpler course was 5. . . . B—K2, developing another piece instead of moving the same one twice. Black must not waste time holding on to the extra Pawn but continue bringing pieces into the field.

6. P x P !

Initiating an attack troublesome to meet. This is superior to 6. B—R4, which gives Black time to reply 6. . . . P—K5 with good counterplay.

6. . . .   Kt x B

The Knight's excursion has cost Black valuable time, as the Knight has made four moves to capture a Bishop which has only moved once.

7. P—QR4

White attacks the Knight at once to recover the piece he lost.

7. . . .   Kt—Q3

A fifth move by the same Knight! White will surely have a strong attack in return for the Pawn he intends to sacrifice.

Black should have played 7. . . . P—Q3, which leads almost to equality.

8. P x Kt

White's first dividend comes in the form of an open center file leading straight to his opponent's King!

8. . . .   B x P

Not a happy recapture, as the Queen Pawn is blocked, but certainly better than taking with the Pawn when Black's position is even more awkward.

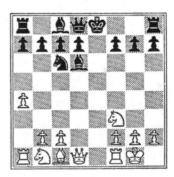

9. Kt—Kt5 !

This move is superior to the natural 9. R—K1ch. It is, as we shall see, both energetic and subtle.

One bit of finesse is directed against Black's castling. White would then play 10. Q—Q3, threatening 11. Q x P mate. Black would be forced to reply 10. . . . P—KKt3 (not 10. . . . P—B4 11. Q—Q5ch, K—R1 12. Kt—B7ch, winning the exchange) and weaken the defensive formation of Pawns. Once the line of Pawns is disturbed, the King is vulnerable to direct attack.

9. . . .   B—K2

An interesting move. In its retreat, the Bishop not only attacks the Knight but manages to unblock the Queen Pawn.

Black hopes either to force the Knight to leave or to bring about an exchange of pieces, ridding himself of the attacking Knight.

10. Q—R5 !

En avant! The obvious threat of mate camouflages the real purpose of this move.

White's last two moves are those of a beginner—or perhaps of a great master! The Knight has moved twice to assist the Queen in an attack, which the books say is premature, as White's development is not complete. Why does Alekhine violate elementary opening principles?

The reason he does so is that routine development ("You get your pieces out quietly and I'll do the same with mine") would give Black time to reorganize his position. Black has committed some indiscretions (such as moving the King Knight five times in the opening!), and the way to punish these lapses is to keep him occupied—face him with problems at every point and give him no time to recover. If it requires unconventional moves to force weaknesses in his position, then play these unorthodox moves! Moves are good or bad by one stand-

ard only—their effect on the position at hand.

10. . . .   P—KKt3

What other choice was there?

If Black castles to avoid 11. Q x BP mate, he falls into 11. Q x RP mate.

Or if he exchanges by 10. . . . B x Kt, then 11. B x Kt forces 11. . . . Kt—K2 when the pin 12. R—K1 wins a piece—as a start!

11. Q—R6 !

White anchors the Queen at once on this square, no longer guarded by Black's Knight Pawn, as the first step in getting control of the black squares.

White now threatens to penetrate further into the heart of the position by 12. Q—Kt7, attacking the Rook. This would force 12. . . . R—B1 in reply, when 13. Kt x RP wins the exchange, a Rook for a Knight.

11. . . .   B—B1

Not only must further invasion be prevented, but the Queen must be driven back.

Black has little choice, as castling is against the law, while 11. . . . B x Kt loses by 12. B x B, P—B3 13. Q—Kt7, R—B1 14. R—K1ch, Kt—K2 15. B—R6, R—B2 16. Q—Kt8ch, R—B1 17. Q x R mate.

12. R—K1ch

Forcing Black to tie himself up in knots.

12. . . .   Kt—K2

Certainly not 12. . . . B—K2 when 13. Q—Kt7, R—B1 14. Kt x RP (threatening 15. Q x R mate), P—Q4 15. Kt—B6 is mate.

At this point, in spite of White's disregard of conventional methods of development, he has three pieces in active play, while Black has none! Black does have one piece off the first rank, but it is held fast by a pin and unable to move.

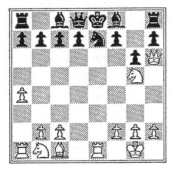

13. Kt—K4 !

Threatening mate on the move!

13. . . .   P—KB4

The only move on the board! If Black plays 13. . . . B x Q, White wins by 14. Kt—B6ch, K—B1 15. B x B mate, or if 13. . . . Kt—B4 with a double attack on the Queen, White retaliates with a double attack on the King by 14. Kt—B6 dble. ch and mate!

14. Kt—B6ch

One way to get at the King is to make him come out into the open.

14. . . .   K—B2

Moving the King forfeits the privilege of castling, but unfortunately it's Black's only move.

15. Q—R4

White's Queen and Knight were both attacked, so the Queen moves where she protects the Knight.

15. . . .   B—Kt2

Now threatening 16. . . . B x Kt. The alternative attack by 15. . . . Kt—Kt1, which pins the Knight and strikes at it with two pieces, is refuted by 16. Q—B4ch, K x Kt (or 16. . . . K—Kt2 17. Kt—K8ch, and Black must give up his Queen) 17. Q—R4ch, and White wins the Queen.

16. B—Kt5

Protects the Knight, which had no flight square.

16. . . .   P—KR3

Threatens the Knight again by hitting out at one of its defenders.

If 16. . . . Kt—Kt1 instead, White has a pretty combination in 17. Kt x Kt, Q x Kt 18. R—K7ch, K—B1 19. B—R6, followed by 20. Q—B6ch, forcing mate. Or he may prefer to win it by 17. Q—QB4ch, P—Q4 18. Kt x QP, Q x B 19. Kt x P dis. ch, K—B3 20. Kt—K8 mate.

17. Q—B4ch !

A happy diversion, as the cry of "Check!" compels the opponent to drop everything and get his King out of check.

17. . . .   K—B1

Practically forced, as 17. . . . P—Q4 18. Kt x P, Q x Kt 19. R x Ktch costs Black his Queen.

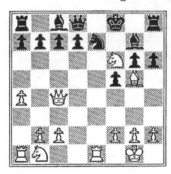

18. R x Kt !

The hallmark of an Alekhine combination! It's the kick at the end of a series of apparently innocuous moves.

White's threat is obvious: mate on the move.

18. ...   Q x R

On 18. . . . K x R, the only other means of preventing mate at B7, White replies 19. Kt—Q5 dble. ch, and wins the Queen next move.

19. Kt—R7ch

Direct attack on the King and discovered attack on the Queen.

19. ...   R x Kt

Black takes all the material he can get for his Queen.

20. B x Qch

The point of the combination: in return for his Rook and Bishop, White gets the Queen—and a lasting initiative!

20. ...   K x B

Black must take the Bishop.

21. Q x P

Simpler than 21. Q—Kt8, K—B3 22. Q x R, K—B2, which, says Alekhine, "puts the Queen to sleep." Of course White can win after that by 23. Kt—B3, P—Q3 24. R—K1, followed by 25. R—K7ch, but the text move is more in keeping with the spirit of the attack. The Queen remains active while Black's Queen side is immobilized.

21. ...   B x P

Black makes trouble. He takes a Pawn and attacks the Rook.

22. R—R2

The Rook steps aside nimbly and turns on his attacker.

22. ...   B—B3

The Bishop retreats to (comparative) safety.

23. P—QB4 !

Clears the way for the Rook, who now can get to the open King file— and the King!

23. ...   K—B2

The King flees from the line of fire. Black hopes to free himself by 24. . . . R—R1 and 25. . . . B— Q1, driving the Queen off and then advancing his Queen Pawn to release his Queen-side pieces.

24. R—K2

White seizes the open file. Controlling it gives the Rook a clear road and access to the enemy camp.

24. ...   R—R1

Black intends either to evict the

Queen by 25. . . . B—Q1 or dispute ownership of the King file by 25. . . . R—K1.

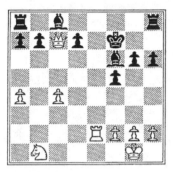

25. Q—Q6 !

Nails the Queen Pawn down and paralyzes the forces on that wing.

25. . . .   P—QR4

What else is there? If 25. . . . R—K1 26. R x R, K x R 27. Q x B wins a piece, or if 25. . . . P—Kt3 26. Q—Q5ch catches the Queen Rook.

Black's idea is to follow up with 26. . . . R—R3, dislodge the Queen, and get his Queen-side pieces rolling.

26. Kt—B3 !

Excellent! White brings another piece up to join in the attack. Notice how the master player selects the move he would like to make, sees that it can't be made (here the Knight is left *en prise*) and then makes the move!

26. . . .   R—R3

Black does not grab the Knight, as after 26. . . . B x Kt 27. R—K7ch, K—B1 (or 27. . . . K—Kt1 28. Q—Q5ch and mate next) 28.

R x QP dis. ch, K—Kt1 29. Q—Q5ch, K—B1 30. Q—B7 mate.

27. Q—Q5ch

The Queen must retreat, but gains time by checking.

27. . . .   K—Kt2

Or 27. . . . K—B1 28. Q—B5ch, K—Kt2 29. Kt—Q5 (threatening 30. Kt x B, K x Kt 31. Q—K7 mate), R—K3 30. R x R, P x R 31. Q—B7ch, and after Black's King moves, White has choice of Bishops!

28. Kt—Kt5

Ready to switch over to Q6 to support the Queen in a mate threat at KB7.

28. . . .   R—K3

Otherwise the Knight goes to Q6 and cuts the Rook off from participating in the defense.

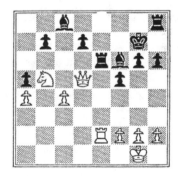

29. Kt—Q6 !

The Knight goes there anyway! The Knight settles down on this fine outpost where it will either take a hand in a combination that will settle matters or simply stay there and choke Black to death.

29. . . .   R—Q1

Naturally, 29. . . . R x R is unthinkable, as 30. Q—B7 mate would
come in a flash.

30. K—B1

Protects the Rook and declares
his intention of winning by 31. Kt x
B, R x Kt 32. Q x QPch, followed by
taking a Rook or two.

30. . . .   Resigns

There is no fight left.

GAME NO. 16
QUEEN'S GAMBIT ACCEPTED

WHITE	BLACK
Tarrasch	Kurschner

NUREMBERG, 1889

1. P—Q4

One of the merits of beginning a
game with 1. P—Q4 is that the
Pawn standing in the center is protected. It is safe from attack, whereas
in openings starting with 1 P—K4,
the King Pawn can be immediately
threatened by 1. . . . Kt—KB3. It
is true that White may then protect
his Pawn or move it up a square, out
of danger, but he is no longer doing
what he set out to do. He is not
playing the opening of his choice.
The fact that he must meet Black's
threat before doing anything else
cramps his style.

In Queen Pawn openings, with
the Queen firmly backing up the
center Pawn, White dictates the
tempo. He has the initiative and

keeps it for a long time against any
defense, any line of play that Black
may select. Right from the start,
White is given the opportunity to
build up his position, with little
danger of being bothered by a counterattack, while Black struggles to
achieve equality. If Black plays tim-
idly—if he fails to dispute the center
by . . . P—QB4 at some stage—his
Queen-side pieces, especially the
Bishop, will be badly cramped and
unable to put up decent resistance.
If he develops carelessly—moving
the same piece several times in the
opening or bringing his Bishops out
before the Knights—punishment
will come swiftly.

The purpose of chess being to
win, not to entertain the gallery with
pretty pictures on the chessboard, it
is no wonder that most players prefer the "dull, safe Queen's Gambit"
to the romantic but risky adventures
of the King's gambits.

I venture to say (and this opinion
has forty years of research behind it)
that the Queen Pawn openings have
contributed as many masterpieces
and as many genuine brilliancies as
did any of the openings of the King
side.

The moral is: Play Queen Pawn
openings if you want to win; if you
are looking for fun in chess, play
King Pawn openings—or Queen
Pawn openings!

1. . . .   P—Q4

This is the best way for Black to
stabilize the pressure in the center.

Each side now has a Pawn firmly
stationed in the middle of the board,
occupying one square and attacking

two others; each side has released two pieces for action.

2. P—QB4

The object of this move is to destroy Black's Pawn center. First, White offers a Pawn to induce Black to surrender the center. If that does not work, White threatens to dissolve it by 3. P x P, Q x P 4. Kt—QB3, Q—QR4 5. P—K4, and White controls most of the center.

2. . . .   P x P

Black's idea with this capture is to avoid the constricted positions that are normally his lot in the Queen's Gambit Declined opening, but in doing so he has given up a beautifully centralized Pawn for one at the side.

Accepting the gambit is perfectly sound, but the resulting play requires great care on Black's part. Above all he must not hold on too long to the extra Pawn.

3. P—K3

A good move, but more to the point is 3. Kt—KB3 to prevent the counterthrust 3. . . . P—K4.

White plays to release his King Bishop and recover the Pawn at once.

3. . . .   B—B4

By this, Black hopes to solve the problem of the shut-in Bishop, one of the evils the defense is heir to. But the solution is not quite so simple! The Bishop's absence from the Queen side weakens that section of the board and endangers the Queen Knight Pawn. Another drawback in Black's move is that it violates one of the precepts for sound development:

Bring out your Knights before the Bishops!

Instead of the text move, Black's best bet is in counterattack, viz.: 3. . . . P—K4 4. B x P (or 4. P x P, Q x Qch 5. K x Q, B—K3), P x P 5. P x P, B—Kt5ch.

Attempting to hold on to the extra Pawn might lead Black into one of the traps prepared for the greedy: 3. . . . P—QKt4 4. P—QR4, P—QB3 5. P x P, P x P 6. Q—B3, and White wins a piece.

4. B x P

The recovery of the Pawn equalizes material force, but White's position is slightly superior.

4. . . .   P—K3

A Pawn move which contributes to the development of a piece, in this case the King Bishop, is always in place.

Developing one of the Knights first is somewhat risky. For instance, if 4. . . . Kt—KB3 5. Q—Kt3 threatens to win a Pawn by 6. Q x P or 6. B x Pch. Or if 4. . . . Kt—QB3 5. Q—Kt3, Kt—R4 6. B x Pch, K—Q2 7. Q—Q5ch, K—B1 8. Q x Bch, K—Kt1 9. Q x Kt, and White has won two pieces.

Even at this early stage White is directing events.

5. Q—Kt3

Why does White move his Queen instead of getting his Knights out?

His purpose is to punish Black

for faulty development. Black's play has not been normal procedure, and the way to take advantage of his sins is not with routine moves.

White's move, developing a piece with a threat (6. Q x P) keeps Black on the run. It does not give him time to consolidate his position with the customary approved methods.

5. . . .   B—K5

This looks attractive, since Black protects his Queen Knight Pawn, and at the same time threatens to play 6. . . . B x P, winning a Rook.

Black's move, however, is abnormal and a serious infraction of the opening principle, which states:

Move each piece only once in the opening; place it at once on the square where it exerts most power and where it has the greatest freedom of movement.

6. P—B3

This move is justified on more than one count. Not only does it parry a threat in an economical way, but it forces Black to lose a move in the retreat of his Bishop. Incidentally, the Pawn at B3 will firmly support a later advance of the King Pawn.

6. . . .   B—B3

Now we see the results of the Bishop's ill-timed expedition. It stands at QB3, depriving the Queen Knight of his natural square of development in the opening. Worse yet, it obstructs the Bishop Pawn. If this Pawn cannot get to B4 to dispute control of the center and to open the Bishop file for Black's

pieces, there is danger that Black will be smothered.

7. Kt—K2

"But Knights belong on B3!" you must be protesting. So they do, but if they cannot develop at B3, get them into the game somehow! Move them, if only to get them off the back rank!

White is ready to castle and get the King Rook working.

7. . . .   Kt—B3

At last a normal, reasonable developing move to which no exception can be made! In nearly every variation of every opening, the King Knight does its job most effectively at KB3.

8. P—K4

With a threefold purpose:

To control the center, by occupying it with his Pawns.

To clear a path for the convenience of his Queen Bishop.

To limit further the activities of Black's Queen Bishop.

8. . . .   B—K2

The only square open to the

Bishop. On 8. . . . B—Q3 instead, the reply 9. P—K5 wins a piece for White.

The back rank is cleared and Black is ready to castle—if White lets him!

ce! In standing at Q5 it occupies :quare that should be reserved for :ces. Pieces have more mobility

He has a Pawn stationed at Q5, which at first glance is doing an excellent job. It prevents Black's Queen Knight from developing at B3, keeps his Bishop from coming to K3, and restrains the King Knight. The Pawn

Brings another piece into play with gain of tempo. The threat is

12. P—Q6 !

This energetic thrust opens the diagonal leading to Black's tender spot, the King Bishop Pawn, clears the Queen file for later exploitation by a Rook, and vacates the strategic square Q5 for the use of a piece. Meanwhile, the attack on Black's Bishop leaves him no time to breathe!

12. . . .   B x P

Better than 12. . . . P x P, hemming the Bishop in.

13. B x Pch

This will smoke the King out! Once the King moves and loses the privilege of castling, he stands on insecure ground to the end of his days.

13. . . .   K—Q1

Black prefers this to 13. . . . K—B1, imprisoning the King Rook.

14. B—Kt5

A pin which paralyzes Black's most useful piece. Meanwhile, and this sums up the miserable state of his game, his mighty Queen is smothered by Black's own pieces!

14. . . .   Kt—B3

Black's idea is to develop a piece and give the Queen and Queen Rook freedom to move—if only to the next square! It is hard to suggest a better move, since every move is inadequate in a losing position. Black might have ventured on a more active defense, such as 14. . . . B—K1, followed by 15. . . . R—B1 or 15. . . . Q—Q2 or 15. . . . Q—

B4. He must try to beat back White's attacking pieces or get rid of them by exchanges.

The formula in such cases is:

In a crowded position try to relieve the pressure by forcing exchanges of pieces.

15. Kt—K4

White puts more strain on the pinned Knight. The threat (and there always is a threat when a pinned piece is attacked more than once) is 16. Kt x Kt, P x Kt 17. B x Pch, and White wins a Rook.

15. . . .   B—K2

Protecting the Knight once again, and at the same time unpinning it. This is a better defense than 15. . . . B—K4, which helps guard the Knight but does nothing to relieve the pin. In such situations, the extra defender itself may be on shaky ground and apt to be upset. For instance, if 15. . . . B—K4 16. P—B4, B—Q5 17. Kt x B (removing one of the Knight's protectors), QKt x Kt 18. Q—QB3, and Black is embarrassed for a plausible continuation.

16. B x Kt

White does well to remove this rock of defense.

16. . . .   P x B

Black takes with the Pawn, as he wants to keep both his Bishops.

With his King so well sheltered by pieces, it looks difficult to penetrate Black's hedgehog defense.

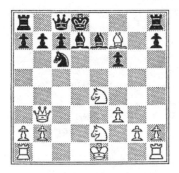

17. O—O—O !

Much more energetic than castling on the other side. White's King is somewhat exposed, but as compensation his Queen Rook has a powerful grip on the open Queen file, putting particular pressure on the unfortunate Bishop, which now is pinned. The maneuver of castling on the Queen side gains a tempo for the attack, while White's King is in little danger, since Black's development is so backward.

White threatens 18. B—K6 or 18. Q—K6, either of which adds pressure to the pin.

17. . . .   Kt—K4

Not only to help the Bishop but to play 18. . . . Kt x B, removing one of his tormentors.

18. Kt—B4

Threatens sudden death by 19. Kt—K6 mate.

18. . . .   Q—Kt1

An unhappy situation for the Queen, but the King needs a flight square.

What else was there? If 18. . . . B—B1, to free the square K2 for the King, then 19. Q—K6 (threatening 20. Q—K8 mate), B—K2 20. Q x Kt !, P x Q and 21. Kt—K6 mates neatly.

19. Q—K6

With the Queen's entrance into the enemy camp, the attack gains momentum. White plans a win by 20. Kt x BP (striking once more at the hapless Bishop and threatening 21. R x Bch and quick mate), B x Kt 21. Q x B(B6)ch, K—B1 22. Q x Rch and mate next move.

19. . . .   R—B1

Hoping to scare off the Bishop, when his Bishop Pawn would be protected by the Rook. The alternative 19. . . . Q—B1 runs into 20. Q x Kt and the previous win.

20. Kt x P

Isn't it remarkable how threats are summoned up as if by magic against a piece that is pinned?

20. . . .   B—Q3

Interfering with the Rook's action on the open file and thereby threatening to take the Queen.

Other defenses promise no favorable results:

20. . . . R x B 21. R x Bch, and mate in two.

20. . . . B x Kt 21. Q x B(B6) ch, K—B1 22. Q x Kt, R x B 23. Q—R8ch.

20. . . . Q—B1   21.   Q x Kt, R x B 22. Kt—K6 mate.

With the text, Black unpins his Bishop, guards the Knight, attacks the Queen and threatens the Bishop.

21. Kt x B

This one hurts a bit. The Knight captures one piece and attacks three others.

21. . . .   Kt x Kt

Black recaptures and disposes of a troublesome piece.

22. KR—K1

The doubling of heavy pieces on the open King file, with the consequent threat of 23. Q—K8ch, R x Q 24. R x R mate, is enough to break anyone's spirit.

22. . . .   Resigns

The Bishop Pawn cannot move to give the King room on account of 23. R x B in reply, and if 22. . . . Kt—B4 23. Q—K7ch, K—B1 24. Q x Rch, B x Q 25. R—K8 mate is the finishing touch.

The Queen's Pawn Opening

At some time in his life every chess player makes a happy discovery —the Queen's Pawn opening.

If it is not *The Weapon that Makes you Invincible*, it is the closest thing to it. The Queen's Pawn offers White a great many advantages, and all of them can be summed up in one word—pressure!

White gets opportunities to control and exert pressure on the Queen Bishop file, and in particular on the square QB5. So powerful can it be as to cause, from this alone, the collapse of Black's game.

Against its dire effects there is only one antidote: the advance of . . . P—QB4, which Black *must* get in, sooner or later. Without it he may be choked to death; with it he frees his position on the Queen side, establishes a state of tension in the center, and is enabled to put up a fight for possession of the Queen Bishop file.

The game Pillsbury-Mason (No. 17) is a classic example of White controlling the Queen Bishop file, while Black fails to free himself by . . . P—QB4. Pillsbury fixes the Bishop Pawn so it dares not move, and then proceeds to attack it with more pieces than Black can summon to its defense. The Pawn falls, of course, and White's continuing control of the vital Queen Bishop file, extending into the ending, makes the winning process look easy.

In Noteboom-Doesburgh (No. 18) neglect of the freeing maneuver . . . P—QB4 allows White to restrain and prevent forever the advance of the Bishop Pawn. Eventually, the Pawn is nailed down so that Black's Queen side is held in an iron grip. The weaknesses on the Queen side of the board lead to collapse on the King side.

Similar difficulties beset Black in Grunfeld-Schenkein (No. 19), where delay in challenging the center leads to a sealing in of Black's Queen Bishop Pawn, and with it his Queen side, by an unprotected Pawn! White's sudden shifting of the attack to the King side leaves Black helpless to resist.

Position play on a grand scale is seen in the Rubinstein-Salwe (No. 20) game. This again shows the consequences of Black's omission of the key move in the defense of this opening . . . P—QB4. White's control of the Bishop file and the square QB5 enables him to demonstrate a remarkable bit of strategy. He blockades QB5 with a Bishop (stopping Black's Queen Bishop Pawn dead in its tracks) and then switches blockaders about, so that this square is occupied in turn by a Bishop, a Knight, a Rook and the Queen! Rubinstein eventually captures the Bishop Pawn that was marked for doom and swings into the final movement, a triumphal march of his own passed Pawn.

In the Chernev-Hahlbohm (No. 21) game, Black gets in the important counterthrust . . . P—QB4, but his center, with an unprotected Knight at Q4, lacks solidity. Chernev gains time for his attack by threats on Black's exposed pieces, and it is these gains of tempo that lend the game its interest.

Pillsbury-Marco (No. 22) is the beau ideal of the Queen's Gambit. In it we see the classic demonstration of what came to be known as the Pillsbury attack. It is a beautiful example of the power of a Knight outpost at K5, and the impetus it furnishes to a whirlwind King-side attack.

In the game between Vliet and Znosko-Borovsky (No. 23) it is Black who wrests control of the Queen Bishop file by a counterattack at the second move with 2. . . . P—QB4. It leads to more advantages, culminating in the Queen Rook's invasion of the seventh rank

and the establishment of a Knight outpost at K5. Eventually, Black doubles Rooks on the file and maneuvers his King in among the adverse Pawns. This leads to his winning a Pawn, and the rest is a delightful little lesson in the art of simplification.

GAME NO. 17

QUEEN'S GAMBIT DECLINED

WHITE	BLACK
Pillsbury	Mason

HASTINGS, 1895

1. P—Q4

White opens with one of the strongest possible first moves:

The Queen Pawn occupies an important square in the center and attacks two valuable points, K5 and QB5. Control of these squares keeps the opponent from making use of them for his pieces.

The Queen and Queen Bishop are enabled to leave the first rank.

The King is safe from some of the surprise attacks which occur in King Pawn openings. These come about when Black develops his King Bishop at QB4 and sacrifices it for White's King Bishop Pawn to force the King out into the open and subject him to assault by the other pieces.

1. . . . P—Q4

Black equalizes the pressure in the center, prevents White from continuing with 2. P—K4, and also releases two of his own pieces for action.

2. P—QB4

This is a threat and an offer! The threat, a positional one, is 3. P x P, when after the recapture by 3. . . . Q x P, 4. Kt—QB3 drives the Queen off and leaves White dominating the center.

The offer of a Pawn has as its purpose the removal of Black's Queen Pawn from its fine position in the center. This offer, unlike the one in the King's Gambit, involves no risk. White regains the Pawn easily and remains with the superior position. It is in effect an exchange of a flank Pawn for Black's center Pawn. The point of playing 2. P—QB4 so soon is that *it disputes the center at once, without endangering the safety of the King.*

There is also another purpose—a strategic one. An exchange of Pawns must come, sooner or later, resulting in the opening of the Queen Bishop file. *Ownership of this file is of paramount importance in the Queen's Gambit.* White generally tries to get full possession of it by posting his Queen at QB2, and his Queen Rook at QB1.

Control of this file and of the square B5 on this file is equivalent to control of the game. Of such peculiar significance is this square QB5 that it is almost enough simply to plant a piece securely there to get a paralyzing grip on Black's game.

2. . . . P—K3

Black defends the center Pawn by supporting it with another Pawn.

He does not care to capture by 2. . . . P x P, as that means surrendering the center to gain a Pawn which he can not hold onto. White, in reply to this, would play 3. Kt—KB3 (to prevent 3. . . . P—K4), follow up with 4. P—K3, and then get the Pawn back by 5. B x P with an impressive position.

Defending the Queen Pawn with 2. . . . Kt—KB3 is weak. White would play in response 3 P x P, *and Black would have to recapture with a piece.* On 3. . . . Q x P 4. Kt—QB3 banishes the Queen from the center and costs Black time, while 3. . . . Kt x P lets White seize the center with 4. P—K4 and evict the Knight in the process.

After the actual move, Black is set to meet 3. P x P by 3. . . . P x P, keeping his hold on the center by maintaining a Pawn there.

3. Kt—QB3

A commendable developing move, as it settles a minor piece on its most suitable square without loss of time. The Knight bears down on the square K4 and adds its pressure to that of the Bishop Pawn in the attack on Q5.

3. . . . Kt—KB3

This Knight carries out his part of the job in the early proceedings by simply leaving the back rank. Naturally, his development is toward the center, where he counteracts the influence of White's Knight on two of the important squares there.

4. B—Kt5

A highly efficient move as it combines rapid development of a piece with a threat. This latter consists of 5. P x P, P x P 6. B x Kt, P x B (or 6. . . . Q x B 7. Kt x P, and White wins a Pawn) and Black's King-side Pawn position is shattered.

The opening thus far had been given sporadic trials by various players before this game was played, but Pillsbury was the first to appreciate its enormous winning possibilities. He pictured the Bishop move (most masters brought the Bishop quietly into the game at B4) as a sort of Ruy Lopez on the other side of the board! With this particular sequence of moves, which he perfected and popularized, he achieved some remarkable victories, notably in his debut at the Hastings 1895 tournament.

In this game we see him applying the great power of the Queen's Gambit to crush an opponent who is not familiar with its fine points and who puts up less than flawless defense. He beats Mason, "like a child," as Marshall used to express it.

4. . . . B—K2

If nothing else, the development of the Bishop *anywhere* furthers Black's progress, as the decks are cleared for King-side castling. At K2, the Bishop is happily placed for defense, and if need arises can be transferred quickly to a more aggressive position. Incidentally, the Knight is unpinned and White's threat nullified.

5. Kt—B3

In Queen Pawn openings the King Knight's job is the control and

sometimes the occupation of the outpost K5. In fact, entrenching the Knight at this square and supporting it solidly with the Queen Pawn and the King Bishop Pawn is the motif of what later came to be known as the Pillsbury attack, a tremendously effective assault on the King side.

5. . . . P—QKt3

At first glance, this seems to be a simple and natural way to develop the Queen's Bishop, as it is hemmed in on the other side by the King Pawn. It took many years, and a great many losses by the Black pieces, to discover that fianchettoing the Bishop was not an easy solution to the problem of the Bishop's development.

After a great deal of trial and error, one method was hit on which consisted of playing . . . QP x P at an early stage, followed after suitable preparation by an attack on White's Queen Pawn by . . . P—QB4 or . . . P—K4. The first of these moves (. . . P—QB4) is intended to dispute control of the center, open the Queen Bishop file for the use of Black's pieces and in general free his cramped position. The attack by . . . P—K4 is meant to take away the control of K4 from White's Queen Pawn, and to open as well a diagonal for Black's Queen Bishop. In short, Black first puts up a fight for the center before he thinks of developing the Bishop.

It is of almost vital importance that Black play . . . P—QB4 sooner or later. This move strikes at White's Queen Pawn, establishes tension in the center, opens the

Queen Bishop file for his own Queen and Queen Rook and frees the crowded position on the Queen side. Failure to make this move permits White to seize control of the Queen Bishop file and the square QB5 (counting from his side of the board). Should White manage to post a piece on that square, it will exert terrific pressure on Black's entire position, reducing resistance so effectively as to make the technique of completing the win ridiculously easy.

6. P—K3

White strengthens his center and clears a path for his King Bishop.

6. . . .   B—Kt2

Black completes the fianchetto development of the Queen Bishop.

7. R—B1

The Rook hurries over to the important Queen Bishop file. This is only partly open now, but an exchange of Pawns will clear the file and aggravate the Rook's power all along the length of it.

7. . . .   P x P

Black usually waits until White moves his King Bishop before making this capture as then the Bishop loses a move in recapturing. Apparently Black is anxious to give his Queen Bishop more scope on the long central diagonal.

8. B x P

White recaptures the Pawn and gets another piece into the field.

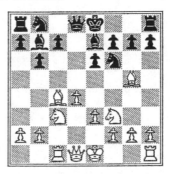

8. . . .   QKt—Q2 !

This disposition of the Knight is characteristic in Queen Pawn openings. The Knight must not go to QB3, blocking the Bishop Pawn. *The Pawn must be free to advance and challenge the center.*

At Q2, the Knight is situated ideally: it supports an advance by . . . P—B4 or . . . P—K4 attacking the center, it participates in the fight for possession of these squares, and it co-operates with the King Knight.

9. O—O

The King disappears from the scene while the Rook is made available for duty.

9. . . .   O—O

The advantage of castling is that the King is safer in the corner, sheltered by the three Pawns in front of him and the doughty King Knight, than in the center of the board, while the Rook is brought toward the center files in the most convenient way possible.

10. Q—K2

The two most effective squares that White's Queen can occupy in this opening are K2 and QB2. At QB2, the Queen supplements the Rook's action in exploiting the Queen Bishop file, while in another direction guards the strategic square K4 from invasion by Black's King Knight. At K2, the Queen prevents Black from breaking up the Kingside Pawn position by 10. . . . B x Kt, supports an advance of the King Pawn which would monopolize the center, and clears the way for the King Rook to reach Q1.

Developing the Queen to K2 offers another advantage: attack on the Queen side. By playing 11. B—QR6, White can force an exchange of Bishops and then bring pressure to bear on Black's white squares, weakened by the removal of the Bishop controlling those squares.

10. . . .   Kt—Q4

Black's purpose in this is to free his cramped position by bringing about an exchange or two.

11. B x B

White is willing to simplify by clearing away some pieces, as he can then return to his theme of exerting painful pressure on the Queen Bishop file.

The alternative, retreat by 11. B—B4, offers Black too many good continuations: He could play 11. . . . Kt x B (leaving himself with the two Bishops) and after 12. P x Kt, move 12. . . . Kt—B3, followed by 13. . . . Kt—Q4, keeping a piece permanently on a square where no adverse Pawns could dislodge it. Or, Black might attack the center at once with 11. . . . P—QB4. Fi-

nally, he could swing the Queen Knight over to KB3 with a respectable game.

White's actual move has the merit of restricting Black's choice of reply.

11. . . .   Q x B

This is preferable to capturing by 11. . . . Kt x B, as Black gets his Queen into play and unites his Rooks.

Naturally, he cannot go in for 11. . . . Kt x Kt 12. B x Q, Kt x Qch 13. B x Kt, KR x B 14. R x P (triumph of the Rook on the open file) as it loses a Pawn and the game.

12. Kt x Kt

This time the exchange suits White, who now can dictate the course of events.

12. . . .   P x Kt

Black must capture this way, as 12. . . . B x Kt 13. B x B, P x B 14. R x P costs a Pawn.

In forcing Black to take with the Pawn, White has compelled the closing of the long diagonal so that Black's Bishop is now terribly limited in scope.

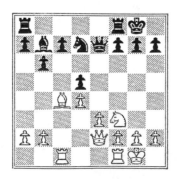

13. B—Kt5 !

Presto! The file is suddenly cleared, and action begins along there with the Rook's attack on the Bishop Pawn.

13. . . .   Q—Q3

Guards the Pawn and prepares for 14. . . . P—QB3 to dislodge White's Bishop.

It is already too late to advance the Pawn to B4 as after 13. . . . P—QB4 (seemingly a safe move as the Pawn is triply defended and only twice attacked) 14. B x Kt, Q x B (note how White disposes of two of the defenders with one stroke) 15. P x P, P x P 16. R x P, White wins a Pawn.

14. R—B2

White makes room for the King Rook at QB1, to add to the pressure.

The device of doubling Rooks on an open file more than doubles their strength on that file.

14. . . .   P—QB3

Black tries to evict the annoying Bishop.

15. B—Q3

This is much stronger than 15. B—R4, when Black gets some troublesome counterplay by 15. . . . P—QKt4 16. B—Kt3, P—QR4 (threatening to win the Bishop by 17. . . . P—R5) 17. P—QR3, Kt—Kt3, and the Knight settles itself firmly at QB5.

15. . . .   Kt—B3

Blissfully unconscious of impend-ing danger, Black goes about his business, which in this case consists of bringing the Knight over to attack, and perhaps to occupy K5. Ordinarily, this is commendable procedure, but all strategy must be conditioned by the circumstances, the position at hand. All moves must be made with respect to the threats of the opponent, not to arbitrary judgments which declare that certain moves are always "good" or "bad." *All moves must be measured by their worth in the one particular position being played.*

White has declared his intention of piling up as much pressure as possible on the Queen Bishop file and on the Queen Bishop Pawn. Black must meet that threat by bringing all his resources to bear on defense of the file, or institute a counterattack vigorous enough to divert White's forces from the assault.

Black must do something to resolve his immediate difficulties, and he must do it at once, before his opponent gets a death grip on the open file.

With his last move, Black misses a golden opportunity—his last chance to play 15. . . . P—QB4, establish a state of tension in the center, and give his pieces more room to move around in.

16. KR—QB1

This fixes Black's Bishop Pawn by preventing it from moving. If 16. . . . P—B4 17. P x P, P x P 18. R x P, and White wins a Pawn.

16. . . .   QR—QB1

Rushing to the defense of the

Pawn and renewing (now that Black realizes his peril) the possibility of pushing the Pawn.

17. B—R6 !

Very fine strategy! White wants to remove Black's Bishop, since minor pieces are excellent defenders of Pawns that are attacked by the heavy pieces. White's Rooks could never seriously threaten the Bishop Pawn while the Bishop protected it.

17. . . .   B x B

Was there anything else Black could have done? If 17. . . . R—B2, White wins by 18. B x B, R x B 19. R x P, or if 17. . . . Q—B2 18. P—QKt4 further restrains the Pawn, after which White intensifies the pressure by 19. Kt—K5, simplifies by exchanging Bishops and then takes the Pawn off.

18. Q x B

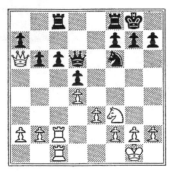

The Queen comes closer, menacing not only the Rook Pawn but also the Bishop Pawn by the threat 19. Q—Kt7, R—B2 20. R x P, R x Q 21. R x Q, and White wins.

18. . . .   R—B2

Looks good, as Black saves the Rook Pawn, keeps the Queen out of Kt7, and prepares to double Rooks and supply the wretched Pawn with another defender.

19. Kt—K5

White's strategy is simple: he piles up more pressure on the Bishop Pawn. It is now attacked by three pieces and defended by two.

19. . . .   P—B4

The planned 19. . . . KR—QB1 lets White win nicely by 20. Kt x QBP, R x Kt 21. Q x Rch !, R x Q 22. R x Rch, Q—B1 23. R x Qch, K x R 24. R—B7, P—QR4 25. R—Kt7, and the rest is child's play.

20. R x P

From now on White simply removes anything that isn't nailed down.

20. . . .   R x R

Black is not wild about exchanging pieces when he is a Pawn down, but what can he do? If he disputes the Bishop file by 20. . . . KR—B1, then 21. Q x Rch wins, as in the earlier note, while on 20. . . . R—K2 (the Rook's only flight square) 21. R—B6, Q—Q1 (or 21. . . . Q—Kt5 22. Kt—Q3, Q—Q7 23. R(B6)—B2, Q—R4 24. Q x Q, P x Q, and the forced exchange of Queens leaves Black's position in ruins) 22. P—QR3, and White's threat of winning the Queen by 23. R—B8, Q—Q3 24. R(B1)—B6 is hard to meet.

21. R x R

The Rook recaptures, disdainful

of the pinned Pawn helpless to remove it, and remains in control of
the valuable open file.

21. . . .   Kt—Q2

This looks attractive as the
Knight attacks two pieces. If White
replies 22. Kt x Kt, then 22. . . .
Q x Kt leaves a Queen and Rook
ending which is not easy to win.
White would eventually have to advance his Pawn majority on the King
side and expose the King to a possible perpetual check and a draw.

If the Rook retreats, Black continues by 22. . . . Kt x Kt 23. P x
Kt, Q x KP, again with drawing
chances.

22. R—B6

Neatly sidestepping either offer of
a Knight exchange, the Rook gains
time by attacking the Queen.

22. . . .   Kt—Kt1

Black is forced into making this
"combination" as the retreat by 22.
. . . Q—K2 is disastrous after 23.
R—B7 (pinning the Knight), R—
Q1 24. Q—Kt5 (triple attack!), and
White wins a piece.

23. R x Q

Simplify! That's the magic word
to remember in endings where one
side has an advantage in material.

*With a Pawn ahead, reduce the
material (and your opponent's
chances) by exchanging pieces, if it
does not weaken your position.*

23. . . .   Kt x Q

Forced, of course.

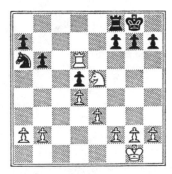

24. Kt—B6 !

A master move! You or I might
grab the Queen Pawn in order to be
two Pawns ahead. This could win,
but why complicate matters? Why
let Black seize the Bishop file with
24. . . . R—B1 and start a counterattack?

Note that Pillsbury retains his attack on the Queen Pawn with the
text move, adds to it a threat against
the Rook Pawn and prevents Black
from moving 24. . . . R—B1,
where the Knight check at K7 would
annihilate him!

It is not Queen sacrifices but
moves such as this, in the conduct of
an apparently simple position, that
mark the master player.

24. . . .   P—Kt3

Sooner or later the King will need
some air. The King is also anxious
to lend a hand in the ending by moving toward the center, by way of Kt2.

25. Kt x P

Another Pawn falls, while two
more are menaced by the Rook.

25. . . .   R—R1

Unable to get to QB1, the Rook

makes frantic efforts to get into the fight.

26. Kt—B6

The Knight withdraws, still in position to penalize 26. . . . R—QB1 by 27. Kt—K7ch winning the Rook.

26. . . .   K—Kt2

Black moves the King out of range of the Knight check and closer to the center.

27. P—QR3

There is no hurry about taking the Queen Pawn. White guards his Rook Pawn from any discovered attack on it by the Rook hidden away at R1, and also stops Black's Knight from later emerging at Kt5.

White avoids this possibility: 27. R x QP, R—QB1 28. R—Q6 (the Knight cannot move on account of the mate threat), Kt—Kt5, and Black wins the helpless Knight.

27. . . .   R—QB1

Finally posting his Rook on the coveted file. But can Black make use of it?

28. P—KKt4

White's King too needs an escape square. Black was threatening to win a piece by 28. . . . Kt—Kt1, twice attacking the Knight which could not run away.

The breakup of the Pawn position around the castled King is of no consequence in the ending. It is in the opening and midgame that these moves endanger the health of the King, as then he may be assaulted by every piece on the board.

28. . . .   Kt—B2

Protects his Queen Pawn, but at the cost of blocking the Rook. There was little choice as White was threatening 29. Kt—K7 (attacking the Rook and a couple of Pawns), R—B8ch 30. K—Kt2, R—QKt8 31. R x KtP, and the two connected passed Pawns assure White an easy win.

29. Kt—K7

Once again chasing the Rook from the file. To the threat on the Rook, White adds an attack on the Queen Knight Pawn and a double attack on the Queen Pawn.

29. . . .   R—QKt1

Black must hang on to the Knight Pawn as long as possible, as with its loss White's Pawns on the Queen side are free to go on to Queen.

30. R—Q7 !

Pressure must not be relaxed! Pillsbury prefers this to the Rook ending resulting from 30. Kt x QP, Kt x Kt 31. R x Kt, though that would also win.

30. . . .   Kt—K3

The Knight must leave, as the

effort to protect it by *30. . . . R—Kt2* fails after *31. Kt x QP* winning a piece.

31. Kt x QP

The Pawn falls at last, giving White a passed Pawn on the Queen file and a Rook on the seventh rank (in addition to the Pawns he picked up).

31. . . .   R—QB1

Rather than be gradually crushed to death, Black gives up another Pawn to get some sort of counterplay on the open file. If his Rook can get behind White's Pawns it might gather up a couple of them.

32. Kt x P

White can play safe and keep the Rook out by playing *32. Kt—B3,* but capturing the Knight Pawn leaves him with three passed Pawns—an offer hard to resist!

32. . . .   R—B7

Occupation of the seventh rank is the logical consequence of play on an open file by a Rook. This could mean trouble for White except that he has powerful antidotes in all those Pawns ready to rush up the board to become Queens!

33. P—Kt4

The Pawn lightly evades the Rook's attack.

33. . . .   Kt—Kt4

White's Pawns are not readily hindered from advancing, but perhaps White's deserted King might be sensitive to an attack by Knight and Rook.

34. P—QR4 !

White goes calmly about his business of pushing the passed Pawn and getting a Queen.

It was tempting to drive the Knight off with *34. P—B4,* but this move, believe it or not, enables Black to draw the game! After *34. P—B4, Kt—B6ch, 35. K—B1* (definitely not *35. K—R1, R x P mate!*), *R—Q7 ! 36. Kt—B4, Kt x Pch 37. K—Kt1, Kt—B6ch 38. K—B1, Kt—R7ch 39. K—K1, Kt—B6ch,* and Black draws by perpetual check.

34. . . .   Kt—K5

Black tries another means of entry.

35. P—R5

Again Pillsbury resists the impulse to get in a dig at the Knight. If *35. P—B3, Kt—Kt4* renews the threat of *36. . . . Kt x Pch* and a draw by perpetual check.

35. . . .   Kt x P

Can Black conjure up a mating attack?

36. P—R6

White pays no attention to his opponent's gestures as the best way to demonstrate their futility.

The passed Pawn has only two more squares to cover and cannot be stopped in its march.

36. . . .   Resigns

Black decides that it would be too much to hope for this bit of luck:

36. . . . Kt—R6ch 37. K—R1, Kt—Kt4 38. P—R7, Kt—B6 39. P—R8(Q), R x P checkmate!

GAME NO. 18

QUEEN'S GAMBIT DECLINED

WHITE	BLACK
Noteboom	Doesburgh

HOLLAND, 1931

1. P—Q4

In the opening it is advantageous to occupy the center with a Pawn and to develop the pieces with a view to controlling the center.

White begins by placing a Pawn where it takes complete possession of one important square and attacks two others. Control of these two squares K5 and QB5 makes it impossible for Black to place pieces there. White can hope to use K5 and QB5 as outposts for his pieces, which will have the support of the Queen Pawn.

The advance of the Queen Pawn serves an additional purpose in opening lines for White's Queen and Queen Bishop.

1. . . . P—Q4

This is the simplest way for Black to get an equal grip on the center and to prevent White's acquiring more territory with 2. P—K4.

2. P—QB4

White offers a Pawn to divert Black's Queen Pawn from the center. In effect, it is an offer to exchange a flank Pawn for a center Pawn, as White can regain the Pawn without any trouble.

Concealed in White's proposal is a threat of destroying Black's Pawn center by 3. P x P, Q x P 4. Kt—QB3 (gaining a tempo, as White develops a piece while Black must move the same one again), Q—QR4 5. P—K4, and White's centralization is imposing.

2. . . . P—K3

Black defends the center by supporting the Queen Pawn with another Pawn. If White plays 3. P x P he can recapture with a Pawn and maintain a Pawn in the center.

Black does not capture the Bishop Pawn as that means surrendering the center and his grip on K5.

The shutting in of his Queen Bishop (after 2. . . . P—K3) and the consequent difficulty in developing that piece effectively is one of the reasons for the popularity of the Queen's Gambit—for White.

3. Kt—QB3

A good move, as the Knight attacks two center squares K4 and Q5, adding its influence to the Pawn's pressure on the latter.

3. . . . Kt—KB3

Black's Knight develops toward the center, where its mobility is greatest and where it can equalize the pressure exerted by White's Knight.

4. B—Kt5

A pin which threatens to win a Pawn or break up Black's King-side Pawn position: 5. P x P, P x P 6.

B x Kt, and Black must either submit to being left with a badly doubled Pawn by 6. . . . P x B or lose a Pawn after 6. . . . Q x B 7. Kt x P.

The threat is actually of minor importance. White does not pin the Knight to institute a threat which can so easily be parried. What White is interested in is the most effective placement of his pieces, and the development of the Bishop at Kt5 is extremely strong. The restraint it places on Black's Knight and the cramping effect it has on Black's whole game is not easily shaken off.

4. . . .   QKt—Q2

In Queen Pawn openings, Black's Queen Knight does its best job at Q2, not QB3. At Q2 it supports the King Knight and helps prepare the advance of the Queen Bishop Pawn to B4. The Queen Knight must not move to B3, where it obstructs the Bishop Pawn. *The Queen Bishop Pawn must be free to advance and attack White's center.*

Black incidentally sets a trap with the text move, which is designed to catch the greedy player.

5. P—K3

Why not win a Pawn? This is what would happen: 5. P x P, P x P 6. Kt x P, Kt x Kt! (the Knight breaks the pin by brute force) 7. B x Q, B—Kt5ch 8. Q—Q2, B x Qch 9. K x B, K x B, and Black has gained a piece.

White could not fall into the trap if he followed the principle which covers these cases:

Do not chase after Pawns at the expense of your development.

White's last move supports the center Pawn and creates an outlet for the King Bishop.

5. . . .   P—B3

Black strengthens the base of his Queen Pawn and opens a diagonal for his Queen's use. He plans a counterattack beginning with 6. . . . Q—R4 and 7. . . . B—Kt5.

6. P—QR3

This puts a stop to any such maneuver, as Black's Bishop can never get to Kt5 to pin the Knight.

6. . . .   B—K2

Black develops a piece, unpins the Knight and clears the back rank for castling.

7. Q—B2

An ideal development for the Queen in this opening. At B2, the Queen exerts pressure on the Bishop file (which will be strongly evident after center Pawns are exchanged) and controls the square K4. The latter circumstance is the reason for the Queen's coming into play at this point, instead of the expected mobilization of the King-side pieces. It is vital to guard the square K4 so that Black can not free himself easily by playing 7. . . . Kt—K5 and exchanging some pieces.

7. . . .   O—O

Black moves his King to safer quarters.

He cannot free his crowded posi-

tion by the Lasker maneuver of
7. . . . Kt—K5 as White responds
by 8. B x B, Q x B 9. Kt x Kt, P x Kt
10. Q x P and wins a Pawn. Notice
that White's Pawn at QR3 prevents
Black from regaining the Pawn by
10. . . . Q—Kt5ch, so that White's
sixth move was not a waste of time.

Instead of the passive King-side
castling, Black should have tried for
counterplay by 7. . . . P x P 8.
B x P, P—K4 !, which disputes control of the center and helps clear a
diagonal for his Queen's Bishop.

8. Kt—B3

Brings the King Knight to its best
post and attacks the square K5
again, putting an end to any contemplated break by . . . P—K4.

8. . . .   P—QR3

A preparatory move for the ma-
neuver 9. . . . P x P 10. B x P, P—
QKt4 11. B—Q3, B—Kt2, followed
by an eventual 12. . . . P—QB4.
This would serve to develop the
Queen Bishop, free his Queen side
and start action against White's
Pawn center.

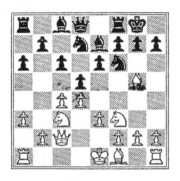

9. R—Q1 !

If Black is going in for an attack
on the wing, White is prepared to
meet it with the recommended
specific—play in the center!

The position of the Rook at Q1
acts as a deterrent to exchanges of
center Pawns by Black, as any
clearances on the file increase the
pressure of the Rook on the file.

9. . . .   R—K1

Black brings his Rook to the King
file as the center is usually the
theater of action.

10. B—Q3

With the entrance of this Bishop,
White's development is nearly complete. Notice that he plays no combinations of any sort, either to win
material or to start an attack on the
King until most of his pieces are
brought off the back rank and into
the field. It is only after these pieces
are posted where they are most
effective—where they control the
center, enjoy their greatest mobility,
and take possession of a good part
of the important territory—that
White looks around for a combination, a stroke that will decide the
game quickly.

10. . . .   P x P

Black has delayed taking this
Pawn until White's King Bishop
made a move, so that the Bishop
will now lose a move in recapturing.

11. B x BP

The recapture is forced.

11. . . .   P—Kt4

Black makes the Bishop lose time

in retreating and vacates the square QKt2 for his Queen Bishop's development.

12. B—Q3 !

From this square, the Bishop manages to be remarkably useful:

It reaches out in two directions to attack, it helps guard K4 from invasion, it threatens Black's King-side position and prevents Black from freeing himself by 12. . . . P—B4.

12. . . .   P—R3

If 12. . . . P—B4 13. P x P, B x P (certainly not 13. . . . Kt x P 14. B x Pch, and White wins the Queen by discovered attack) 14. B x Pch, and White wins a Pawn, as the pinned Knight is helpless to touch the Bishop.

With the text move, Black moves the Rook Pawn out of the line of fire (of the above note). Now he hopes to be able to proceed to free his Queen side and establish a state of tension in the center by 13. . . . P—B4. Incidentally, he would like White's Queen Bishop to declare its intentions.

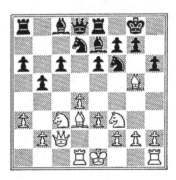

13. B x Kt !

A very fine concept! White does not waste time holding on to the two Bishops but plays to prevent any counterplay by . . . P—B4. If he can keep the Bishop Pawn from advancing, Black's game will be fearfully cramped, and he may never solve the problem of getting his Queen Bishop settled on a decent square.

The immediate object of 13. B x Kt is to divert one of Black's recapturing pieces, the Knight or the Bishop from its surveillance of Black's QB4 square and the support of a Pawn moving to that square.

13. . . .   Kt x B

This is probably better than taking with the Bishop, as Black's Queen and Queen Bishop now have more freedom.

14. O—O

The King (who must be secure from danger at all costs) goes into hiding, while the Rook (that must take part in the fighting) comes closer to the scene of action.

14. . . .   B—Kt2

With Rook and Queen on the same file, it would be foolhardy to venture on 14. . . . P—B4. White simply takes the Pawn and penalizes the recapture 15. . . . B x P with 16. B—R7ch winning the Queen.

Black's idea, besides that of developing the Queen Bishop, is to bring his Rook to QB1 and then push the Bishop Pawn.

15. Kt—K4 !

White clears the Bishop file so

that he now has three pieces
(Queen, Knight and Queen Pawn)
concentrating their power on QB5,
with the object of making an advance of Black's Bishop Pawn to
that square impossible.

Notice too how White has re-
sisted the temptation to play P—K4
filling up the center with Pawns.
Instead he keeps the square K4 free
and utilizes it as a springboard for
his pieces.

15. . . .   Kt x Kt

Otherwise, White might swing
the Knight over to QB5 and completely smother Black's Queen side.

16. B x Kt

Still keeping Black under restraint: he may not play 16. . . .
P—QB4 as his Queen Bishop would
be snapped up.

16. . . .   P—KB4

Black must drive the Bishop off
at once, even at the cost of weakening the Pawn position on his King
side. A delay gives White time to
play 17. Kt—K5 (intensifying the
pressure on the Queen Bishop Pawn
and incidentally providing the
square KB3 as a square of retreat
for the Bishop) followed if need be
by 18. R—B1.

17. B—Q3

Third visit of the Bishop to this
square.

White must not be hasty and
play 17. B x QBP, as the reply
17. . . . R—QB1 pins the Bishop.

17. . . .   Q—Kt3

Once again preparing for the liberating Pawn push.

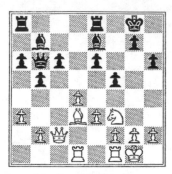

18. R—B1 !

The position demands that
White devote all his efforts to sustaining the blockade of Black's
Queen Bishop Pawn. White must acquire undisputed control of the
square QB5, so that the Pawn may
never advance. He must not relax
for a moment, as *domination of the
key square QB5 assures him of a
positional win.*

18. . . .   QR—B1

Black persists in his plan to push
the Pawn. If he does not get this
move in, his Queen Bishop will
never have any air.

19. P—QKt4 !

Nails the Pawn down! White has
a won game, strategically. What remains is to apply the proper tactical
touches to compel the opponent to
yield. The time is ripe for the combinations to appear!

19. . . .   Q—Q1

Ready to parry 20. Q—Kt3
(threatening 21. Q x Pch or 21.
B x BP) with 20. . . . Q—Q4.

20. Kt—K5

A powerful blow! White attacks the unfortunate Queen Bishop Pawn (which must stay where it is) a third time. Against passive resistance, White plans 21. P—B4 (to give his Knight additional support and to stabilize the center), followed by 22. B—K2 and 23. B—B3, after which the Bishop Pawn must perish.

20. . . .   P—QR4

Black attacks one of the Pawns hemming in his Queen side.

Against 20. . . . B—B3, White sticks to the script with 21. P—B4, then 22. B—K2 and 23. B—B3.

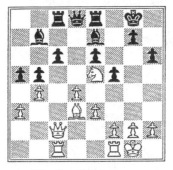

21. Q—Kt3 !

Renews the threat of 22. Q x Pch or 22. B x BP.

White probably gave no more than a glance to 21. P x P, to which Black can reply 21. . . . Q x RP or 21. . . . B x P or 21. . . . P—B4, any of which gives him far too much freedom—from White's point of view!

21. . . .   B—Q3

The defense that Black had relied on is ruled out: if 21. . . . Q—Q4

22. Q x Q, KP x Q 23. B x BP, and White wins a Pawn. Or if Black recaptures the Queen with the Bishop Pawn, then 23. B x KtP wins for White.

22. B x BP

The first bit of actual violence brings in a Pawn.

22. . . .   Q—B3

With an attack on the Bishop and a double attack on the Knight, Black hopes to get his Pawn back.

23. B—Kt1

The idea of this withdrawal to the back rank is to support the Queen in an attack along a diagonal, either by moving the Queen to B2 or by shifting the Bishop to R2 behind the Queen.

23. . . .   B x Kt

Black does not care to part with the services of an active piece, but he must do so in order to recover the Pawn he lost.

24. P x B

Forced.

24. . . .   Q x KP

Material is even, and Black seems to have survived the worst.

It is true that White can win a Pawn by 25. P x P, but he would be left with doubled Pawns, isolated on the Rook file, and it is doubtful that he could get any advantage from the extra Pawn. There must be a better reward for fine position play than this dubious bounty!

25. R—B5!

White spurns the Pawn, in favor of putting on more pressure. The Rook now holds Black's Queen side in a paralyzing grip. The strength of White's move is evident in the fact that the Rook can never be dislodged!

25. . . .   P—R5

An intervening move, whose purpose is not only to save the Pawn, but to gauge White's plans by his next Queen move.

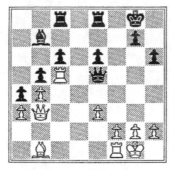

26. Q—R2!

A remarkable retreat! One would expect 26. Q—B2, so that the Queen, backed up by the Bishop, might penetrate Black's King-side position. But Black refutes this cleverly by 26. . . . Q—B3, when the check at R7 is met by 27. . . . K—B2, and White has no means of furthering the attack. Or, if after 26. Q—B2, Q—B3 27. P—K4 (intending to banish the Queen by 28. P—K5 and then pierce the position), P—K4 by Black repels any invasion.

26. . . .   Q—Q3

The defense by 26. . . . Q—B3 succumbs to 27. P—K4! (now we see the point of 26. Q—R2—it is to pin Black's King Pawn and prevent 27. . . . P—K4 at this point), QR —Q1 28. P—K5, Q—B5 29. Q—B2 (threatening 30. Q—R7ch, K—B1 31. B—Kt6, R—K2 32. Q—R8 mate), Q—Kt4 30. P—B4, Q—Kt5 31. R—QB3, and the entrance of the Rook at KKt3 followed by 33. Q—R7ch is conclusive.

Notice that the move 31. R—QB3, relaxing the pressure on the Queen side is not an infraction of principle. An attack which leads to mate or to resignation takes precedence over positional considerations.

27. Q—B2

Now this grouping has more effect! White threatens 28. Q—R7ch, K—B1 29. B—Kt6, KR—Q1 30. Q—R8ch, K—K2 31. Q x KtP mate.

27. . . .   R(B1)—Q1

If 27. . . . P—K4 (to guard his KKt3 square with the Queen) 28. Q—R7ch, K—B2 (on 28. . . . K—B1 29. B—Kt6 wins easily), 29. P—B4 (threatens 30. P x P dis. ch) P—K5 30. B—R2ch, K—B3 31. Q—B5ch, K—K2 32. Q—B7ch, and White takes the Bishop off, as a start.

28. Q—R7ch

Control of the white squares leading to Black's King makes this a decisive invasion; the cramping of Black's Queen side and the smothering of his Bishop makes it difficult for Black to hold out.

28. ... K—B1

On 28. ... K—B2, White can either win the exchange by a Bishop check or pursue the attack by 29. P—B4, when the continuation might be 29. ... R—KR1 30. Q—Kt6ch, K—B1 31. P—B5, P—K4 (or 31. ... Q—K2) 32. P—B6, and White wins.

29. B—Kt6

Further confines the King while attacking the Rook. The threat is 30. Q—R8ch, K—K2 31. Q x KtP mate.

29. ... Resigns

Black can only delay the execution at great cost in material.

White's play is a fine example of the value of preventive strategy. In paralyzing Black's Queen side he demonstrates the extraordinary fact that weaknesses on one wing can lead to complete collapse on the other! Once Black is held in restraint, his efforts to make some sort of stand seem little more than feeble flutterings.

GAME NO. 19

QUEEN'S GAMBIT DECLINED

WHITE   BLACK
Grunfeld   Schenkein
VIENNA, 1915

1. P—Q4

Beginning the game with this Pawn move releases two pieces at one stroke. This is as much advantage as White can get in one move, in the business of getting the pieces off the back rank and onto the field of battle. The Pawn itself plays an important part in the struggle for domination of the center and the control of key squares.

1. ... P—Q4

Probably Black's best reply. With it he offsets White's pressure on the center.

2. P—QB4

This is an attack, as well as an offer of a Pawn. It is an attack in that White threatens by 3. P x P, Q x P 4. Kt—QB3, Q—QR4 5. P—K4 to establish two Pawns abreast in the center. It is an offer, since Black can gain a Pawn (temporarily, it is true) by 2. ... P x P.

Either way you look at it, White's purpose is to destroy White's Pawn center, either by removing Black's Queen Pawn from Q4, or enticing it away from there.

2. ... P—QB3

Black is ready to meet 3. P x P with 3. ... P x P, *recapturing with a Pawn* in order to maintain a Pawn in the center.

Black's second move has the merit of not shutting in the Queen Bishop, as the alternative 2. ... P—K3 does. On the debit side though, if Black does develop his Bishop freely, he must be prepared to beat off troublesome attacks on his Queen Pawn and his Queen Knight Pawn, occasioned by the absence of the Bishop. Another and more important consideration is that while the Bishop Pawn standing at B3 makes a fine support for the

Queen Pawn, it is not fulfilling its main purpose in life, which is to challenge White's control of the center. It must be available to advance to B4 in order to attack White's Queen Pawn and to open the Bishop file at the same time for the use of Black's heavy pieces.

3. Kt—KB3

Why doesn't White play 3. P—B5 and stifle his opponent completely on the Queen side? These are some of the reasons he does not do so:

a) It is good strategy to maintain tension in the center—to keep the Pawn position fluid, not static.

b) In advancing to B5, White gives up his attack on the Black center, and the option of exchanging Pawns when it is worth while to do so. Such an exchange might be the means of demolishing Black's whole center!

c) The square QB5 should be an outpost for a piece, not a Pawn. A piece posted there exerts a tremendous effect on Black's whole Queen side.

d) Placing a Pawn at QB5 closes the Bishop file and makes it useless for the operations of the Queen or the Rooks.

e) In the opening, pieces, not Pawns, should be moved.

All the foregoing explains why a chess master "instinctively" finds the right moves. It is not that he can analyze twenty moves ahead, or that he bothers to examine the effects of every possible move. Sometimes he does not even look one move ahead! He saves time by dismissing from consideration any move which his instinct (or more accurately his experience and judgment) warns is contrary to principle and cannot possibly lead to favorable results. By discarding moves which offend his feeling for what is proper, by avoiding artificial expedients which are distasteful to his position judgment, he plays stronger, sounder chess at ten seconds a move than does the average amateur in his serious tournament games.

3. . . .   P—K3

A quiet but not a waiting move. It strengthens the center and frees the King Bishop.

Black's intentions are still indefinite. He might capture the Pawn next move and then try to hold on to it by . . . P—QKt4. Or he might go in for the Stonewall arrangement, by playing 4. . . . P—KB4 followed by 5. . . . Kt—KB3 and 6. . . . Kt—K5.

4. P—K3

So White plays safe by protecting the Bishop Pawn. He releases one Bishop at the expense of another, but one cannot have everything.

4. . . .   Kt—B3

The Knight takes up a good post, extending powerful influence on Q4 and K5, two of the four strategic squares in the center.

5. B—Q3

The Bishop occupies a diagonal where it can operate with great effect, while the King side is cleared for speedy castling.

Broadly speaking, it is good policy to develop the King-side pieces first, so that the King can find safer quarters. Most players are familiar enough with this procedure and its benefits to carry it out faithfully, some even to the extent of completely forgetting about releasing the Queen-side pieces!

5. . . .   QKt—Q2

Excellent, as the Knight supports an eventual thrust at White's center by . . . P—B4 or . . . P—K4. Being in touch with the other Knight also has its uses, as it can replace the King Knight at B3 if the need arises.

6. QKt—Q2

The chief object of this move is to back up an advance of the King Pawn as in the Colle system. A second purpose of the Knight's development at Q2 instead of B3 is to recapture with the Knight if Black plays 6. . . . P x P, and then anchor one of the Knights at K5, strongly supported by the other one.

6. . . .   B—K2

A good defensive move—perhaps too much so! The Bishop is well placed at K2, and progress is made toward castling, but no attempt is made to prevent White from expanding and acquiring more territory. Black must get in the counterthrust . . . P—B4 or be slowly crowded back and confined to a small area.

7. O—O

The King flees to a safer part of the board, while the King Rook takes a more active position.

7. . . .   Q—B2

Another quiet developing move, which might better have been replaced by the aggressive 7. . . . P—B4. Black cannot temporize but must fight for equal rights. Chess is no game for cowards!

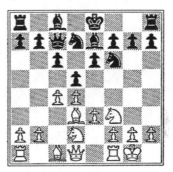

8. P—K4 !

This resembles the Colle device for breaking up the position in the center and opening lines of attack for the pieces crouched in the background.

8. . . .   P x KP

Black cannot allow the Pawn to go to K5. There it would dispossess his King Knight and put it completely out of action.

9. Kt x P

More energetic than recapturing with the Bishop. The Knight gets out of the way of the Queen Bishop and puts the question to the adverse Knight.

9. . . .   Kt x Kt

Black must exchange to relieve his constricted position.

10. B x Kt

The exchange of pieces suits White too. The more material disappears from the board, the more scope there is for the activities of his pieces, especially the wide-ranging Bishops.

10. . . .   Kt—B3

The attack on the Bishop gains a tempo for Black while giving his Queen-side pieces a bit more room.

11. B—B2

The Bishop retreats, but to a fine point of vantage. It is poised for a King-side attack but can quickly shift to the Queen's wing if necessary.

White's position is distinctly superior. He enjoys these advantages:

His Bishops have a great range of attack.

He dominates the center with his Pawns.

He controls the strategic square K5.

His major pieces can operate with great effect on the center files.

11. . . .   P—QKt3

To develop the Bishop at Kt2, since it is shut in by the King Pawn on the other side.

12. Q—K2

White develops another piece and intensifies the pressure on K5. Control of this square will make it difficult if not impossible for Black to free his position by advancing the King Pawn.

12. . . .   B—Kt2

With the development of this Bishop, Black seems to be finding a way out of his troubles. He is now set to play 13. . . . P—B4 next move, operate on the long diagonal with his Queen Bishop and establish a proper state of tension in the center. Will he have time for this, or has he missed the right moment to hit out with . . . P—B4?

13. Kt—K5 !

A magnificent outpost for the Knight! From this center station the Knight radiates power in eight directions, accentuating Black's difficulties in gaining freedom for his pieces.

13. . . .   R—Q1

This looks plausible, as Black mobilizes the Rook with a threat on a Pawn.

It is too late, alas, to play the liberating 13. . . . P—B4. White's reply 14. B—R4ch would force his King to move (interposing the Knight or Bishop instead costs a piece) and forfeit the right to castle.

14. R—Q1

White defends without loss of time. The King Rook guards the Pawn and develops simultaneously, going to the file it would have chosen in any event.

Rooks belong on open files, or on files likely to be opened.

14. . . .   O—O

The advance 14. . . . P—B4 is still premature, being met by 15. B—R4ch, and Black must either move the King and lose the castling privilege or play 15. . . . Kt—Q2, losing the exchange after 16. B x Ktch, R x B 17. Kt x R.

Before White makes his next move, let us sum up his advantages:

His Pawn position in the center, restraining the free movements of the enemy pieces, is definitely superior to Black's.

His Queen attacks nine squares while Black's is limited to five.

His Bishops control thirteen squares, whereas Black's dominate seven.

His Knight enjoys wonderful mobility, while Black's Knight can only retreat.

Clearly White has established a definite superiority in position. His pieces have greater mobility, as simple arithmetic shows, and their power to attack is definitely greater than is Black's. White has earned the right to look for a decisive combination that will exploit to the full his positional advantages.

It is interesting to see what form of attack will succeed in breaking through Black's strongly intrenched position.

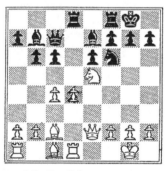

15. B—B4!

The Bishop develops with a threat against the Queen. White intends to play 16. Kt—Kt6 next move, discovering an attack on the Queen by the Bishop. After the Queen moves away, White will capture the Rook, winning the exchange.

15. . . .   B—Q3

The alternative 15. . . . Q—B1, moving the Queen out of the Bishop's range, does not look appetizing. With the text, Black prevents the Knight from leaving and uncovering an attack.

16. P—B5 !

This begins a series of vigorous blows which do not let up until Black surrenders. White's idea is twofold: he will dislodge the Bishop and permanently seal up Black's Queen-side position.

16. . . .   P x P

This is forced, as on 16. . . . B x Kt White can win by 17. B x B, Q—B1 18. B x Kt, P x B 19. Q—Kt4ch, K—R1 20. B x P, K x B 21. R—Q3 followed by 22. R—R3 mate.

17. P x P

Another Pawn springs up to stab at the Bishop.

17. . . .   B x Kt

Or 17. . . . B x P 18. Kt—Kt6, and White wins the exchange.

18. B x B

The recapture again menaces the Queen and keeps Black on the run.

18. . . .   Q—R4

If 18. . . . Q—B1, White wins

by *19.* B x Kt, P x B *20.* Q—Kt4ch, K—R1 *21.* Q—KR4 (threatening mate), P—B4 *22.* Q—B6ch, K—Kt1 *23.* P—KR4 (intending to push the Pawn to R6 and then to mate at Kt7), R—Q2 (to follow with *24.* . . . Q—Q1 driving White's Queen off) *24.* R x R, Q x R *25.* R—Q1, Q—B2 *26.* P—R5, and the threat of winning by *27.* P—R6 as well as by *27.* R—Q3 followed by *28.* R—Kt3 ch is decisive.

19. B x Kt !

White does away with the Knight, the best defender of a castled position, as a prelude to breaking into the stronghold of the King.

19. . . . P x B

After this, Black's position on the King side is torn apart, where it should be barricaded. On the Queen side, where his pieces need room for their movements, his position is nailed up—and by an unprotected Pawn at that!

20. Q—Kt4ch

This is more accurate than *20.* Q—K4. It leaves Black with only one reply.

20. . . . K—R1

The King must go to the corner.

21. Q—KR4

Now threatening mate on the move.

21. . . . P—B4

Black's only defense.

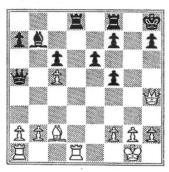

22. Q—K7 !

Penetrating into the heart of the enemy's position. The attack on Black's Bishop is a device whose purpose is to occupy the opponent, even if only for a moment, with the problem of saving the Bishop. This will give White the time he needs to carry out his real threat, an attack on both the Rooks.

22. . . . B—B1

If Black moves *22.* . . . R—QKt1 to protect the Bishop, White wins it this way: *23.* Q—B6ch, K—Kt1 *24.* R—Q3, P—B5 *25.* R—KR3 (threatening *26.* B x P mate), KR—Q1 *26.* R x P, and mate follows next move.

23. P—QKt4 !

A knockout blow! The Queen is forced off the diagonal leading to the Rook at Q1—which needs her protection!

What can Black do? If *23.* . . . Q x KtP *24.* R x R, R x R *25.* Q x Rch wins. Or if *23.* . . . KR—K1 *24.* Q—B6ch, followed by *25.* P x Q is the reply. Finally, if *23.* . . . R x Rch *24.* R x R in response leaves two strong threats on tap: *25.* Q x R mate and 25. P x Q, both of which cannot be parried at the same time.

23. . . .   Resigns

QUEEN'S GAMBIT DECLINED

WHITE	BLACK
Rubinstein	Salwe

LODZ, 1908

1. P—Q4

A hundred years ago players began their games almost automatically with 1. P—K4. And if they could offer a gambit, they did so too.

Today, when everyone wants to win with the minimum of risk, it's 1. P—Q4 nearly every time. The Queen Pawn openings lead to positions which are safe and sound. They offer security, and as additional inducement let White have a slight advantage right from the start.

With his first move, White occupies and exerts pressure in the center with a Pawn *which is protected* and frees his Queen and Queen Bishop at the same time.

1. . . .   P—Q4

The classical reply, this equalizes the pressure in the center. It also prevents White from playing 2. P—K4 and monopolizing most of the best squares.

2. P—QB4

With several objects in mind:

To induce Black to surrender the center, by offering him a Pawn.

To exchange Pawns (if Black doesn't) and open the Bishop file for his Rooks.

To institute an attack on Black's Queen Pawn, and the square Q5.

2. . . .   P—K3

Black supports the Queen Pawn with another Pawn. He is prepared, if White plays 3. P x P, *to recapture with a Pawn* and maintain a Pawn in the center.

3. Kt—QB3

A good development for the Knight, now that it does not block the Bishop Pawn and the opening of that file. It is a bit sharper than 3. Kt—KB3, since it augments the pressure on Q5, an important square in this opening.

3. . . .   P—QB4

This move has the unqualified endorsement of Tarrasch. He held that Black had no better means of developing his pieces freely and easily, even if exchanges of Pawns in the center left him with an isolated Pawn.

One advantage of 3. . . . P—QB4 is that it disputes possession of the center at once by the attack on the Queen Pawn. Another is that it enables Black to post his Queen Knight at QB3, instead of at Q2 where it interferes for a long time with the career of the Queen Bishop.

4. BP x P !

The best way to keep the initiative! The purpose of this exchange is to saddle Black with an isolated Queen's Pawn.

4. . . .   KP x P

The safest recapture. Black can offer a Pawn by 4. . . . BP x P 5. Q x P, Kt—QB3 6. Q—Q1, P x P 7. Q x P, B—K3, but the gambit is dubious.

5. Kt—B3

White's Knights now have all four of the strategic central squares (K4, K5, Q4 and Q5) under surveillance.

5. . . .   Kt—KB3

More to the point is 5. . . . Kt —QB3 first, intensifying Black's pressure on Q5. He would then be ready to meet 6. P x P with 6. . . . P— Q5, giving him a wedge in the center.

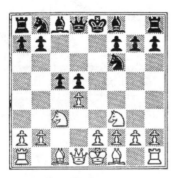

6. P—KKt3 !

Probably the best of the many good moves White has at his command. He can play the placid 6. P— K3 or 6. B—B4, either of which gives him a safe, substantial position. Or he can attack at once by the aggressive 6. B—Kt5, with which Alekhine beat Kussman brilliantly in 1924.

With the quiet text move, Rubin-

stein intends to fianchetto his King Bishop and increase the pressure on Q5.

6. . . .   Kt—B3

Black attains one of the objectives which actuated him to select the Tarrasch Defense. His Queen Knight enjoys some influence in the center, while the Queen Bishop (usually restrained by a Knight at Q2) is free and untrammeled.

7. B—Kt2

The Bishop commands the long diagonal and will devote special attention to Black's Queen Pawn. For the moment, the Knight obstructs its path, but a Knight can readily leap aside.

7. . . .   P x P

Black exchanges to give his pieces more scope (note the increased mobility of his King Bishop) but this is not without its dangers. Open lines favor the player whose development is superior, and in this case it is White.

Somewhat better is the quiet 7. . . . B—K2, developing a piece. Or, if Black feels pugnacious, the sharp 7. . . . B—Kt5, putting more pressure on the Queen Pawn by striking at one of its defenders.

8. KKt x P

The recapture leaves Black with an isolated Pawn in the center of the board. Such a Pawn must depend on pieces to defend it from attack, as there are no Pawns on either side that can come to its support. Another consideration is that an adverse piece can be posted firmly on the square directly in front of the isolated Pawn, in this case White's Q4, without any fear of being driven off by a Pawn.

All this is very discouraging, but in return for these shortcomings, the possessor of the isolated Pawn is rewarded with open files and diagonals —room for the activities of his pieces. The Pawn itself, in spite of its forlorn appearance, often becomes the spearhead that pierces and breaks up a fortified position.

The theorists themselves are not in complete agreement on the merits or demerits of an isolated Pawn. Many years ago, Philidor said in his *Chess Analyzed: or Instructions by Which a Perfect Knowledge of This Noble Game May in a Short Time Be Acquired:* "A Pawn, when separated from his fellows, will seldom or never make a fortune." For the defense, we have Tarrasch, who said, "He who fears to have an isolated Queen's Pawn should give up chess."

There are arguments for both sides:

Black has in his favor: increased mobility for his pieces, possible outposts for his pieces at K5 and QB5 (supported by the Queen Pawn) and open files for his major pieces (the King and Queen Bishop files).

White has advantages in the fact that he can station a piece permanently at Q4 and can keep Black busy warding off threats on the Queen Pawn. Not that the Pawn can easily be captured, since the number of pieces attacking it can always be equaled by the number of pieces defending it, but by virtue of the fact

that the Pawn needs constant care, White can switch the attack to another section of the board. Black must not only be prepared to fight back there but also keep in close touch with the Pawn.

8. . . .   Q—Kt3

Urging his opponent to exchange Knights or defend by 9. P—K3 blocking the path of his Queen Bishop.

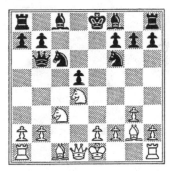

9. Kt x Kt !

A suggestion White is delighted to fall in with! He relieves Black of the isolated Pawn, but in return fixes him with other weaknesses. From now on White will forget about the square Q5 and turn his attention to dominating Q4 and QB5 completely. By anchoring pieces on those squares he can prevent Black from advancing his Queen Pawn or his Queen Bishop Pawn. The effect of blockading these Pawns will be to shut in all of Black's pieces behind the Pawns.

9. . . .   P x Kt

The alternative capture by 9. . . . Q x Kt loses the Queen Pawn at once.

10. O—O

Before pursuing the attack, White conveys the King to safer quarters. The King Rook meanwhile becomes available for action on the center files.

10. . . .   B—K2

Unfortunately, Black may not advance either of the Pawns marked for doom: if 10. . . . P—B4 11. Kt x P wins a Pawn, or if 10. . . . P—Q5 11. Kt—R4 forces the Queen to desert one of the threatened Pawns.

There were better chances of resistance with 10. . . . B—K3, protecting the Queen Pawn once more so as to get in the freeing . . . P—B4 as quickly as possible. Black cannot rely on passive measures or he will be crushed to death.

11. Kt—R4 !

White is not interested in scaring the Queen. The Knight does not move to attack but to get a grip on the square QB5 so that a White piece may settle itself securely there.

11. . . .   Q—Kt4

The Queen stays in the neighborhood to help beat off the invaders.

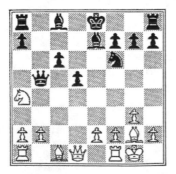

12. B—K3 !

You would expect this Bishop to go to B4, where its range is long and where it does not obstruct the King Pawn's movements; or you might consider Kt5 where it cramps Black's game an effective spot for the Bishop's development. These are good moves and natural moves, but they do not fit in with the strategic concept governing this position. Once there is a definite, logical plan to follow, we must play moves that conform to that plan, so that the improvement of our own position or the undermining of the opponent's is conducted systematically and not as a result of desultory development. Development, at this point, must not be carried on for its own sake.

It may seem strange that control of one square can cause a position to collapse, but it is true. It is one of the fine points in the Queen's Gambit that such domination (resulting from Black's neglect to dispute the center and also free his Queen side by . . . P—QB4) enables White to confine his opponent's pieces to a small area and drive them back step by step, while he (White) either starts escorting a Pawn to the Queening square or turns to the other side of the board and beleaguers the King.

12. . . .   O—O

Not having read the previous note, Black is content to make "good" developing moves.

Black should concentrate his energies to advancing the Bishop Pawn one square before it is permanently fixed at B3. Pushing the Pawn at once is premature, as after 12. . . . P—B4 13. B x QP, Kt x B 14. Q x Kt, Q x Kt 15. Q x R, White has won the exchange. But he could put up more fight with 12. . . . B—K3 (protecting the Queen Pawn and preparing to move the Bishop Pawn) followed by 13. . . . Kt—Q2 and 14. . . . R—QB1, all of which is designed to help the Pawn to advance one square.

13. R—QB1

White seizes the open file, puts more pressure to bear on QB5, and prepares to post a piece there.

13. . . .   B—KKt5

A double attack on the King Pawn, which may be embarrassing to meet. How does White answer it?

If 14. R—K1, the Rook's development is wretched.

If 14. Kt—B3, Q x KtP costs a Pawn.

If 14. R—B2, Black snaps up the Knight.

If 14. P—B3, White loosens the Pawn position around his King and hems in his own Bishop.

In spite of all these arguments in favor of Black's move, Tarrasch used to dismiss such demonstrations with: "Beginning of an attack . . .

14. P—B3

. . . and end of attack!"

The hemming in of the King Bishop is only temporary, and as for the weakness of the King-side Pawns, it is of no consequence if Black cannot exploit it.

14. . . .   B—K3

The Bishop finds the right square, but it is late—much too late!

15. B—B5 !

Now that the strategic squares Q4 and QB5 are under his control, White stations a piece where it will immobilize Black's Pawns and restrict the movements of his pieces.

15. . . .   KR—K1

Black must either protect his Bishop or submit to an exchange of pieces. The latter option does not appeal to him, as after 15. . . . B x B 16. R x B replaces one blockader with another, with gain of tempo, by the attack on the Queen.

16. R—KB2 !

A very fine move! The Rook prepares to switch over to QB2, to help exploit the Queen Bishop file. It also vacates KB1, so that the Bishop can get to a more useful diagonal.

16. . . .   Kt—Q2

Black attacks the Bishop a third time, with the hope of forcing it to retreat.

17. B x B

The Bishop does not withdraw, as that lets Black get in the thrust 17. . . . P—QB4, breaking the bind on the position. Nor does White support the Bishop by 17. P—QKt4, the kind of move many players make instantly. The consequence would be 17. . . . B x B, forcing recapture by the Pawn, since 18. R x B costs the exchange, and 18. Kt x B allows 18. . . . Q x KtP. After 18. P x B though, the Pawn stationed at B5 is not only immobile and useless but itself closes the file to White's pieces. This would negate the whole strategy of the position, which is to occupy the weak squares in the opponent's position with pieces, not Pawns. Pieces can be freely moved about, so that lines are kept open for the attack. Pieces can be shifted around, permitting one blockader to make room for a different one, if occasion requires it.

17. . . .   R x B

Black must recapture.

18. Q—Q4 !

Excellent! The centralization of the Queen is tremendously effective. Not only does the Queen exert its influence to every part of the board, but it prohibits Black from getting in the freeing 18. . . . P—QB4 move and prepares as well the posting of the Knight at QB5. Notice how, from its new position, the Queen still guards the Knight and keeps an eye on the Knight Pawn. The Knight is free to leave, while the King Pawn, abandoned by the Queen, is now under the Rook's care.

18. . . .   KR—K1

This Rook retreats to help defend the Queen Bishop file against White's attack, since a move by the Queen Rook costs a Pawn.

19. B—B1

A subtle means of activating the Bishop. The alternative 19. P—B4 is not nearly as good, because it gives Black's pieces much more room in which to maneuver, his Bishop and Knight then having access to White's K4 square.

19. . . .   KR—QB1

Reviving the possibility of playing 20. . . . P—QB4. Black must have realized by this time that if he does not get this move in, he might just as well sit back and wait for the ax to fall.

20. P—K3 !

Such a little move, but it accomplishes a great deal! It gains a tempo or two as it uncovers an attack on the Queen (forcing Black to lose a move by its retreat), opens up a diagonal for the King Bishop, and clears a pathway on the second rank, so that the King Rook can switch over to QB2 and increase the pressure on the Bishop file.

20. . . .   Q—Kt2

Discretion is the better part of valor, as Beaumont and Fletcher said, anticipating Shakespeare.

The desperate thrust 20. . . . P —QB4 is refuted by 21. R x P, and Black dare not touch the Rook, his Queen still being under attack.

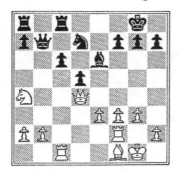

21. Kt—B5 !

Blockade! The Knight settles down on QB5 and barricades Black's position.

21. . . .   Kt x Kt

Black removes the Knight, not only to get rid of an active blockader but on the theory that exchanges help relieve a cramped position.

22. R x Kt

Not so agile as its predecessor, the new blockader enjoys the privilege of immunity to harassment by Pawns or threats by the Bishop, which is confined to squares of opposite color to the one the Rook occupies.

22. . . .   R—B2

Black cannot counterattack. All he can do is sit tight and await events.

But how does White profit by his opponent's lack of mobility? How does he overcome passive resistance?

23. KR—B2

First by doubling Rooks on the open file, *which more than doubles the strength of the Rooks.*

At present, the Rooks seem to be biting on granite, but there are ways and means! Have faith!

23. . . .   Q—Kt3

Black sticks to noncommittal moves, until his opponent declares himself by a threatening gesture.

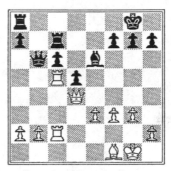

24. P—QKt4 !

This is the point! While the Rooks keep a grip on the enemy, the Pawn will spearhead an attack on the position.

White's immediate threat is 25. P—Kt5, striking a third time at the immobilized Bishop Pawn.

24. . . .   P—QR3

Black must not allow the Pawn to advance.

25. R—R5 !

Shifting the attack so as to keep Black occupied guarding all the weak points. Transferring the Rook does not relinquish pressure on the Bishop Pawn, which must remain where it is.

25. . . .   QR—Kt1

Protects his Queen, which was

threatened with capture. Other courses offered bleak prospects:

If 25. . . . Q x Q 26. P x Q, B—B1 (to save the Rook Pawn) 27. R x QP wins a Pawn for White.

If 25. . . . Q—Kt2 26. Q—B5 followed by 27. P—QR4 and 28. P—Kt5 engineers a decisive breakthrough.

26. P—QR3

Protects the valuable Knight Pawn (which is destined to bring the enemy to his knees) before proceeding with the attack.

26. . . .   R—R2

Saves the Rook Pawn, which was under double attack, but loses a different Pawn. However, there was no way for Black to safeguard all the vulnerable points. Had he tried 26. . . . B—B1, White would have won a Pawn by 27. Q x Q, R x Q 28. R x QP, taking advantage of the Bishop Pawn's being pinned.

27. R x BP !

This bit of plunder is the first tangible evidence of the merit of White's positional strategy. It is no more than justice that the Bishop Pawn, the cause of Black's troubles, should be the first to fall.

27. . . .   Q x R(B3)

Better than retreating to Kt2 or exchanging Queens: if 27. . . . Q—Kt2 28. R(R5) x RP wins another Pawn and leaves White with two connected passed Pawns ready to race to a Queening square. Or if 27. . . . Q x Q 28. P x Q, and White will then gather up the triply attacked Rook Pawn.

28. Q x R

The recapture keeps Black on the *qui vive*. His Rook is attacked and so is the Rook Pawn.

28. . . .   R—R1

Rescues the Pawn, as 29. R x RP, R x Q 30. R x Q, R x P nets Black a Pawn in return.

29. Q—B5

Again taking possession of the Bishop file and the key square, this time with the Queen.

29. . . .   Q—Kt2

Black avoids the exchange of Queens, since it leads to this: 29. . . . Q x Q 30. R x Q, K—B1 31. R—R5, and Black can save the Rook Pawn only by abandoning the Queen Pawn.

30. K—B2

Not only to fortify the King side but to move the King closer to the center for the end game, in the event that Queens are exchanged.

30. . . .   P—R4

A demonstration which does not intimidate White or divert him from his purpose of effecting a decision on the Queen side.

31. B—K2

White shelters the King from any annoying checks that might ensue once the position is opened up.

31. . . .   P—Kt3

Black's pieces are tied down to the defense of the two isolated

Pawns, so he makes a waiting move with a Pawn.

32. Q—Q6

White responds vigorously by attacking the Rook Pawn with a third piece. The Queen's further infiltration into Black's territory also clears the square QB5 so that the Rook can use that as a springboard to get to the seventh rank.

32. . . . Q—B1

Black cannot guard all his Pawns (on 32. . . . B—B1 33. Q x QP), so he deserts the Rook Pawn to try to get at White's King by way of the open Bishop file.

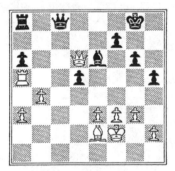

33. R—B5 !

Not through the iron Duke! It is more important to retain control of the Bishop file and to keep Black's pieces off it than to pick up stray Pawns.

33. . . . Q—Kt2

The Queen hasn't a bewildering choice of squares to fly to, from the Rook's attack.

34. P—KR4

This immobilizes Black's Pawns on the King side and also guards against any surprise attack on that wing.

34. . . . P—R4

Black tries to open a file for his Queen by main force.

What else is there? If 34. . . . K —Kt2 35. R—B7, Q—Kt1 36. B x P, K—Kt1 (or 36. . . . R x B 37. R x Pch, winning the Queen) 37. B— Kt7 !, R—R2 38. R—B8ch, B x R 39. Q x Q, and White wins easily.

35. R—B7

This reduces the Queen's flight squares to the minimum—one square!

White is now in full control of all the strategic areas—the Queen Bishop file, the all-important square QB5, the Queen file, the sixth rank and the seventh rank.

35. . . . Q—Kt1

The only hiding place! The Queen is driven further and further back.

36. P—Kt5

A new source of trouble! White has a passed Pawn moving up the board.

36. . . . P—R5

Black must give his Rook more room.

37. P—Kt6

Threatening to continue with 38. P—Kt7, R—R2 39. R—B8ch, B x R 40. Q x Q, winning everything in sight.

37. . . . R—R4

The Rook accomplishes nothing here, but there is no plausible defense.

38. P—Kt7 !

Renewing the threat of winning the Queen by 39. R—B8ch.

38. . . .   Resigns

There is no holding out any longer:

If 38. . . . K—Kt2, R x Pch wins the Queen at once by discovered attack.

If 38. . . . Q—K1 39. Q—Kt6 wins the Rook in an odd way.

If 38. . . . Q—R2 39. Q—Q8ch, K—Kt2 40. P—Kt8(Q) faces Black with mate on the move to avert which he would have to give up his Queen.

The whole game is a remarkable example of the systematic exploitation of a positional advantage. The manner in which the square QB5 is used as a springboard for White's pieces—the Bishop, Knight, Rook and then the Queen occupying it in turn—contributes a bit of sleight of hand to an artistic achievement of the highest sort.

GAME NO. 21

QUEEN'S PAWN GAME
(*Colle System*)

WHITE   BLACK
Chernev   Hahlbohm
NEW YORK, 1942

1. P—Q4

This is the best move on the board—and so is 1. P—K4 !

Either move establishes a Pawn in the center, while permitting two pieces to come into play.

Which move should you adopt? The choice is a matter of taste. Broadly speaking, P—K4 leads more often to wide-open attacking games, while P—Q4 tends to a struggle for positional advantage. Blackburne says, "The first piece of advice I would offer to the young student who wishes to improve his chess is that in the formation of his style he should try to follow his own aptitude and temperament. One player derives pleasure in working a game out accurately like a sum in mathematics, another cares for nothing but ingenious combination and brilliant attack. It is by far the best for each to develop his own qualities."

1. . . .   P—Q4

An excellent reply, as it prevents White from continuing with 2. P—K4, when the two Pawns abreast dominate the center. Black, too, frees his Queen and a Bishop.

2. Kt—KB3

Instead of this, White often plays 2. P—QB4 at this point, offering a Pawn. This is a gambit only by the grace of definition, since White recovers the Pawn easily while maintaining a strong position.

The Knight move has the virtue of developing a piece to its most useful post while retaining the option of transposing into the Queen's Gambit.

2. . . .   P—K3

Perfectly safe, but somewhat

modest. I would prefer 2. . . . Kt—KB3, which does not commit Black to defensive play and does not interfere with the Queen Bishop's development.

The text move is the best way to support the Queen Pawn *after White has attacked it by P—QB4,* but White has not yet made this threatening gesture!

3. P—K3 !

This quiet move is the prelude to the Colle attack, a vicious King-side assault.

The general plan of the Colle is to advance the King Pawn to K4, *after suitable preparation.* This consists of the following maneuvers:

a) Developing the King Bishop at Q3, to strengthen the pressure on the vital square K4 and to attack Black's King Rook Pawn, a tender point after he castles.

b) Posting the Queen Knight at Q2 (not at B3, as the Bishop file must not be obstructed), to bear down on K4 and lend support to the King Pawn when it reaches that square.

c) Castling on the King side, to mobilize the King Rook.

d) Developing the Queen at K2 and/or the Rook at K1, to add further weight to the contemplated Pawn push.

e) Advancing the Pawn to K4. The Pawn moves only one square, but it sets all the machinery in motion: the position in the center will be ripped apart and lines opened up for White's attacking forces.

3. . . . P—QB4

This thrust at the Pawn center is practically compulsory for Black in Queen Pawn openings.

Black *must fight* for an equal share of the center.

Black *must dispute* possession of the important squares.

4. P—B3

Ready to recapture with the Bishop Pawn if Black should decide to exchange Pawns. White's King Pawn must not be diverted from K3, as its future is marked out for it at K4.

4. . . . Kt—KB3

Natural and strong. This is the best possible disposition of the King Knight. It is developed *toward the center,* so as to take part in the events there. It is in the center that most of the fighting takes place, and whatever happens there affects the rest of the chessboard. Superiority in the center is essential for positional advantage, and control of the center is indispensable to the successful conduct of a King-side attack.

All development should therefore be conducted with a view to the effect on the center.

A plausible move, instead of the text, is the advance 4. . . . P—B5, to prevent White from placing his Bishop at Q3. It is the kind of move many players find irresistible, but it must be avoided. It is an error in strategy, as it relaxes the pressure on White's Queen Pawn and the center.

It is important to keep the Pawn position in the center fluid.

It is important to maintain pres-

sure on White's Queen Pawn in the center.

It is important to retain the option of exchanging Pawns in the center.

5. B—Q3

An ideal development for the Bishop: it controls the long diagonal leading to Black's King (after he castles) and bears down on the key square K4, where the break will come.

5. . . . Kt—B3

The Knight comes into play toward the center, as prescribed. Black has an eye to freeing his game by an early . . . P—K4.

A good alternative is 5. . . . QKt —Q2, in order to recapture with the Knight, instead of with the Bishop, if White should play 6. P x P.

6. QKt—Q2

Offhand this looks unnatural, as the Knight seems awkwardly placed and blocks the path of the Queen Bishop. In reality the Knight performs its two assigned tasks: *it gets into the game,* even if it is only at the modest square Q2, and it also lends support to the coming action at the critical point K4. The Queen Bishop is inconvenienced, but only temporarily.

6. . . . B—K2

This is preferable to the aggressive development at Q3. The Bishop is needed closer to home for defense of the King.

7. O—O

This remarkable *coup,* by means of which the King is spirited away to safety while the Rook magically appears on the scene, is probably the most significant contribution to civilization since the discovery of the wheel.

7. . . . O—O

Black too hurries to safeguard his King and put the Rook to work.

8. Q—K2

A perfect spot for the Queen in nearly every form of Queen's Pawn opening. The Queen supports the contemplated advance of the King Pawn and will add a great deal of weight to the consequent attack.

8. . . . R—K1

Rooks must seize the open files! What if there are none? Then bring your Rooks toward the center! They will then be at the head of files most likely to be opened. That is why the King Rook is usually developed at K1 or Q1, while the Queen Rook goes to Q1 or QB1.

9. P x P !

The thrust by 9. P—K4 would be premature: after 9. . . . QP x P 10. Kt x P, P x P, White would either lose a Pawn or be left with an isolated Queen's Pawn. The text move was made with these further considerations in mind:

a) Black's Bishop, which has moved once, will have to waste a move in recapturing the Pawn.

b) This Bishop, needed for defense of the King side, will find itself on the wrong side of the board.

c) At QB4, the Bishop will stand unprotected and subject to a surprise attack.

d) White's Knight at Q2 will gain a tempo later by moving to Kt3, where it threatens the exposed Bishop while simultaneously clearing a way for his own Queen Bishop.

e) In the ending, if it comes to that, White will have the favorable arrangement of three Pawns to two on the Queen side.

9. . . .   B x P

Black must recapture or be a Pawn down.

10. P—K4 !

The key move in the Colle attack! It is the forcible break which releases all the fury of the pent-up pieces.

How shall Black reply? If he exchanges by 10. . . . P x P, then after 11. Kt x P, Kt x Kt 12. Q x Kt, he is threatened with loss beginning with 13. Q x Pch. No longer does he have a Knight at KB3 (the best defender of a castled position) so he would have to weaken himself by moving one of the Pawns in front of the King.

If he avoids exchanging Pawns

and plays 10. . . . P—Q5 instead, then comes 11. Kt—Kt3, B—Kt3 (the Bishop must stay in touch with the Queen Pawn) 12. P—K5, Kt—Q4, and White has the pleasant choice of winning "accurately like a sum in mathematics," as Blackburne puts it, by 13. P x P, or through "ingenious combination and brilliant attack" by 13. B x Pch, K x B 14. Kt—Kt5ch, K—Kt3 15. Q—K4ch, P—B4 16. P x P e.p. ch, K x P 17. Q—B3ch, K—K2 (if 17. . . . K—K4 18. Kt—B7 mate) 18. Q—B7ch, K—Q3 19. Q x KtP, and the threats of winning the Queen by 20. Kt—B7ch, or the King by 20. Kt—K4 mate are decisive.

10. . . .   P—K4

Black avoids both pitfalls and plays to prevent 11. P—K5, dislodging the Knight. Meanwhile, the Rook has more elbowroom, and the Queen Bishop can take part in the action.

11. P x P

Work in progress! White continues the process of opening lines for the attack. The square K4 is now available as a jumping-off spot for his pieces.

11. . . .   Kt x P

Black did not care to capture with his Queen, as these attacks might result:

11. . . . Q x P 12. B—B4, Q—Q3 13. Kt—Kt5 (threatening 14. B x Pch, winning the exchange), R—K2 14. Kt(Q2)—K4, Kt x Kt 15. Kt x Kt, and White wins the Bishop.

11. . . . Q x P 12. B—B4, Q—

Q2 13. Kt—Kt5, R—K2 14. Kt(Q2)—K4, Kt x Kt 15. Q x Kt (threatening the Rook Pawn), P—KKt3 16. Q—R4, P—KR4 17. Kt—K4, and Black must give up his Bishop to avert loss of his Queen by a Knight fork.

11. . . . Q x P 12. B—B4, Q—Q1 13. Kt—Kt3, B—Kt3, and White will have a happy time weighing the effects of various attacks beginning with 14. B—KKt5, or 14. R—Q1 or 14. Kt—Kt5.

12. Kt—Kt3

Gaining a tempo by the attack on the exposed Bishop. Note too that White's Queen Bishop now has lots of room.

12. . . .   Q—Kt3

A move with deceptive aspects. It is true that the Queen has made a developing move and that the Bishop is now protected, but other factors appear in the reckoning. Black's King side lacks pieces for defense, and his Knight at Q4 is loose (unguarded by another piece or a Pawn).

Is there a combination? Is there a check or capture—a move that smites? Yes, indeed there is!

13. B x Pch !

Such opportunities must be seized at once, before the opponent has a chance to catch his breath.

13. . . .   K x B

Refusing to capture is even worse: the Bishop can run away with his booty or stay put while the attack continues with 14. Q—B4, and the Queen pounces down on the stranded pieces in the center.

14. Q—K4ch

The point! By means of a double attack White regains his piece, with a Pawn as interest on his investment.

14. . . .   K—Kt1

There is nothing to be gained by interposing a Pawn by 14. . . . P—B4 or 14. . . . P—Kt3, either of which moves further disrupts the King-side Pawn position.

15. Q x Kt

Wins the piece back and gains another tempo by the double attack on the Bishop. Black is kept busy defending and is given no time to consolidate his position. Without having made any moves that were obviously bad, the Western master has a theoretically lost game.

15. . . .   B—B1

Abject retreat, but the alternative 15. . . . B—K2 lets White take the King Pawn.

16. Kt—Kt5

Threatening 17. Q x Pch, and mate in two more moves. Black must be given no respite!

16. . . .   B—K3

At last the Queen Bishop comes into the game. Black's move looks effective as mate is warded off, the adverse Queen driven back, a piece developed, and another one (the Queen Rook) released.

17. Q—K4

The Queen retreats, but no time is lost as mate threatens at R7.

17. . . .   P—Kt3

Black has little choice, and this is a better defense than 17. . . . P—B4, after which the play would be 18. Q—KR4, B—Q3 (or 18. . . . B—B4 19. KKt x B, R x Kt 20. Q—QB4 winning a piece) 19. Q—R7ch, K—B1 20. Kt x Bch, R x Kt 21. Q—R8ch, and Black's Queen Rook falls.

18. Q—KR4

Again threatening mate on the move. Black is kept on the run and has to place his pieces where White's

mating threats compel them to go.

18. . . .   B—Kt2

White cannot be kept from checking at R7, but this prevents the Queen's further inroad at R8. Failure to keep the Queen out, say by 18. . . . B—Q3 instead, would lead to loss by 19. Q—R7ch, K—B1 20. Kt x B, R x Kt (if 20. . . . P x Kt 21. B—R6 mate) 21. Q—R8ch, and White wins a Rook.

With the actual move, Black seems to have built up a bomb-proof shelter for his King.

19. B—K3

So White brings up the reserves! The Queen Bishop comes into active play with a gain of tempo. The attack on the Queen is incidental to the Bishop's real purpose, which is to gain control of QB5 for itself or the Knight. A Knight planted there would dominate the center and the Queen side; a Bishop would be useful to guard against Black's King escaping by way of KB1.

19. . . .   Q—R3

Black rejects 19. . . . Q—B2, as he visualizes the consequence: 20. Q—R7ch, K—B1 21. B—B5ch, Kt—K2 22. Q x P!, P x Q (or 22. . . . Q x B 23. Kt x Bch, P x Kt 24. Q x Rch, K x Q 25. Kt x Q, winning easily) 23. Kt x Bch, K—Kt1 24. Kt x Q, and Black's Rooks are impaled on a Knight fork.

20. Kt—B5 !

Once more one of White's pieces invades the enemy's half of the board by the time-saving expedient of attacking the Queen.

20. . . .   Q—B5

Hoping to get some peace by effecting an exchange of Queens.

21. Q—R7ch

With the object of smoking the King out and ripping away his Pawn protection.

21. . . .   K—B1

The only move left.

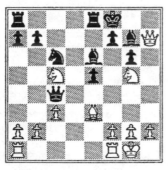

22. Kt(B5) x Bch

There is often more than one way to win, *after a positional superiority has been established*. A pretty windup would be 22. Kt(Kt5) x Bch, P x Kt 23. B—R6, R—K2 (if 23. . . . B x B 24. Kt—Q7 mate) 24. Q—R8ch (if only to show that the Queen *can* get to R8), K—B2 25. Q x Bch, K—K1 26. Q—Kt8 mate.

22. . . .   P x Kt

Sacrificing the exchange by 22. . . . R x Kt prolongs but does not alleviate the suffering.

23. Q x P

Threatening 24. Q—B7 mate.

23. . . .   Kt—Q1

I was hoping for 23. R—K2 when I could have forced the win by the "excelsior" idea, a Pawn march up the board as follows: 24. P—B4 (threatening 25. P x P dis. ch, K—Kt1 26. Q—R7 mate), P—K5 25. P—B5 (again threatening discovered check), P—K4 26. P—B6, and White wins.

24. Kt—R7ch

Here I was sorely tempted to go in for the flashy win by 24. P—B4, P—K5 25. P—B5, P—K4 26. P—B6, B—R1 27. Kt—R7 mate, but common sense prevailed. One must win in the quickest possible way. One must play the simple, brutal move if thereby it shortens the struggle.

24. . . .   Resigns

If 24. . . . K—Kt1 25. Kt—B6ch, K—R1 (or 25. . . . K—B1 26. Q x R mate) 26. Q—R7 mate. Or if 24. . . . K—K2 25. QR—Q1, and quick mate follows after 26. B—Kt5ch or 26. Q x Bch.

GAME NO. 22

QUEEN'S GAMBIT DECLINED

WHITE	BLACK
Pillsbury	Marco

PARIS, 1900

1. P—Q4

Whether for fun, honor or blood, this is the best way to begin the fight. Outlets are created for the Queen and a Bishop while the Queen Pawn itself takes an active part in the struggle for control of the center. It occupies Q4 and stands guard over K5 and QB5, making those squares unavailable for the opponent's pieces.

1. . . .   P—Q4

The simplest way to prevent White from gaining more ground in the center. If White is permitted to play 2. P—K4 freely, the two Pawns abreast in the center will give him the balance of power in that important area.

2. P—QB4

White offers a Pawn in order to eliminate Black's strong point in the center. It is necessary to play this move before developing the Queen Knight at B3, as the Bishop file must not be obstructed.

2. . . .   P—K3

Black is set to reply to 3. P x P with 3. . . . P x P, maintaining a Pawn at Q4. If he were to recapture with a piece, White could attack it, drive it off, and have an advantage in his strong Pawn center.

Accepting White's offer by 2. . . . P x P is not recommended policy. Black could not hold on to the extra Pawn, so that in the end it would amount to exchanging a center Pawn for a side Pawn. It is true that the text move limits the Queen Bishop's scope, but it is a necessary evil of what is probably Black's soundest defense. In this lies the great strength of the Queen's

Gambit (for White) and its popularity with the majority of players who feel happy with an opening which lets them put on pressure with the very first move.

3. Kt—QB3

The Knight develops aggressively, moving in toward the center and intensifying the attack on Black's Queen Pawn.

3. . . .   Kt—KB3

An excellent move: it brings the King Knight to its most suitable square in the opening, exerts pressure on Q4 and K5 (to neutralize the influence of White's Knight on those squares), helps defend the center Pawn and facilitates early King-side castling.

4. B—Kt5 !

This powerful move develops a piece, pins one of Black's and threatens by 5. B x Kt, P x B (if 5. . . . Q x B 6. P x P, P x P 7. Kt x P, and White wins a Pawn) to dislocate the Pawn position on the King side.

Strangely enough, although Pillsbury used this move to great effect in a magnificent victory over Tarrasch at Hastings in 1895, the comment on it by Gunsberg, who annotated the game for the tournament book, was, "No good results from this early sortie of the Bishop. The attack, or perhaps better speaking, would-be attack differs from similar play in the French defense, inasmuch as White has not P—K5 at his command. Generally speaking, both the first and the second player in this opening require their Queen's Bishop on the Queen's side."

This view, it turned out, easily qualified for "the clouded crystal ball department." Pillsbury utilized the attack stemming from 4. B—Kt5 for some of his most marvelous triumphs, defeating such masters of the game as Steinitz, Maroczy, Janowsky, Burn, Marco and Tarrasch. Others who evaded this line, Lasker, Marshall, Tchigorin (to name a few), fell victims to other forms of the Queen's Gambit. Gunsberg, who criticized this form of attack so severely, chose what Lasker called "a peculiar, but not altogether sound, manner of development," with the result that Pillsbury defeated him in an ending which is one of the most beautiful in the literature of chess. In short, it was Pillsbury's great success with the Queen's Gambit that revealed its terrific strength to the other masters and gave it a popularity that has continued to this day.

4. . . .   B—K2

The simplest: Black develops the Bishop where it is best placed for defense—close to home. Incidentally, he neutralizes the pin of the Knight.

5. P—K3

Pawns should be moved sparingly in the opening, but moves which help pieces come into play are developing moves. In playing 5. P—K3, White develops because he creates an outlet for his King Bishop.

5. . . .   O—O

The King finds safer quarters

while the Rook prepares to make itself useful.

6. Kt—B3

With the development of this piece, White's Knights now exert pressure on all the four squares in the center. The King Knight has an eye to utilizing K5 as an outpost. Once firmly stationed there, it will get a death grip on Black's position.

6. . . .   P—QKt3

At the time this game was played, it seemed natural to develop the Bishop at Kt2, especially when it was hemmed in on the other side. But the plight of the Bishop is linked with other problems, and they must be solved first.

A better continuation was 6. . . . QKt—Q2, to support a thrust at White's center by . . . P—B4 or . . . P—K4. The Knight's move would also curb White's ambition to anchor his King Knight at K5.

7. B—Q3

An ideal spot for the Bishop: it commands a long diagonal and aims at Black's King Rook Pawn. This Pawn is in no immediate danger, but it does stand in the line of fire.

7. . . .   B—Kt2

The fianchetto, by means of which Black expects to control the long diagonal with his Bishop. But Pillsbury exposes the weakness of the formation (at this stage of the game) by playing:

8. P x P !

White removes a Pawn and lets

Black recapture in any of four ways
—none of them satisfactory!

8. . . .   P x P

Black wants to maintain a Pawn
in the center. But this Pawn blocks
the path of his Queen Bishop and
prevents it from accomplishing anything useful on the diagonal.

Black could have captured with a
piece instead, but that amounts to
an eventual surrender of the center.
White would evict the piece by P—
K4 and remain in control of all the
strategic central squares.

9. Kt—K5 !

The key move in the famous
"Pillsbury attack." The Knight anchors itself on a square from which
its striking power is terrific! Its attack extends in all directions, affect-
ing the Queen side as well as the
King side.

9. . . .   QKt—Q2

This Knight does what it can: it
makes a developing move, it threatens to do battle with White's
Knight, and it stands ready to support a break by 10. . . . P—B4, disputing control of the center.

10. P—B4

This Pawn not only strengthens
the position of the Knight by providing it with a firm base, but it discourages Black from exchanging
pieces. On 10. . . . Kt x Kt, the recapture by 11. BP x Kt opens wide
the King Bishop file for an attack
by the heavy pieces. The capturing
Pawn itself will then stab at Black's
King Knight and drive it away from
its strong defensive post.

10. . . .   P—B4

This demonstration on the Queen
side is either too soon or too late.
Black wants to attack on the Queen
side where, after playing 11. . . . P
—B5, he will have a three to two
Pawn majority. What he underesti-
mates is the speed and vigor with
which White can get an attack rolling on the King side. It will strike
faster and with more force than any
action of Black's on the Queen side.
He must deprive it of some of its
strength by effecting some exchanges
and then counterattacking in the
center. One possibility was 10. . . .
Kt—K1 11. B x B, Q x B 12. O—O,
Kt x Kt 13. BP x Kt, P—KB3. This
would comply with two important
principles in defense:

An exchange relieves a crowded
position.

An attack on a wing is best met
by play in the center.

11. O—O

A defensive measure (the King
should be sheltered) but primarily
to put the Rook immediately to
work on the partly open Bishop file.

11. . . .   P—B5

With the idea of securing a Queen-side Pawn majority. This is commendable strategy for the ending, but Black has not yet survived the midgame!

The move *11. . . . P—B5* is a strategic error. It removes the pressure on White's Queen Pawn and relieves the tension. As long as Black has the option of capturing the Queen Pawn and disturbing White's center, so long will it be difficult for White to stabilize the center. And until the center is stabilized, the success of a King-side attack for White is doubtful.

The moral is clear: *Keep the Pawn position in the center fluid; reserve the option of capturing the center Pawn.*

12. B—B2

The Bishop retreats but does not relax its grip on the diagonal leading to Black's King side.

12. . . .   P—QR3

Preparing for a sweeping advance of Queen-side Pawns, beginning with *13. . . . P—Kt4* and *14. . . . P—Kt5.*

13. Q—B3

Brings up the heavy artillery. White is not concerned with the petty threat of winning a Pawn by *14. Kt x QBP, P x Kt 15. Q x B,* as it is hardly worth while for this purpose to give up his beautifully centralized Knight for a miserably placed Bishop. White's object with the Queen move is to start a direct attack on the King. To defend himself against White's threats, Black will be forced to move some Pawn near his King. This change in the Pawn formation will loosen the structure and create an irreparable weakness in the King's defenses.

13. . . .   P—Kt4

Marco protects the Bishop Pawn, which Pillsbury had no intention of taking, and proceeds with his counterattack on the Queen side. Note how Black's last three moves, filling up white squares with Pawns, further reduces what little mobility his Queen Bishop has.

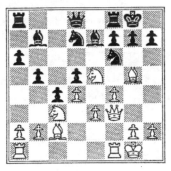

14. Q—R3 !

Threatening *15. Kt x Kt, Q x Kt* (certainly not *15. . . . Kt x Kt 16. Q x P mate*), after which he has a choice of three winning continuations:

a) *16. Q x Q, Kt x Q 17. B x B,* and White gains a piece.

b) *16. B x Pch, K—R1* (if *16. . . . Kt x B 17. Q x Q wins*) *17. B —B5 dis. ch,* and White wins the Queen.

c) *16. B—B5, Q—Q1 17. B x Kt, B x B 18. Q x P mate.*

"All this is very interesting," you might say, "but how does White plan this series of moves? What makes him look at even so much as the first move in the combination?"

Very well! Let's try to follow his line of reasoning:

White attacks the critical point, Black's King Rook Pawn, with Queen and Bishop.

If this Pawn were protected only by the King, White could capture it and announce mate.

But the Pawn has another protector, a Knight.

How about removing the Knight? That would not do. It would only be replaced by another Knight.

How about getting rid of the other Knight? With that Knight disposed of, wouldn't the whole structure collapse?

Once White thinks in this direction and sees the first move in the combination, the rest of it plays itself. In fact, once he finds the key—removing the Knight which protects the Knight which protects against mate—he can win it anyway he pleases.

14. . . .   P—Kt3

Black avoids being mated by making a simple Pawn move. What then has White accomplished, if a mating combination can so easily be frustrated?

It is true that White has not inflicted mate, but the threat of doing so has enabled him to achieve his real objective—a disturbance in the lineup of Pawns near the King. *This change in the Pawn configuration weakens the entire defensive structure.* After Black's actual move, his King Knight, deprived of the Pawn

support, is a vulnerable object of attack, notwithstanding the fact that it is protected by three pieces.

What other defense did Black have? If *14. . . . P—KR3 15.* B x P, P x B *16.* Q x P, Kt—K5 *17.* R—B3 (threatening *18.* R—Kt3ch, Kt x R *19.* Q—R7 mate), QKt—B3 *18.* R—R3, and White wins. Or if *14. . . .* Kt x Kt (to avoid moving the King side Pawns) *15.* B x Kt (threatening *16.* Q x P mate), Kt—Kt3 *16.* B x B, Q x B *17.* P—B5, Kt—R1 (or *17. . . .* Kt—R5 *18.* P—B6, P x P *19.* Q x Kt) *18.* P—B6, and Black must give up his Queen to prevent mate.

15. P—B5 !

A Pawn is a wonderful weapon of attack! This one threatens to break up Black's Pawn cordon by *16.* P x P. The capture will also uncover an attack on Black's Knight by the Rook, an attack which could be augmented by doubling Rooks.

15. . . .   P—Kt5

Clearly *15. . . .* P x P is out of the question. White could recapture with the Queen or the Rook, in either case with a tremendous game.

Black hopes, with his threat on the Queen Knight, to divert White's attention from the course of events on the King side. If he can persuade White to delay the attack for even a moment, he might put up a fight. If, for example, White prudently retreats the Knight to K2, then *16. . . .* Kt—K5 complicates White's task.

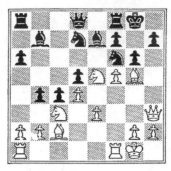

16. P x P !

Rips right into Black's position! The Rook's attacking range is lengthened—he has the whole Bishop file to work on—while the Bishop's attack leads straight to the King!

16. . . .   RP x P

Let's dispose of the alternatives: If *16. . . .* P x Kt *17.* B x Kt, Kt x B *18.* R x Kt, BP x P (or *18. . . .* B x R *19.* Q x P mate) *19.* B x P, P x B *20.* R x P mate!

If *16. . . .* BP x P *17.* Q—K6ch, K—R1 *18.* Kt x Kt, Kt x Kt (or *18. . . .* Q x Kt *19.* B x Ktch followed by *20.* Q x Q) *19.* R x Rch, Kt x R *20.* Q—K5ch, K—Kt1 *21.* B x B, and White wins.

17. Q—R4 !

Concentrating his fire on the King Knight, whose position has been weakened by the loss of the Pawn support.

17. . . .   P x Kt

Black might as well take the Knight. Against the alternative *17. . . .* Kt x Kt, the continuation *18.* P x Kt, P x Kt *19.* P x Kt, B—Q3 *20.* Q—R6 is decisive.

Before White makes his next move, let us look at the object of his attack, the Knight at Black's KB3. Although it has lost the protection of the Pawn, which has had to move to Kt3, it is still immune from capture, since it has a defender for every piece that attacks it. In fact, if White tries something like *18.* B x Kt, B x B *19.* R x B, Q x R *20.* Q x Q, Kt x Q, he finds himself a Rook down. So direct assault doesn't do it! The answer must then lie in indirect means. We have lured away one of the Knight's defenders, the Pawn. Can we get rid of its other protectors? Indeed we can!

18. Kt x Kt !

This removes one of the props supporting the Knight.

18. . . .   Q x Kt

And this recapture draws another one away! Notice the technique of besieging a heavily guarded objective by doing away with the pieces that protect it. In this case, two of the Knight's defenders have disappeared —one removed bodily, and the other lured away by the compulsion to recapture.

Black had no better defense in *18. . . .* Kt x Kt, as after *19.* B x B, Q—R4 *20.* P—QKt4 (faster than *20.* B x R), P x P e.p. *21.* P x P, Q—Kt3 *22.* R—B3, followed by *23.* R—KR3, forces a quick mate.

19. R x Kt !

Stronger than *19.* B x Kt, as Black does not dare take the Rook.

19. . . .   P—R4

If 19. . . . B x R 20. B x B,
threatening 21. Q—R8 mate is conclusive.

Black's actual move prepares for
20. . . . R—R3, to help defend the
Knight Pawn and perhaps to beat off
White's Rook.

> 20. QR—KB1

Doubling the Rooks institutes
two new winning threats.

21. B x P, P x B 22. R x P mate.
21. R(B1)—B3, followed by 22.
R—R3 and 23. Q—R8 mate.

> 20. . . .   R—R3

Hoping to induce an exchange of
Rooks which would divert one of
White's pieces from the attack.
White could still win, but the play
would require care. It might go like
this: 21. R x R, B x B 22. Q x B,
B x R 23. R—B6 (B x P at once is
risky and might even lose), P x P 24.
B x P, P x B 25. R x Pch, K—B2 26.
R—Kt7ch, K—K1 27. Q—K5ch,
K—Q1 28. Q—Kt8ch, B—B1 29.
R x Qch, K x R 30. Q x P, etc.

But Pillsbury is not to be swayed!
He carries out the motif of the attack with admirable consistency by
annihilating the Knight Pawn that
stepped out of line and weakened the
defensive formation.

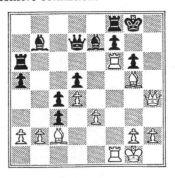

> 21. B x P !

Logic and poetic justice dictate
that this Pawn be destroyed!

> 21. . . .   P x B

White was threatening mate on
the move.

Pillsbury now demonstrated a
forced mate in six moves, as follows:

22. R x Rch, B x R 23. R x Bch,
K x R 24. Q—R8ch, K—B2 25. Q—
R7ch, K—B1 (if 25. . . . K—K1
26. Q—Kt8 mate or if 25. . . . K—
K3 26. Q x P mate) 26. Q x Q, any
27. B—R6ch, K—Kt1 28. Q—Kt7
mate.

More than any other, this game
made the chess world aware of the
terrific potential of the Queen's
Gambit, a positional opening, as an
instrument of attack. The assault on
the King side is carried out with
speed and power, and unlike attacks
stemming from speculative King's
Pawn Gambits, it is founded on a
position sound to the core.

GAME NO. 23

QUEEN'S PAWN GAME

(Stonewall Attack)

WHITE	BLACK
Vliet	Znosko- Borovsky

OSTEND, 1907

> 1. P—Q4

The Queen's Pawn opening, to
paraphrase George Bernard Shaw,
"offers the maximum of security with
the maximum of opportunity."

With the first move, White occupies the center with a Pawn and frees two of the Queen-side pieces.

His general plan of development runs somewhat as follows:

He will establish and maintain at least one Pawn in the center.

This Pawn will act as a support to a Knight outpost at K5 or QB5.

The Bishops are to take charge of long diagonals or pin enemy pieces.

The Rooks are to control the open or partly open files.

The Queen should stand at QB2 or K2, close to home but off the back rank.

The King should find safety in castling, preferably on the King side.

Basically, White's aim is to acquire possession of territory and crowd Black to the wall. With less room to move around in, and with the consequent difficulty of maneuvering his pieces effectively, the enemy will be forced to weaken his position. He will have to make some poor moves, since good moves are not easily available in a cramped position. The weaknesses will come to light, and the opportunity to exploit them will come in the form of a combination, resolving the issue at one stroke.

1. . . .   P—Q4

This is more forthright than 1. . . . Kt—KB3. Either of these moves prevents White from playing 2. P—K4 and establishing two Pawns in the center. The text offsets White's pressure in the center and establishes a state of equilibrium there.

2. P—K3

A strangely passive move in an opening where every moment counts. Usually, White strikes at Black's Queen Pawn by 2. P—QB4, to weaken his grip on the center. Or, if White does not want to show his hand too soon, he simply develops a piece by 2. Kt—KB3.

2. . . .   P—QB4

So Black takes the initiative! He plays this all-important freeing move. It opens the Bishop file for the use of the Rooks and gives the Queen Knight more scope by letting it come out at B3. The Bishop Pawn itself puts up a fight for possession of the center by its attack on White's Queen Pawn.

3. P—QB3

Indicating that he intends to reply to 3. . . . P x P with 4. BP x P. This would keep his Pawn position in the center intact and open the Bishop file for his major pieces.

3. . . .   P—K3

Black must protect the Bishop Pawn. Otherwise White might play 4. P x P, and then hang on to the extra Pawn by supporting it with 5. P—QKt4.

4. B—Q3

The Bishop develops to a useful diagonal, where it exerts pressure on the center and is ready to participate in a King-side attack.

4. . . .   Kt—QB3

A rare opportunity for this Knight, who seldom gets good breaks in Queen Pawn openings. From its post at QB3 the Knight brings considerable influence to bear on K4 and Q5, and as later turns out, on another important sector.

5. P—KB4

White has made four out of five moves with Pawns in order to secure a particular arrangement known as the Stonewall attack. Aside from the fact that making so many Pawn moves in the opening is a flagrant violation of principle, the adoption of a system which calls for the launching of an attack by a preconceived formation of pieces, without regard to the advisability of an attack, without reference to the requirements of the particular position, is contrary to the concept of proper strategy and to the spirit of chess itself. What such an expedition amounts to is undertaking the risk of assuming the offensive against an enemy whose force is equal, whose lineup of power is unknown and who has betrayed no vulnerable points. Under these conditions, an attack is premature and is sure to be repulsed and turned into a disorderly retreat. If any such system worked, it would be fine for White, who would always win, but then who would want to play Black?

5. . . .   Kt—B3

An excellent development while awaiting developments! Black's Knights are poised beautifully, with one watching over K4 and Q5, while the other keeps the two remaining center squares under observation.

6. Kt—Q2

This Knight has the unhappy choice of making its entrance at this square or at R3. At Q2 it blocks the Bishop and itself has no bright prospects in view. At R3 it is only half a Knight, since it reaches at most in four directions instead of eight.

6. . . .   Q—B2

Very good, since the heavy pieces (the Queen and the Rooks) fulfill their functions best when placed on open files, or files likely to be opened.

The Queen develops with a gain of tempo since a positional threat is involved—which White either overlooks, or disregards.

7. KKt—B3

Routine and in this case thoughtless development. White is so intent on carrying out the basic theme of the Stonewall attack (posting of a Knight at K5, stoutly supported by Pawns) that he fails to stop at every move to ask himself, "What does my opponent threaten with his last move? Has he any checks or captures that cut down my choice of reply?"

7. . . .   P x P !

Black wrenches the Bishop file open at one blow!

8. BP x P

The point of Black's move is revealed in this forced recapture. White could not take by 8. KP x P (hoping to maintain a strong Pawn support for the prospective stationing of a Knight at K5) as that permits the brutal reply 8. . . . Q x P, winning a Pawn for Black. The alternative, recapturing by 8. Kt x P, conflicts with the system White had determined to follow before lines of battle were drawn up. In that scheme of things, the Knight belongs at K5 not Q4, while the square Q4 should be occupied by a Pawn.

8. . . .   Kt—QKt5 !

A disturbing attack on the Bishop! Without the services of this piece White can never hope to work up an effective King-side attack.

9. B—Kt1

An unusual square of retreat, but the only one available if the Bishop wants to stay on the diagonal leading to Black's King side.

White is not too troubled by this setback. He expects to drive the adverse Knight off with 10. P—QR3 and then reorganize his troops.

9. . . .   B—Q2

A quiet move, but a subtle one. The Bishop will make its presence felt, even from this modest start.

Black is now prepared to shift his Rook over to B1 to strengthen his grip on that file.

10. P—QR3

Before going about his business, White must dislodge the annoying Knight which disconcerts his entire Queen side.

10. . . .   R—B1 !

A counterattack which must have come as a surprise to White.

What shall he do against the threat of 11. . . . Q x B? If he takes the Knight, there comes 11. . . . Q x B 12. R x P (certainly not 12. Q x Q, R x Qch, and Black wins a Rook), Q x P (threatening 13. . . . R—B8, pinning the Queen) 13. O—O, Q x KtP, and Black is a Pawn ahead and a passed Pawn at that.

11. O—O

Now the Bishop is guarded by Queen and Rook, and safe from capture. The King meanwhile goes into hiding.

11. . . .   B—Kt4 !

The Bishop seizes a fine diagonal with gain of time, as White must move his Rook out of range.

12. R—K1

Clearly forced, since 12. R—B2 loses on the spot by 12. . . . Q x B, while 12. P x Kt, B x R (threatening to continue with 13. . . . Q x B) costs the exchange.

12. . . .   Kt—B7 !

An attack on both Rooks which leaves White no choice of reply. He must remove this terrible Knight.

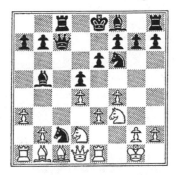

13. B x Kt

The alternative capture 13. Q x Kt leads to 13. . . . Q x Q 14. B x Q, R x B, and Black has a Rook on the seventh rank, as occurs in the actual game.

13. . . .   Q x B

And Black penetrates into the vitals of the enemy's position—the seventh rank.

White's forces are almost paralyzed:

His King Rook and his Queen are prevented from moving by Black's Bishop.

His Bishop cannot move at all.

The Queen Knight must stay at Q2 to prevent 14. . . . Kt—K5.

The Queen Rook can move—but to no avail.

14. Q x Q

So he exchanges his helpless Queen for Black's active one.

14. . . .   R x Q

The upshot of Black's positional combination is that it has given him full control of the open file and a grip on the seventh rank by his Rook. The placement of the Rook at B7

has a terribly constricting effect on White's game. It is especially troublesome here, as the Rook is not easily driven off, while White's pieces are still in each other's way.

15. P—KR3

To prevent 15. . . . Kt—Kt5, an invasion by another piece.

15. . . .   B—Q3

The Bishop develops to a useful diagonal.

16. Kt—Kt1

White's idea is to rearrange his forces so as to get some freedom of movement. He plans the continuation 17. Kt—B3, B—R3 18. R—Q1, followed by 19. R—Q2, to get rid of Black's annoying Rook. By this means, his Bishop might eventually see some action.

16. . . .   Kt—K5 !

The Knight pounces on this excellent outpost! Not only does this throttle any freeing movement of the King Pawn, but it sweeps aside White's plan of reorganization. If White tries 17. Kt—B3, Kt x Kt 18. P x Kt, R x BP wins a Pawn for Black.

17. Kt(B3)—Q2

White therefore tries to exchange or otherwise dispose of Black's powerfully placed Knight. After that, he might arrive at some reasonable development.

17. . . .   B—Q6

Black falls in with this offer, with the stipulation that if Knights are to be exchanged, he wants another piece occupying the outpost K5.

18. Kt x Kt

White has no option but to clear the board of as many pieces as he can. Otherwise he will never be able to extricate his pieces from their tangled position. The move 18. Kt–QB3, which earlier would have lost a Pawn, is worse now as after 18. . . . Kt x Kt(Q7) 19. B x Kt, R x B, Black wins a piece.

18. . . .   B x Kt

Black recaptures with the threat of 19. . . . R x Pch, which gives White no time to play 19. Kt–B3.

19. Kt–Q2

Saves the King Knight Pawn by blocking the Rook, but he cuts off his own Bishop as well—and he's back to the previous entanglement.

Unfortunately, there is nothing else that is promising. If 19. B–Q2, R x P 20. R–B1 (getting an open file for the Pawn and threatening 21. R–B8ch), K–Q2, and White will be driven off the file by the threat of 21. . . . B x Kt winning more material, or 21. . . . R–QB1 opposing Rooks on the file.

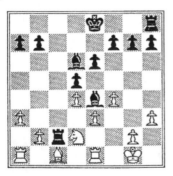

19. . . .   K–Q2

Much more energetic than castling. Mating threats are not likely with so few pieces on the board, so the King comes out into the open. The King's power increases with every reduction of force, and, as becomes a fighting piece, the King heads for the center to assist in the attack. Meanwhile, a whole avenue has been opened for the benefit of the King Rook.

20. Kt x B

White's only hope is to keep clearing the board.

20. . . .   P x Kt

After the recapture, a survey shows the inferiority of White's position:

The Bishop is undeveloped, preventing communication between the Rooks.

The Pawn cluster in the center is completely immobilized.

All the pieces are still on the first rank.

Aside from the features of this particular position, it is important to appreciate the peculiar strength with which a Rook is imbued when it dominates (as Black's does) the seventh rank:

For one thing, it attacks the Pawns still on the rank, striking all along the line, so that defending them is difficult.

For another, the Rook can get behind Pawns that have moved off the rank and maintain constant pressure, since the Pawns are always under attack by the Rook, no matter how far up the file they move.

Finally, the Rook restrains the enemy King from coming out to take a hand in the ending, by guarding the line of exit.

The moral is:

In the opening, shift the Rooks toward the center, on files likely to be opened.

In the midgame, seize the open files and command them with your Rooks.

In the ending, post your Rooks on the seventh rank. Doubled Rooks on the seventh rank are almost irresistible in mating attacks. If there is little material left on the board, the seventh rank is a convenient means of maneuvering a Rook behind enemy Pawns.

21. R—Kt1

Preparing to play 22. P—QKt4 followed by 23. B—Kt2, to let the Bishop finally see daylight.

It is useless to attempt to dislodge Black's Rook. If for example 21. K—B1, KR—QB1 22. R—K2, R x Bch, and White wins a piece.

21. . . .   KR—QB1

The doubling of Rooks on an open file more than doubles their strength on that file.

Their power is clearly manifest here, where they reduce White's resistance to the feeble hope of developing his Bishop. White's Rooks may not leave the first rank until the Bishop does so first.

22. P—QKt4

This makes the square Kt2 available to the Bishop.

22. . . .   KR—B6

Discourages that project! Against 23. B—Kt2, Black plays 23. . . . R—Kt6, with a double attack on the Bishop. This forces 24. B—R1 when 24. . . . R x RP wins a Pawn for Black, who then doubles Rooks on the seventh rank for an easy win.

23. K—B1

The King comes closer to guard the Rook which will protect the Bishop when it comes off the rank. Stated in chess language, White intends 24. B—Kt2, R—Kt6 25. R—K2 (a move previously impossible) when all points are secure.

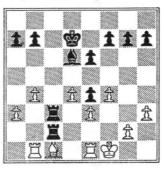

23. . . .   K—B3

The King takes a hand in the ending, making its way in along the weakened white squares.

Tarrasch's recipe in similar cases is "The King must be moved (in the ending) as far as is compatible with his safety, right into the enemy camp, where he can capture Pawns, hold up hostile Pawns and lead his own Pawns on to Queen."

Reuben Fine says clearly and simply, "The King is a strong piece —use it!"

24. B—Kt2

The Bishop manages to emerge, but is it too late?

24. . . .   R—Kt6

Immediately pinning the Bishop and forcing White's next move.

25. R—K2

Clearly the only way to save the Bishop without losing the Rook Pawn. If instead 25. KR—B1, R(Kt6) x B wins a piece for Black.

25. . . .   R x R

Black is happy to exchange Rooks and simplify the ending. He retains a positional advantage in the superior mobility of his pieces, including his King, who plans to get in among the adverse Pawns and wreak havoc there.

26. K x R

White recaptures and threatens to extricate himself by 27. R—B1ch, K—Kt4 28. R—B2, and the Bishop is unpinned while the Rook (after 29. B—B1) might even utilize the open file!

26. . . .   K—Kt4

Lightly stepping aside, the King evades the check. He is headed for R5, to get a good grip on White's Queen side before starting to undermine the Pawns on that wing.

27. K—Q2

White's Rook and Bishop are immobilized, so he is reduced to King moves. And not too many at that, as the King Pawn needs protection.

27. . . .   K—R5

Before starting the decisive combination, Black renders the opposing Pawns impotent too.

28. K—K2

All that White has left, aside from meaningless moves by the King-side Pawns.

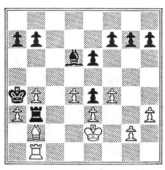

28. . . .   P—QR4 !

Pawns, as we shall see, are unexcelled as spearheads of an attack. They can break through almost any barrier.

Black's threat is 29. . . . P x P 30. P x P, K x P, winning a Pawn.

29. K—B2

On 29. P x P, B x RP regains the Pawn and then wins the Bishop. Or if 29. K—Q2, P x P 30. P x P, B x Pch 31. K—B2, B—R6, and Black exchanges all the pieces to leave himself with an extra Pawn and an elementary win.

29. . . .   P x P

The first bit of booty.

30. P x P

Otherwise Black's Pawn slays right and left, first another Pawn and then the Bishop.

30. . . .   K x P

Black does not take with the Rook or the Bishop. Either would give White time for 31. R—R1ch and freedom for his Bishop.

31. K—K2

White is restricted to waiting moves.

31. . . .   K—Kt4 !

Here, too, moving the King to the Rook file or the Bishop file allows a check by the Rook.

Black now threatens to double the pressure on the pinned Bishop by 32. . . . B—R6 and win a piece.

32. K—Q2

The King moves closer to save the Bishop.

32. . . .   B—R6

Forcing the issue by attacking the Bishop again.

33. K—B2

The only move.

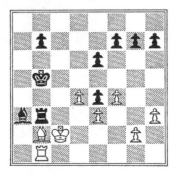

33. . . .   R x Bch !

Clearing the board of pieces and reducing it to a Pawn ending. This is the simplest way of winning an ending with a Pawn up.

34. R x Rch

White must recapture.

34. . . .   B x R

Continuing the simplification.

35. K x B

The only move.

35. . . .   K—B5

Threatening to get at the King-side Pawns by way of Q6.

36. K—B2

Prevents the planned invasion.

36. . . .   P—QKt4

Passed Pawns must be pushed! This clinches the win, as White cannot stop the Pawn without letting Black's King come in among his deserted Pawns. The continuation might be 37. P—Kt4, P—Kt5 38. P—R4, P—Kt6ch 39. K—Q2, P—Kt7 40. K—B2, P—Kt8(Q)ch 41. K x Q, K—Q6 42. K—B1, K x KP 43. K—Q1, K—B7, and the new passed Pawn moves up to become a Queen.

37. Resigns

The Chess Master Explains His Ideas

Let us imagine ourselves sitting beside a master player who reveals his thoughts in the course of a game. We can then thrill to the excitement of combination play and revel in the pleasure of watching ideas come to life. We can see how the tactical themes, the pin, the Knight fork, the double attack and the mating combination (the sort of thing we could always spot if similar opportunities only presented themselves) are prepared for by the strategy of setting the scene for their appearance.

The games that follow are not primarily displays of pretty fireworks, nor do they feature explosive (and sometimes unpredictable) attacks. They may not conform to the popular concept of brilliancy, but they do show how circumstances can be shaped by iron control of the forces involved. And they do show what can be accomplished by applying the three great principles that Capablanca advocated and himself utilized so successfully:

1. In the opening, rapid and efficient development.

2. In the midgame, co-ordination of pieces.

3. In the ending, accurate and time-saving play.

These games are wonderful illustrations of the efficacy of Capablanca's principles in practical play. In *my* book, games such as these are brilliancies.

In the game Capablanca-Mattison (No. 24) White does nothing but develop his pieces, but it's enough to summon up all sorts of piquant little combinations. What makes the feat impressive is that all the combinations are in White's favor, even unto the mere threat of one (a smothered mate), which is enough to persuade Black to resign. A Capablanca jewel!

Janowsky-Alapin (No. 25) is undoubtedly the most beautiful game Janowsky ever played. His maneuvering on the open Queen file leads to the creation of a passed Pawn. The Pawn must be blockaded, and Black shows ingenuity in shifting blockaders so that a weaker piece keeps replacing a stronger one. Then comes an interesting phase where Janowsky's Pawns reach out to the black squares on the seventh rank, gripping them like so many fingers at the throat of an adversary. And the finale includes an amusing shifting of attack to various files, which Black must try to imitate in defense.

"Étude on the Black Keys" might be a title for the Bernstein-Mieses (No. 26) game. Bernstein fastens on the weaknesses of his opponent's black squares and plants pieces in these holes in the position. After a remarkable tour by his King, the Pawns begin to fall and a pathway is cleared for Bernstein's passed Pawns.

An unknown masterpiece is Chekhover-Rudakowsky (No. 27) in which the themes we discussed in the King-side attack and the Queen's Pawn opening are beautifully blended. Black omits the freeing . . . P—QB4 move, a circumstance which his opponent promptly exploits. Chekhover, who controls the Queen Bishop file, restrains and then blockades the adverse Queen Bishop file. With Black tied up on the Queen side, he switches the attack suddenly to the King side, giving his opponent the job of defending on both wings, to say nothing of the center. Black is forced to play . . . P—KKt3 and weaken his black squares KB3 and KR3. White's Queen pounces on one of the weak squares. Then begins a series of mating threats on the King side which culminates in winning the Queen—on the Queen side!

Tarrasch-Mieses (No. 28) is notable for Tarrasch's skillful refu-

tation of a premature attack. His gains of tempo in the opening are carried over into the ending, so that what remains is a clear-cut demonstration in the technique of converting a Pawn majority on the Queen side into a passed Pawn.

The game Marshall-Tarrasch (No. 29) is a little-known masterpiece which features a duel between a genius of attack and a virtuoso of defense. The methods of the position player prove superior, his continued acquisition of territory driving White to the wall. Against Tarrasch's steady accumulation of positional advantages, any attack by his opponent seems futile.

There follow three games in which the motif is: Get a passed Pawn, move it up the board, and win! In the first, Capablanca-Villegas (No. 30) offers to sacrifice his Queen. But where in most games such an offer is the high point in a combination, here it is subordinate to the grand strategy of securing a positional advantage. It leads to control of the Queen file, and this in turn is converted to a Queen-side majority of three Pawns to two. Skillful play resolves this into a lone passed Pawn, heavily blockaded, until another Queen sacrifice opens wide the gates.

Havasi-Capablanca (No. 31) is a superb specimen of position play featuring the art of squeezing the most out of a tiny advantage. Capablanca secures a Pawn majority on the Queen side and sets to work to translate it into a passed Pawn. This he does by getting control of the open Queen Bishop file and then exploiting the weakness of his opponent's white squares. The rest consists of escorting the passed Pawn safely to the Queening square.

Canal-Capablanca (No. 32) is a game for the connoisseur. Canal surprises Capablanca by a combination that wins two pieces for a Rook. Or was it a surprise? Apparently Capablanca anticipated the combination and, looking further into the position than Canal, saw resources that were not revealed to his opponent. The endgame that follows is a fascinating study and illustrates a "domination" theme rare in actual play. There is a Pawn to be Queened, but it would take an eagle eye to find the particular Pawn that will be crowned.

Rubinstein-Maroczy (No. 33) is a splendid all-around performance. Rubinstein's economic development in the opening results in a magnificent midgame centralization, and this in turn is a prelude to a Kingside attack in the ending. Not the least of this game's attractions is the remarkable use of Q5 as a pivot for the maneuvers of Rubinstein's Knight, Bishop, Rook and Queen, who each utilize this square in turn as a landing field!

GAME NO. 24

QUEEN'S PAWN GAME
(Nimzo-Indian Defense)

WHITE	BLACK
Capablanca	Mattison

CARLSBAD, 1929

1. P—Q4

The popular concept of King Pawn openings is that they offer all sorts of opportunities for whipping up a quick attack. A variety of gambits can be played, pieces may be sacrificed to open lines, combinations ventured on, and speculation indulged in—anything for the sake of mate. Sometimes these tactics succeed, but very often the gambit player finds himself at the wrong end of the attack. The wide-open positions are as dangerous for one side as for the other.

In Queen Pawn openings, the ideal to strive for is development for its own sake. The attack is not "the be-all and the end-all." It is not deliberately played for, but, strangely enough, the very fact that all the pieces are developed economically, that they are put to work as quickly as possible on the squares where they function best, seems to imbue them with marvelous powers of attack. Combinations come into life out of nothing! Can it be that the simple posting of pieces where they have the greatest freedom of movement and the greatest command of the board generates in them so much dynamic energy that it must be released somehow? And can it be that knowledge of this fact is what makes the virtuosi of position play repress their instinct to attack until the time is ripe for an attack to be unleashed?

White's move of the Queen Pawn begins the process of getting *all* the pieces into play as quickly as possible. Two of them are now free to make their debut, while the Pawn which released them occupies the center of the stage.

1. . . .   Kt—KB3

A developing move, whose object (besides the commendable one of bringing a piece to its most suitable square) is to prevent White from gaining too much ground with 2. P—K4.

2. P—QB4

This move does many things:

a) It begins an attack on the square Q5.

b) It keeps the Bishop file open for the use of the heavy pieces.

c) It offers the Queen a diagonal.

d) It hinders Black from establishing a Pawn in the center by 2. . . . P—Q4. White's reply 3. P x P, compelling a recapture with a piece would leave Black with no Pawn in the center.

2. . . .   P—K3

Clears a path for the King Bishop and indicates that Black will go in for an active defense.

3. Kt—QB3

White's motive is evident: he develops the Queen Knight first, to support an advance of the King Pawn.

3. . . .   B—Kt5

To this, Black counters by clamping a pin on the Knight. If White were to play 4. P—K4, the reply 4. . . . Kt x P leaves him helpless to recapture.

4. Q—B2

With a twofold purpose: to meet 4. . . . B x Ktch with 5. Q x B, keeping the Pawn position intact, and to threaten again the advance 5. P—K4.

There is a prevalent concept that in the opening there is a "best move" at every point. The belief is that the chess master memorizes every one of these best moves and its proper reply. That such reasoning is specious is obvious: the very fact that millions of games have been played without duplication of moves is proof enough in itself.

Let us consider the position on the board. Besides the text move (4. Q—B2) there are at least seven excellent alternatives, each of which has enthusiastic advocates. They are:

4. Q—Kt3
4. B—Q2
4. P—QR3
4. B—Kt5
4. P—K3
4. P—KKt3
4. Kt—B3

Which of these is best? No one can say for sure, but the move that leads into positions congenial to your style is the best move, and the one you should play.

4. . . .   P—B4

Black too can conduct the defense (or the counterattack) in the manner that suits his style and temperament. The move he plays immediately disputes White's control of the center. It does other things, too: it gives the Queen more scope, opens the Bishop file, protects the Bishop, etc.

But there are other moves, equally effective, at Black's disposal. He can select from these replies, each of which has something to recommend it:

     4. . . . Kt—B3
     4. . . . B x Ktch
     4. . . . P—Q3
     4. . . . P—Q4
     4. . . . O—O
     4. . . . P—QKt3

There is something for every taste.

5. P x P

Strongest for various reasons: White does not lose time in taking the Pawn, as Black in recapturing will return the lost tempo. The open Queen file resulting from 5. P x P will benefit White, who will occupy Q1 with a Rook and exert pressure along the length of it, especially endangering the backward Queen Pawn.

Other continuations are less energetic. For instance, after 5. P—K3, Black frees himself by 5. . . . P—Q4, or if 5. Kt—B3, P x P 6. Kt x P,

Kt—B3, and White has the initiative to defend.

5. . . .   Kt—B3

Black develops another piece before recapturing the Pawn.

6. Kt—B3

Somewhere about this stage, the amateur wants things to happen. He begins to look around for surprise moves. There *must* be a brilliancy in the position! The great master, in the same situation, is content to make simple moves. He knows that if he keeps on bringing pieces into the field, there will be no need to look for winning combinations. They will evolve naturally out of the position and spring up all over the place!

6. . . .   B x P

Further delay in recovering the Pawn might be dangerous.

7. B—B4

More usual is the aggressive 7. B—Kt5, to pin the Knight and keep Black under pressure, but no fault can be found with this method of development. It looks mild, but the Bishop surveys an important central diagonal and bears down on Q6, a tender spot in Black's position.

7. . . .   P—Q4

Vigorously challenging possession of the center.

8. P—K3

Another quiet move which liberates one Bishop and strengthens the position of the other.

8. . . .   Q—R4

Black spies a chance to start an attack which will result in saddling White with an isolated Bishop Pawn—a slight positional weakness. So he begins an action against the Knight, but "such artificial maneuvers," says Tartakover, "can hardly succeed against a Capablanca."

Black should instead do something to get his Queen Bishop into play, possibly like this: 8. . . . P—QR3 9. B—K2, P x P 10. B x P, P—QKt4 *11*. B—K2, Q—Kt3 (not at once *11*. . . . B—Kt2 on account of *12*. Kt x P) *12*. O—O, B—Kt2.

9. B—K2

Still another of these modest moves, which is packed with more energy than you might suspect. It accomplishes these objects:

a) It activates a piece, by getting it off the first rank.

b) It develops the Bishop at K2 so that it can swing over to KB3 and attack the center.

c) It clears away the King side, making early castling possible.

d) It prepares the co-operation of the Rooks on the first rank, subsequent to castling.

What was wrong with playing the more aggressive-looking 9. B—Q3? For one thing, the reply 9. . . . Kt —QKt5 enables Black to force an exchange of Knight for Bishop. White would lose the services of a piece valuable for its potential influence on the center. Why not then prepare for developing the Bishop at Q3 by playing 9. P—QR3 first? The answer is that time is too valuable in the opening to waste on unnecessary Pawn moves. *Only those Pawn moves that are essential to the development of pieces should be made.* The additional circumstance that 9. P—QR3 weakens the white squares on the Queen side is more proof that such strategy is artificial and time-wasting.

9. . . .   B—Kt5

In contrast to White's classically simple method of development, Black moves the Bishop a third time in the opening, in order to inflict his opponent with an isolated Pawn. Such an attempt is premature in view of Black's incomplete development.

Instead of this, a plausible continuation was 9. . . . O—O 10. O—O, P x P *11*. B x P, B—Q2, and Black has a fair game.

10. O—O

The King is made secure, while the King Rook moves closer to the center, the theater of action. The Rook, of course, will try to seize an open file, or if none is available, one which is likely to be opened.

10. . . .   B x Kt

The Bishop has moved four times to make this exchange for a Knight which has moved only once! So much shifting around of one piece indicates that the strategy impelling it must be faulty.

11. P x B

Despite the doubled Bishop Pawn, White enjoys these advantages:

a) He has two active Bishops against Black's Knight and Bishop.

b) All of his minor pieces are in play while Black has a Bishop still on the first rank.

c) His Rooks are in touch with each other and ready to seize the open Knight file and the half-open Queen file.

d) His King is safely tucked away in a corner while Black's is out in the open.

e) His Queen is ideally posted and has more influence on the center than does Black's, standing at the side of the board.

f) An exchange of Pawns in the center (which looks inevitable) will open lines of attack—a circumstance which favors the player whose development is superior—in this case, White.

g) He maintains the initiative.

11. . . .   O—O

One of Black's difficulties is resolved with his King's escape to safer quarters.

Developing the Bishop instead was somewhat risky, as after 11. . . . B—Q2 12. QR—Kt1 (attacking the Knight Pawn), P—QKt3

13. B—Q6 (stops King-side castling and threatens 14. R—Kt5, Q—R3 15. P x P, P x P 16. R x QP, and the discovered attack on the Queen wins a Pawn for White).

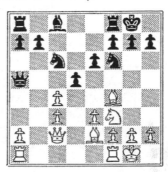

12. QR—Kt1 !

Another of those subtle moves, whose purpose the average player usually fails to see. "What use is it," he says, "to waste a Rook move in attacking a Pawn which is adequately protected?"

True, the Pawn is defended, but by a Bishop which cannot develop without abandoning the Pawn. Sooner or later, Black will be compelled to play . . . P—QKt3, or have three pieces on his first rank interfering with each other. There are drawbacks to . . . P—QKt3, though. Black's Queen will be cut off and prevented from returning to the King side and the defense of the King. Added to that, his Queen Knight's position will be insecure, once the prop (the Knight Pawn) is removed from under it.

White's move is simple and quiet, but it manages to exert uncomfortable pressure on Black's Queen side, makes normal development difficult, and creates perma-

nent weaknesses which lend themselves to exploitation.

12. . . .   Q—R6

Black wants to develop his
Bishop, and for that purpose he
must play . . . P—QKt3. But to do
so at once might endanger the
Queen by cutting off her line of re-
treat. For instance, if 12. . . . P—
QKt3 13. B—Q6, R—Q1 14. R—
Kt5, Q—R3 15. P x P wins at least a
Pawn, as 15. . . . P x P permits 16.
R x QP discovering an attack on the
Queen, while 15. . . . R x B 16.
P x Kt, R x P 17. R—Q5, attacking
the Queen and also threatening
mate is even worse.

13. KR—Q1 !

With the posting of this Rook on
the partly open Queen file, development has been completed in an ideal
way, every piece taking its best post
in no more than one move. White
has not so much as hinted at an attacking combination until every
piece has been put to work.

13. . . .   P—QKt3

To enable the Bishop to come
out, but the advance of the Pawn
takes away the Knight's support and
weakens its position.

Guarding the Knight Pawn by 13.
. . . Q—K2 instead does not help
much, since the Bishop cannot develop at Q2 next move without cutting off the Queen's protection of
the Pawn. Nor can Black try to
simplify by 13. . . . P x P, as the
reply 14. B—Q6 wins the exchange.

14. P x P

The attack begins! The first blow
destroys Black's Pawn center.

14. . . .   Kt x P

The recapture with the Pawn
would be fatal: if 14. . . . P x P 15.
P—B4 ! is the key move to the win.
Black could not then avoid loss by
15. . . . P x P since 16. B—Q6 attacks Queen and Rook, while protecting the Pawn by 15. . . . B—K3
yields to 16. P x P, B x P 17. R x B,
Kt x R 18. Q x Kt, and White has
won two pieces for a Rook.

15. Kt—Kt5 !

A master stroke! The brutal
threat of 16. Q x P mate disguises
the two real purposes of the move:
the strategical concept of forcing
Black to move one of his King-side
Pawns, thereby loosening the defensive structure, and the clearance of
the square KB3 for the benefit of
the King Bishop, who will bear down
heavily on the long diagonal.

15. . . .   P—KB4

Black had two alternatives:
If 15. . . . Kt—B3, to avoid
moving one of the Pawns, 16. B—
Q6 wins the exchange.

If *15*. . . . P—Kt3, Black's position is riddled with weaknesses on the black squares.

So Black moves the King Bishop Pawn, staving off the mate. But it weakens his King Pawn and ties the Bishop down to its defense.

16. B—B3 !

This arrangement of Bishops gives them tremendous raking power along the two parallel diagonals.

White's chief threat is *17*. R x Kt, P x R *18*. B x Pch, K—R1 *19*. B x Kt followed by *20*. B x R, sweeping away a good part of Black's army.

16. . . . Q—B4

The Queen rushes to the aid of the vulnerable Knights. This is what happens on other defenses:

a) *16*. . . . Kt(Q4)—K2 *17*. B —Q6, Q—R4 *18*. B x Kt(K7), Kt x B *19*. B x R, and White wins a whole Rook.

b) *16*. . . . Kt(B3)—K2 *17*. P —B4, Kt—Kt5 *18*. R x Kt, Q x R *19*. B x R, and White wins a piece.

c) *16*. . . . Kt x B *17*. B x Kt, R—Kt1 *18*. P x Kt, and White has won a piece.

d) *16*. . . . Q x BP *17*. Q x Q, Kt x Q *18*. B x Kt, Kt x R(Q8) *19*. R x Kt, B—R3 *20*. B x R, R x B, and White is a piece ahead.

After Black's actual move he seems to have escaped the worst, but White has an ingenious way to get at the Knights:

17. P—B4 !

This stab at the Knight looks harmless, the Pawn being pinned

and helpless to capture. But the point of *17*. P—B4 is to have the Pawn support an attack by *18*. R—Kt5. This will drive the Queen off and make the capture *19*. P x Kt possible.

The combinations now appear in quick succession.

17. . . . Kt(Q4)—Kt5

Counterattack on the Queen. All other attempts at defense fail, viz.:

a) *17*. . . . Kt—B3 *18*. B—Q6, Q—R4 *19*. B x Kt, and both Black's Rooks are *en prise*.

b) *17*. . . . Kt x B *18*. R—Kt5 ! (a pretty in-between move), Q—K2 (or *18*. . . . Kt—Kt5 *19*. Q—Q2, Q x BP *20*. R x Kt and White wins) *19*. B x Kt, Q x Kt *20*. P x Kt, and the attack on the Queen leaves Black no time to save his Rook.

c) *17*. . . . Kt(Q4)—K2 *18*. B —Q6, Q—R4, and White can take either Knight and win the exchange after Black recaptures.

18. Q—Kt3

White's Queen must leave, but the threat of *19*. B—Q6 still hangs over Black like the sword of Damocles.

18. . . . P—K4

Not only because there is no other specific against *19*. B—Q6, but with the hope of curbing the terrible Bishops by putting obstacles in their paths.

19. P—QR3 !

This starts a beautiful combination at one end of the board which culminates in a Queen sacrifice followed by a smothered mate away over at the other end!

19. . . .   Kt—R3

The only other possibility, 19. . . . P x B, allows White to force the game by 20. P x Kt, Q—K2 21. B x Kt, R—Kt1 22. P x P, and the extra piece wins easily.

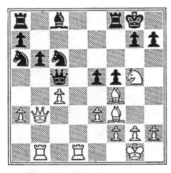

20. B x Kt

After the recapture 20. . . . Q x B, there comes 21. P—B5 dis. ch, K—R1 22. Kt—B7ch, K—Kt1 (if 22. . . . R x Kt 23. R—Q8ch, and White forces mate) 23. Kt—R6 dble. ch, K—R1 24. Q—Kt8ch !, R x Q 25. Kt—B7 mate!

20. . . .   Resigns

Black did not wait to be convinced by a demonstration over the board but turned down his King in surrender.

An exquisite game, played with elegance and precision. Capablanca's own comment on it was "I made a few little combinations in this game."

QUEEN'S GAMBIT DECLINED

WHITE	BLACK
Janowsky	Alapin

BARMEN, 1905

1. P—Q4

White opens by stationing a Pawn in the center. This Pawn performs various services:

It releases two pieces.

It occupies an important square.

It controls K5 and QB5, hindering the opponent from placing pieces on those squares.

It stands ready to give firm support to a friendly piece making use of K5 or QB5 as an outpost.

1. . . .   P—Q4

Black follows suit, establishes a Pawn in the center, and prevents White from continuing with 2. P—K4.

2. P—QB4

White offers a Pawn to induce Black to surrender the center.

White's move is also an attack on the Queen Pawn, by means of which he hopes to uproot it and its hold on the center.

2. . . .   P—K3

The customary device for maintaining a Pawn in the center. In the event of White's playing 3. P x P, *Black must be ready to replace the Queen Pawn with another Pawn.* It would not do to recapture with a piece. The piece could be driven off by White's King Pawn, leaving White in full possession of the center squares.

For instance, if 2. . . . Kt—KB3 3. P x P, Kt x P 4. P—K4, Kt—KB3 5. Kt—QB3, and White holds all the trumps.

3. Kt—QB3

This is more enterprising than the passive 3. Kt—KB3. Pressure is added to the attack on Q5, and the Knight also takes a hand in the battle for control of K4.

One of the objects in Queen Pawn openings is to effect a subsequent advance of the King Pawn, just as in King Pawn openings an effort is made to gain more ground with a later P—Q4.

3. . . . B—K2

The usual move at this point is 3. . . . Kt—KB3, but Black transposes moves to prevent his Knight being pinned. (To such extremes does fear drive a player!)

4. Kt—B3

White is content with simple development and places the King Knight at its most suitable post.

An Alekhine would have penalized this switch in the order of moves and thrown Black on his own resources by playing 4. P—K4 immediately, a move which 3. . . . . Kt —KB3 prevents.

4. . . . Kt—KB3

Black postponed this move, excellent though it is, and now makes it reluctantly. But how else can he develop the King side and prepare for castling?

5. B—Kt5

This is not really a pin, but its effect is somewhat similar. Pressure is exerted on the Knight, the Bishop behind it and even on the last in line, the Queen.

5. . . . P—KR3

Alapin can't stand pins or pseudo-pins! He attacks the Bishop at once, to force it to a decision.

6. B—R4

Whether objectively this is the strongest move is immaterial. The fact that the Bishop's pressure bothers Black is enough reason for Janowsky to maintain the pin!

6. . . . P x P

Black opens the position to give his pieces more elbow room, but with this capture he gives up his hold on the center.

7. P—K3

The simplest way to regain the Pawn. The King Bishop will capture it and make its developing move at the same time.

7. . . . P—QR3

Ready to meet 8. B x P with 8. . . . P—QKt4, attacking White's Bishop and gaining a tempo for the development of his own Bishop.

8. B x P

Material is now equal, but White's prospects are better: he has two more pieces in active play than Black, and his Pawn position in the center is superior.

8. .... P—QKt4

Black's chief purpose in this Pawn attack is to vacate the square QKt2 for his Queen Bishop.

9. B—Kt3

Nobody has yet decided whether this or Q3 is the better retreat for the Bishop. At Kt3 the Bishop strikes at Black's center, but those who favor Q3 reason that from there the Bishop helps control the vital K4 square and is aimed at the King's whereabouts when he castles.

9. .... QKt—Q2

Naturally, the Knight does not go to B3 where it obstructs the Bishop Pawn. The Pawn must not be hindered from carrying out its mission in life, which is to attack White's center and open a file for Black's Rooks.

The Knight's development looks clumsy, but it does back up the King Knight, and it is ready to support a thrust at the center by . . . P—B4 or . . . P—K4.

10. Q—K2

Notice how an expert player puts all his pieces to work before starting any decisive action! This does not look like much of a move for so powerful a piece as the Queen, but the simple act of getting a piece off the back rank advances the cause of development and constitutes progress.

Two more points: in the early stages of the game, the Queen is most happily placed close to home, say at QB2 or K2. A more aggressive development (generally for the sake of picking up a stray Pawn) is courting danger; in getting off the back rank, the Queen permits the Rooks (after the King castles) to get in touch with each other.

10. .... P—B3

It is hard to tell exactly what Black had in mind with this move. He may have feared the advance 11. P—Q5 by White, or perhaps he wanted to create an outlet for the Queen on the Queen side. In any case, the move is definitely inferior to 10. . . . P—B4, disputing the center without any more delay.

11. O—O

Castling by White is an aggressive measure, to press the Rook into active service.

11. .... O—O

Castling by Black is defensive in purpose, to get the King out of harm's way.

12. QR—B1

The Rook comes to the head of the Queen Bishop file. Control of this file is one of White's chief objectives in this opening.

12. ...   B—Kt2

With the development of the Queen Bishop, Black seems to have solved one of the problems that besets the defender in Queen Pawn openings. But he isn't out of the woods yet!

13. KR—Q1

Excellent play! The Rooks are now beautifully posted. The pressure on the Queen file makes it dangerous for Black to try to free himself by 13. ... P—B4, as the reply 14. P x P opens a file for the King Rook.

13. ...   R—B1

Black gives the Bishop Pawn more support in an effort to get in the break by 14. ... P—B4 and the consequent exchange of Pawns. This would free his position and let him put up a fight for the Bishop file.

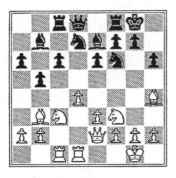

14. Kt—K5 !

White is now ideally developed, with every one of his pieces taking an active part in the game. Black, on

the contrary, is hampered by the restricted mobility of his pieces.

White's Knight move prevents a freeing attempt by 14. ... P—B4, when the continuation 15. P x P, R x P (if 15. ... B x BP 16. Kt x Kt leaves Black helpless to recapture) 16. B x Kt, B x B 17. Kt x Kt wins a Knight and menaces a couple of Rooks.

14. ...   Kt x Kt

Black tries to relieve the pressure by exchanging whatever pieces he can.

15. P x Kt

The exchange suits White in that he has opportunities for attack along the Queen file which has been opened up. Another effect arising from the Pawn's recapture is the creation of a strong point at Q6, a circumstance which White hopes to exploit by planting a piece on that square.

15. ...   Kt—Q4

The Knight must block off the Rook's attack on the Queen. If instead 15. ... Kt—Q2 16 B x B (to remove the guardian of Black's Q3 square), Q x B 17. P—B4, and White will either entrench his Rook at Q6 and double Rooks on the file or maneuver his Knight there by way of K4.

16. B x B

In order to benefit by the weakness of Black's Q3 it is necessary to remove the Bishop which defends the black squares.

16. . . .   Kt x Kt

Black destroys the Knight before it does him any damage. The alternative 16. . . . Q x B lets White swing his Knight over to K4 and then anchor it either at Q6 or QB5.

17. R x Kt

Certainly not 17. R x Q (or 17. B x Q), Kt x Qch 18. K—B1, Kt x R, and Black wins. The text gains a tempo for White in his plan to double Rooks on the Queen file.

17. . . .   Q x B

Material is even after this recapture, but White has a slightly superior position. But how much advantage does a master need to squeeze out a win?

White's specific advantage consists in his possession of the only completely open file, and the pressure he exerts on the strategically important square Q6.

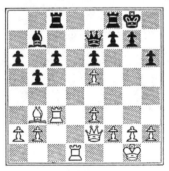

18. R(B3)—Q3 !

Much stronger than the plausible 18. R—Q6. The reply to that would be 18. . . . P—QB4, whereupon doubling the Rooks by 19. R(B3)—Q3 allows the Pawn fork 19. . . . P—B5, and Black wins a piece.

White's actual move doubles the Rooks without loss of time and includes a threat of winning a piece by 19. R—Q7.

18. . . .   KR—Q1

The dilemma which the weaker side always faces in this sort of situation is this: if he does not dispute the enemy at every point and fight for control of every important file, diagonal or square, he will slowly be driven back and crushed to the wall; if he does oppose him at every turn, the resulting exchanges will simplify the position without improving his chances.

In this particular position, Black could hardly delay opposing Rooks, as he was threatened with invasion on the seventh rank by 19. R—Q7, as well as with 19. Q—Q2, tripling the heavy pieces on the file. Such a massing of power on the open file would of course be overwhelming!

19. R—Q6 !

White stakes out a claim to the square Q6 by settling a piece firmly there.

19. . . .   R x R

Otherwise, White plays 20. Q—Q2 next, with intolerable pressure on Black's position.

20. P x R

This gives White a passed Pawn which exerts a terrific influence on the opponent's way of life. Nimzovich calls particular attention to "the lust to expand in a passed Pawn" and says that it must be regarded as "a criminal who should be kept under lock and key."

To prevent any further advance of the passed Pawn, Black must blockade it by placing a piece in its path. In effect, to keep the Pawn under surveillance, he must lose the services of one of his four remaining pieces! If constant vigilance is necessary to keep the Pawn quiescent, it is obvious that Black will be too busy defending to think of counter-attack. But White is free to switch the attack from one point to another!

20. ...   Q–Q2

This is practically forced, as the Pawn must be blockaded, and at once! Another forward step by the Pawn might be fatal! Witness this possibility: If 20. ... Q–Q1 21. P–Q7, R–B2 22. Q–Q2 (threatening to win by 23. Q–Q6 followed by 24. Q x R and Queening the Pawn), P–QB4 23. Q–R5, R x P 24. Q x Qch, and White wins.

After Black's actual move, the Pawn is stopped. But in blockading it, Black is tieing up the Queen, his strongest piece!

21. P–K4

Indicating that he intends to play 22. P–K5, supporting the Queen Pawn and further cramping Black's game. White's pieces, relieved of the necessity for watching over the Queen Pawn, could then move freely about the board.

21. ...   P–QB4

Black opens a diagonal for his Bishop and gives his Rook more air.

An effort to prevent 22. P–K5 might have lead to one of these continuations: 21. ... P–B3 22. Q–Kt4, K–B2 23. P–K5, P x P 24. Q–B5ch, K–K1 25. B x P, Q–Q1 26. Q–B7 mate, or 21. ... P–B3 22. Q–Kt4, R–K1 23. B x Pch, R x B 24. Q x Rch !, Q x Q 25. P–Q7, and White wins.

22. P–K5

Assisting the Queen Pawn to the next stage in its career:

First, a Pawn undistinguished from its fellows, then a passed Pawn, now a protected passed Pawn, and finally (if it fulfills its brilliant promise) a Queen.

22. ...   P–B5

Back to sober reality! Black fights every step of the way to institute countermeasures which will keep his opponent busy on the Queen side.

23. B–B2

The Bishop though thrust back now overlooks a new diagonal with interesting prospects.

23. ...   Q–B3

Black does not like to have his strongest piece tied down to the job of watching a passed Pawn, so he diverts White's attention by threatening mate. While White is occupied with stopping the mate, Black will have time to switch blockaders.

24. P–B3

This puts an end to attacks on the long diagonal, as it leaves Black's Queen and Bishop biting on granite.

24. . . .   Q—B4ch

The chief purpose of the check is to prevent White from playing 25. Q—K3, seizing control of the black-squared diagonals.

25. K—R1

White keeps the Queens on the board. Apparently he wants to win the game by direct attack, in preference to offering an exchange of Queens by 25. Q—B2.

Such decisions are a matter of style more than anything else. A player who has choice of more than one way of winning should select a method that is congenial to his temperament and aptitudes. In the present position, I imagine that a Rubinstein or a Capablanca would unhesitatingly offer to exchange Queens and simplify, confident in his ability to turn a slight advantage in an uncomplicated setting into a win and leave the victories by brilliant attack to other masters. It is to these varying techniques that we must be grateful for the creation of a wealth of masterpieces in so many colors and moods.

After 25. Q—B2, if Black avoids the exchange of Queens and plays 25. . . . Q x KP, White wins elegantly by 26. P—Q7, R—Q1 27. Q—Kt6 (attacking Rook and Bishop), R x P (if 27. . . . Q—Kt1 28. B—K4 wins a piece) 28. Q—Q8 ch !, R x Q 29. R x R mate.

25. . . .   R—Q1

The Rook takes over the job of keeping the Pawn covered.

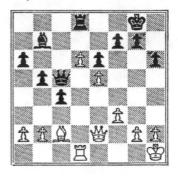

26. Q—K1 !

A very fine move! The Queen threatens to invade Black's King side by way of 27. Q—R4 or his Queen side by 27. Q—R5.

26. . . .   R—Q2

Nailing down the passed Pawn for the time being.

27. P—KR3

An outlet for the King in case of need. If White's Queen and Rook leave for the attack, his King must not be caught by surprise and mated on the first rank.

27. . . .   B—B3

Another regrouping so that the Rook may leave its post, and the Bishop (a lesser piece) stand guard.

28. P—B4

Preparing for a break-through by 29. P—B5. Pawns make excellent instruments of attack. They can break into almost any stronghold and make gaps wide enough for an invasion by the pieces.

28. . . .   R—R2

The Rook vacates Q2 for occupation by the Bishop.

29. P—B5 !

To this vigorous thrust Black may not reply 29. . . . P x P as 30. P— K6, P x P (otherwise he leaves White with two connected passed Pawns on the sixth rank) 31. Q x Pch, K—R1 (if 31. . . . R—B2 32. P—Q7 wins) 32. P—Q7 wins for White.

29. . . .   B—Q2

Black completes the changing of the guard. Since one of his pieces must act as blockader, he assigns the task to the least important, the Bishop.

30. P—B6

This battering ram of a Pawn will force a breach in the defensive structure. White's threat is 31. Q—Kt3 (intending 32. Q x P mate), P—Kt3 32. B x P, P x B 33. Q x Pch, and mate in two.

30. . . .   P—Kt3

On 30. . . . P x P White wins by 31. Q—Kt3ch, K—B1 32. Q—B4, P—B4 (or 32. . . . Q x KP 33. Q x RPch, K—Kt1 34. Q—R7ch, K—B1 35. Q—R8 mate) 33. Q x RPch, K —Kt1 34. Q—Kt5ch, K—B1 35. Q —B6, K—Kt1 36. P—KR4, Q—B1 37. P—R5, Q—KB1 38. P—R6, K— R2 39. R—Q4 (threatening 40. R— Kt4 and 41. R—Kt7ch), Q x Pch 40. R—R4, and the Queen is pinned.

After the actual move, the change in the Pawn configuration provides White with objects of attack. One

thing he must watch out for though is the preservation of his invaluable King Pawn which so stoutly supports the two advanced Pawns. Note that the position of these Pawns gives them a powerful grip on the black squares QB7, K7 and KKt7. These squares are in the enemy's camp and close to his King, but he (Black) cannot place pieces on those squares. With less facilities at his disposal, it will be difficult for Black to beat back the invaders.

The play for the win from this point comes under the heading of instruction and entertainment.

31. Q—Kt3

Threatening to win at once by 32. B x P, P x B 33. Q x Pch, followed by quick mate.

31. . . .   K—R2

The only way to protect the Pawn. Advancing it instead by 31. . . . P—Kt4 allows White a winning reply in 32. P—KR4.

32. P—KR4

Now that Black's Knight Pawn is pinned, White prepares to hit it again by 33. P—R5.

32. . . .   Q—B1

Hastening to bring the Queen over to the danger zone. If Black tries to stop the Pawn's advance by 32. . . . P—KR4, then the Queen works her way in by 33 Q—Kt5 (threatening 34. Q x RPch), K—Kt1 34. Q—R6, and 35. Q—Kt7 mate does the trick.

33. P—R5

Concentrating his fire on a vulnerable spot.

33. . . .   Q—KKt1

But not 33. . . . B—K1, which protects the Pawn but gets in the Queen's way. The Queen is the only piece agile enough to defend against White's attack as it shifts from one point to another.

34. R—Q4

White makes use of all his resources. The Rook will take part by switching over either to the Rook file or the Knight file.

34. . . .   B—K1

The Bishop helps defend the Knight Pawn so that the Queen is free to protect the Rook Pawn, White's next target of attack.

35. R—R4

Revealing the plan, mate in three by 36. P x Pch, P x P 37. R x Pch, K x R 38. Q—R4 mate.

35. . . .   Q—B1

The only possible defense.

36. R—Kt4

A pretty maneuver! White's last move lured the Queen away from the Knight Pawn. Now that this Pawn has one piece less defending it, White attacks it with a fourth piece, the Rook.

36. . . .   Q—Kt1

The Queen rushes back to defend.

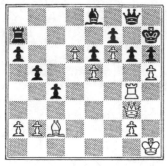

37. Q—K3 !

The threat on the Rook gains time for White's real purpose, an attack on the King Rook Pawn at the other end of the board.

37. . . .   R—Q2

The Rook flees but cannot get over to help defend the King.

38. R—R4

Renews (and shortens) the earlier threat: 39. P x Pch, P x P 40 Q x P mate.

38. . . .   Q—B1

Once again the Queen shifts over to protect the Rook Pawn.

39. P—KKt4 !

Bringing up the infantry! White throws everything into the attack, now threatening 40. P—Kt5 followed by 41. RP x Pch, P x P 42. R x Pch, K—Kt1 43. Q—KR3, with an easy win. If after 40. P—Kt5, Black tries 40. . . . RP x P then 41. P x P dble.ch, K—Kt1 42. R—R8ch, K x R 43. Q—R3ch forces the mate.

39. . . .   K—R1

Unpins the Knight Pawn and pre-

pares for 40. . . . P—Kt4 41. Q—
K4, Q—Kt1, and White will have
trouble breaking in.

40. P x P

Tearing apart the cordon of
Pawns guarding the King.

40. . . .   P x P

The lesser evil, as otherwise
White's next move, 41. P—Kt7ch, is
fatal.

41. R x Pch

Killing off another bodyguard.

41. . . .   R—R2

If 41. . . . K—Kt1 42. Q—KR3,
doubling pieces on the open file, is
conclusive.

42. R x Rch

Certainly not 42. P—Kt5, R x
Rch 43. P x R, and the Rook file is
closed and useless to White.

42. . . .   K x R

White is only one Pawn up, but
his attack has lost none of its viru-
lence.

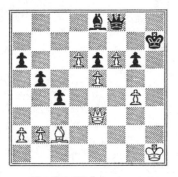

43. Q—Kt5

Now White plans to penetrate by
44. Q—R5ch (exploiting the plight
of the pinned Pawn), K—Kt1 45.
B x P, and the last barrier is destroyed.

43. . . .   Q—B2

Black avoids an exchange of
Queens, as after 43. . . . Q—R3ch
44. Q x Qch, K x Q 45. P—B7,
B x P 46. P—Q7 results in White's
getting a new Queen.

44. Q—R5ch

Beginning of the final movement!

44. . . .   K—Kt1

The King is driven back and the
Knight Pawn loses a protector.

45. B x P

White sacrifices a piece to bring
about a position where the passed
Pawns will decide the issue.

45. . . .   Q x B

An attempt to counterattack by
45. . . . Q—Kt2ch is futile. White
simply replies 46. K—R2, and the
King seemingly exposed, is not in
the slightest danger.

46. Q x Qch

And White wins, 46. . . . B x Q
yielding to 47. P—Q7.

The whole game is a marvelous
blend of clear-cut positional play and
ingenuity in attack. The opening is
sound and simple, the midgame is a
lesson in attacking technique, and
the ending is artistic.

SICILIAN DEFENSE

WHITE　　　　BLACK
Bernstein　　Mieses

COBURG, 1904

1. P—K4

Nowadays it takes daring to venture on this move. It is rarely met by the classic reply 1. . . . P—K4. What one gets is the French, the Sicilian, the Caro-Kann, the Alekhine or some other defense on which the player of Black has written a treatise.

Nevertheless, regarded objectively, 1. P—K4 is one of the strongest possible opening moves. It establishes a Pawn in the center and permits two pieces to come into play. More could hardly be asked of one move.

1. . . . P—QB4

Black will not come out and fight like a man as they did in the good old days. Instead of letting his opponent play whatever is his favorite gambit or opening attack, Black insists on naming the weapons.

Theoretically, Black's response is inferior to 1. . . . P—K4 in that only one piece is released, and the Bishop Pawn itself has less influence on the center than White's King Pawn. Practically, though, the Sicilian Defense is perfectly sound. It leads to a fighting game in which Black has many winning chances, especially against an overambitious opponent, too intent on a King-side attack.

Black aims at Queen-side counterattack, and for this, control of the Queen Bishop file is essential. He must try to offset White's superiority in the center and on the King side.

2. Kt—QB3

A normal developing move. A piece is brought into play which exerts influence on the center—but what a placid move this is!

More to the point is the energetic 2. Kt—KB3. This develops a piece on the King side (facilitating early castling) and prepares for 3. P—Q4 —action in the center and release of the Queen-side pieces.

2. . . . P—K3

Black's move is quiet but effective! Diagonals are opened for the King Bishop and the Queen, and preparation is made to occupy the center with 3. . . . P—Q4.

3. Kt—KB3

An excellent move, it places the Knight at once on its most suitable square, increases the pressure on the center, and makes early King-side castling feasible.

Moving 3. P—Q4 instead leads to 3. . . . P x P 4. Q x P, Kt—QB3, and Black gains a tempo by the attack on the Queen.

3. . . . Kt—QB3

Black misses his chance! Now was the time for the thrust 3. . . . P—Q4, giving him a fine, free game. In almost all King-side openings, Black equalizes if he can get in this . . . P—Q4 move.

4. P—Q4!

The characteristic break in the Sicilian, by means of which the mobility of White's pieces is increased. A diagonal is opened up for the Queen Bishop, while the Queen gets some more air.

4. . . .   P x P

Black exchanges to kill off one of the two center Pawns in return for his side Pawn. Meanwhile he opens the all-important Queen Bishop file for the use of his Queen and Queen Rook.

5. Kt x P

The recapture centralizes the Knight and increases the attacking range of White's pieces.

5. . . .   Kt—B3

By a devious route, the players have arrived at "the Sicilian four Knights game," a tricky position in spite of its tranquil appearance.

What shall White play now? The choice is a matter of style, mood and temperament more than anything else—and this is what makes chess so fascinating.

White can decide to be methodical and stick to straightforward development by 6. B—K3 or 6. B—K2. He can be bold and combinative with 6. Kt(Q4)—Kt5, or cautious with 6. P—QR3, preventing a powerful pin. He can be patient and devote his efforts to securing a positional advantage either by 6. P—KKt3 or 6. Kt x Kt.

Whatever he does, the play will reflect something of his own personality. The turn he gives to events will mirror the thoughts, the moods, and the instincts of an individual as shown in the way he directs the activities of a small army.

6. Kt x Kt

White is content with the slight advantage in position that results from the exchange of Knights. Let us take a quick look at some of the alternatives:

a) If 6. B—K3, B—Kt5 (pinning the Knight and threatening 7. . . . Kt x P) 7. B—Q3, P—Q4 !, and Black has overcome most of his difficulties.

b) The quiet 6. B—K2 (certainly not 6. B—Q3, leaving the Knight *en prise*) is also met by 6. . . . B—Kt5 with good counterplay.

c) Preventing the pin by 6. P—QR3 is not attractive. It is answered by 6. . . . P—Q4, and White must fight to retain the initiative. Time is too valuable in the opening to waste on Pawn moves.

d) The double-edged 6. Kt(Q4) —Kt5 is not to everybody's taste, leading as it does to wild complications after 6. . . . B—Kt5 7. B—KB4, Kt x P 8. Kt—B7ch, K—B1 9. Q—B3, P—Q4 10. O—O—O, B x Kt 11. P x B, R—QKt1.

One merit in the text move is that Black, in recapturing with a Pawn closes the Bishop file, his chief avenue of attack in the Sicilian.

6. . . .   KtP x Kt

This is probably superior to 6. . . . QP x Kt. For one thing, it is usually better strategy to capture toward the center. In this case, it keeps a cluster of Pawns in the center and opens up the Knight file for the benefit of the Queen Rook.

The continuation after 6. . . . QP x Kt might be 7. Q x Qch, K x Q 8. B—KKt5, B—K2 9. O—O—Och, and Black is kept on the move.

7. P—K5

Not only does this evict the King Knight from its fine post, but it strengthens White's grip on the square Q6.

7. . . .   Kt—Q4

Little thought was required to make this centralizing move. The only other spot available to the Knight was KKt1, home base.

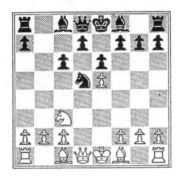

8. Kt—K4

Exchanging Knights would forfeit any advantage White enjoys. The move actually made intensifies the pressure on Q6.

8. . . .   P—KB4

No loitering on the premises! Either the Knight leaves or it declares its intentions!

Black had another defense in 8. . . . Q—B2, and if 9. Kt—Q6ch, B x Kt 10. P x B, Q x P 11. P—QB4, Q—K4ch, and he wriggles out of the pin.

9. P x P e.p.

The Knight must stay where it is for White to carry out his purpose, which is to take possession of the critical square Q6.

9. . . .   Kt x P

Black does not take with the Pawn, as that is answered by 10. Q—R5ch. This would compel his King to move and thereby deprive him of the privilege of castling.

10. Kt—Q6ch

Compelling an exchange of pieces which leaves Black with a "bad" Bishop, one which is ineffective because of the Pawns standing on squares of the same color as the Bishop. A Bishop can accomplish little if its pathway is cluttered up by Pawns.

10. . . .   B x Kt

The only other move, 10. . . . K—K2, is not inviting.

11. Q x B

The recapture gives White a stranglehold on his opponent's position. Not only is the Queen Pawn blockaded, preventing the freeing . . . P—Q4 maneuver, but the King may not flee to safety by castling. In addition, White exerts a great deal of pressure on the black squares, a pressure which is accentuated by the fact that Black's King Bishop, operating on those squares, is off the board.

11. . . .   Kt—K5

The Queen must be driven off, or Black will choke for lack of air.

There is no relief in 11. . . . Q—K2 12. B—KB4, Q x Q 13. B x Q, Kt—K5 14. B—R3!, and White still bears down with a heavy hand.

12. Q—Q4

In retreating, the Queen manages to attack in two directions, threatening the Knight and the Knight Pawn.

12. . . .   Kt—B3

The only move to parry both threats.

13. Q—Q6

White tries again as he hates to relinquish this dominating position. Meanwhile, he hints that he can always draw if he wants to, by a repetition of moves.

13. . . .   Kt—K5

Black cannot let the Queen stay at Q6, and delay in evicting her might prove to be fatal.

That Black's difficulties are not insuperable was demonstrated by Alekhine, who suggested this continuation: 13. . . . Q—Kt3 (threatening 14. . . . Q x P ch 15. K x Q, Kt—K5 ch) 14. B—Q3, P—QB4 15. B—KB4, B—Kt2 16. O—O, QR—B1.

14. Q—Kt4!

Very strong! If the Queen cannot establish permanent residence at Q6, this square is the next best thing. At QKt4 (odd place though it is) the Queen attacks the Knight, controls a diagonal which makes castling for Black impossible, and in a third direction prevents Black's Queen Rook from seizing the open file.

14. . . .   P—Q4

Protects the Knight and prepares to challenge White's Queen by 15. . . . Q—Q3. Black's Pawn center is some compensation for his troubles.

15. B—Q3

An ideal move, as a piece develops with a threat—16. B x Kt, P x B 17. Q x P winning a Pawn.

15. . . .   Q—Q3

An offer to exchange, which will either rid the board of White's attacking Queen or induce her to retreat from a dominating position.

16. Q x Q

White is willing to simplify. He will still have advantages in his two powerful Bishops and an enduring grip on the black squares.

16. . . .   Kt x Q

Black is content with his part of the bargain: both his Rooks have open files on which to operate, and he has a group of Pawns in the center with which he expects to limit the scope of the Bishops.

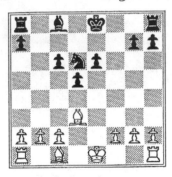

17. P—KB4 !

"An eye for the microscopic betokens the master," says the great Marco.

The square K5 is now controlled by White, while Black's King Pawn is restrained from advancing. One effect of this Pawn's inability to move is that it fearfully circumscribes the mobility of Black's Bishop.

17. . . .   P—QR4

Black must do something about getting the Bishop into play. With this move he plans to develop it at QR3 and exchange it for White's more powerful Bishop.

18. B—K3 !

Excellent! This holds back Black's Bishop Pawn, while two more black squares, Q4 and QB5, come under White's domination.

18. . . .   B—R3

Black hopes to clear the board of one of White's menacing Bishops.

19. K—Q2 !

The King is a strong piece and should be used aggressively in the ending. As the number of pieces on the board becomes smaller, so is the danger lessened of the King being exposed to a mating attack, and its own power as a fighting piece magnified. In the ending, the King is unexcelled as a means of causing damage by getting in among the enemy's Pawns.

That is why, in the present position, the King comes closer to the center, where he is most useful, instead of castling and then working his way there.

19. . . .   Kt—B5ch

Black's plan becomes manifest: he wants to force an exchange of Knight for Bishop. This would leave Bishops commanding squares of different colors on the board, a circumstance generally leading to a drawn game.

Another alternative worth considering was 19. . . . Kt—Kt2, in order to play 20. . . . P—B4, and get his Pawn phalanx in the center rolling.

20. B x Kt

Practically forced, as Black was threatening 21. . . . Kt x B as well as 21. . . . Kt x Pch.

20. . . .   B x B

Let us size up the situation:

White's Bishop enjoys far more freedom than does Black's. The latter is greatly hampered in its movements by the many Pawns standing on white squares, the color of the squares on which the Bishop operates.

White's King, being nearer the center and the critical squares Q4 and K5, is much better situated for the endgame than Black's.

Black's center, the heart of his game, is held fast. The three Pawns he has in that area are fixed and unable to move.

21. P—QR4 !

Blockade! The Rook Pawn is stopped dead in its tracks. It is now a fixed target, always in danger of being attacked by B—Kt6. In order to make sure it is not captured (for its removal gives White a passed Rook Pawn) Black must watch over it constantly with his Queen Rook. Because of the need to guard this one Pawn, Black is thereby deprived of the services of his Queen Rook.

21. . . .   K—Q2

Black brings his King toward the center for the endgame.

The Rooks are now united, while the King himself heads for Q3, where he hopes to support an advance by the King Pawn or the Bishop Pawn.

22. P—QKt3

An attack on the Bishop to force it to the side of the board. You will note that the Bishop's scope is cut down as Pawns *belonging to either side* are placed on white squares, the color of the diagonal on which the Bishop must travel.

22. . . .   B—R3

The only flight square open to the unhappy Bishop!

23. B—Kt6 !

And now an attack on the Pawn!

23. . . .   B—B1

Which can only be met by further retreat!

24. K—K3

Continuing the trek to Q4, K5, and, as we shall see, points north!

A bit more cruel was 24. B—B5, to prevent any demonstration by 24. . . . R—B1.

24. . . .   R—R3

No better was 24. . . . K—Q3, to back up a Pawn push, as the reply 25. K—Q4 nips that little idea in the bud.

Black's best chance was with 24. . . . R—B1, to get some counterplay by getting his King Rook into the game by way of the open file. The move he does make is an attack on the Bishop which succeeds in its object of driving it off from a good square—but only on to a better one!

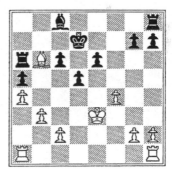

25. B—B5 !

Dominates every important square on the board! The Bishop stops the King Rook from getting to KB1, the Queen Rook from moving to QKt3, the King from Q3, the Queen Pawn from advancing and the Bishop Pawn from moving at all! Compare its control of eight squares with that of Black's Bishop whose influence is confined to one square! This difference in their potential accounts in great measure for the extent of White's attacking opportunities, and for the consequent difficulty Black will have in defending. Every gain or control of territory by White will result in more and more cramping of Black's position.

25. . . .   K—B2

Stepping aside, the King makes the square Q2 accessible to the Bishop.

26. K—Q4 !

Tightening the noose! This King also makes way—for the benefit of the King Rook, who will turn the King file to account.

26. . . .   B—Q2

Black will try to maneuver the Bishop over to the King side, say to KKt3.

His King Rook seems to have a great deal of scope, but what does it avail him? If it moves to QKt1 (as good a file as there is) at what point can it penetrate? It cannot get to any useful square on that file.

27. KR—K1

Much stronger than the immediate occupation of K5 by the King. White intends to use this key square as a transfer point for his Rook on its way to the King Knight file. After it gets there, White will settle his King at K5 and tighten his grip on the black squares.

27. . . .   P—R4

Black prepares a Pawn barricade against the Rook's threatened attack.

28. R—K5

Second stop on the trip to Kt5.

28. . . .   P—Kt3

Battening down the hatches. Black gets ready for a hard winter.

29. R—Kt5

Attacks the Knight Pawn and simultaneously makes room for the King.

29. . . .   R—KKt1

The Pawn must be protected, and this of course is more elastic than 29. . . . R—R3, and the Rook has no mobility to speak of.

30. K—K5

Further penetration along the convenient black squares. The threat is *31. K—B6, B—K1 32. R—K1* (even stronger than *32. K x KP*), followed by *33. R x KP*.

30. . . .   B—K1

Abandons the King Pawn, as he cannot hope to save all his Pawns. There is a slight chance, if White takes the Pawn at once, of putting up some resistance by *31. . . . B—Q2ch 32. K—B6, B—B4.*

Black's poor Bishop is sadly hemmed in by the five Pawns firmly fixed on squares of the same color.

31. R—K1

Before committing himself to decisive action, White applies more pressure. Notice how a master player puts every piece to work before he strikes a blow.

31. . . .   R—QR1

To get back into the game, this Rook has to return home!

There was no satisfactory defense in 31. . . . K—Q2, as the reply 32. K—B6 uncovers the Rook's attack on the King Pawn.

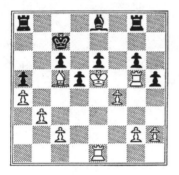

32. K—B6 !

Completes the concept of encirclement. Notice the effects of the arrangement of Black's Pawns at K3, Q4 and QB3. Black's own pieces are kept under restraint, while White's can utilize the weakened black squares QB5, Q4, K5 and KB6 to effect an entrance into the vitals of the enemy position. Notice also that these black squares are "holes," squares from which pieces can not be dislodged by the opponent's Pawns.

White does not resort to brutal attack or to intricate combination to accomplish his purpose but puts his trust in the dynamic power inherent in a crushing positional superiority.

32. . . .   B—Q2

Black reveals another reason for his previous move. In the continuation 33. R x KtP, R x Rch 34. K x R, R—Ktlch 35. K x P, R x P, Black suddenly turns on his foe.

33. P—Kt3

To guard against this possibility, and to lessen any chance of a breakthrough by one of Black's Rooks, White fashions a chain of Pawns on the King side.

33. . . .   R(R1)—K1

Black can do nothing to strengthen his position, so this amounts to no more than a waiting move.

34. R(K1)—K5

White could play 34. R x KtP and have little trouble winning, but he makes assurance doubly sure. He blockades the King Pawn first, to quell even a shadow of resistance!

34. . . .   R—KR1

"While there's life . . ."

35. R x KtP

The first tangible gain. The rest interestingly displays the art of winning a won game.

35. . . .   R—R2

Fearing threats against his isolated Rook Pawn, Black prepares to double Rooks and try to save it.

36. R—Kt7

White keeps on gaining ground. Now he invades the seventh rank.

36. . . .   R(K1)—KR1

Black holds on grimly.

37. R x R

Simplest, hence the scientific way to force the win. In endings where one side has a material advantage, the prescribed strategy is to exchange pieces, not Pawns, and bring it down to a Pawn position. *Endings with Pawns only on the board are the easiest to win.*

37. . . .   R x R

The recapture leaves Black only a Pawn down—for the time being!

38. K—Kt6 !

With every reduction of pieces from the board, the King's power increases! Now the King threatens the Rook and helps attack the Rook Pawn.

38. . . .   R—R1

Strangely enough, the Rook has only one move on the board!
Does White now settle the issue by removing the Rook Pawn?

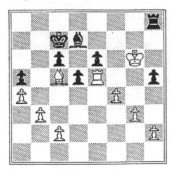

39. K—Kt7 !

No, no, a thousand times no! If 39. R x RP, B—K1ch, and Black wins a whole Rook and the game. How easy it is to go wrong in a simple ending!
White's actual move first banishes the Rook from the premises.

39. . . .   R—Q1

The Rook must leave the file, abandoning the Pawn.

40. R x RP

Now the capture is safe.

40. . . .   B—K1

Hoping to bring the Bishop over to the King side and in back of White's Queen-side Pawns.

41. R—R7

The Rook hastens to the seventh rank, a Rook's proper post in the ending.

41. . . .   R—Q2ch

Otherwise, White's procedure is 42. K—B6 dis. ch, B—Q2 43. P—KKt4, and the Pawn cannot be stopped.

42. K—R6

The King must stay near his Rook.

42. . . .   R x Rch

The exchange of Rooks cannot be avoided, so Black captures first to draw White's King away from R4. If the Bishop can get there, it might still stir up some trouble.

43. K x R

This meets White's approval. His King-side Pawns are mobile, while Black's Pawns either can not or dare not make a move.

43. . . .   B—R4

Now to get in back of the Queen-side Pawns!

44. P—R4

The Queen-side Pawns can not be rescued, so White starts his King-side Pawns rolling.

44. . . .   B—Q8

After so much inactivity, this Bishop not only threatens the lives of all the Pawns on white squares but restrains (for the time being) all the Pawns on the King's wing.

45. P—B3 !

To save itself, this Pawn flies to a black square.

45. . . .   B x P

Black takes a Pawn, more to distract White than anything else, since he has no real threats.

46. P—Kt4

Ready to refute 46. . . . B x P with 47. P—B5, K—Q2 (if 47. . . . B—B7 48. K—Kt6, and the Rook Pawn walks up, or if 47. . . . P—K4 48. P—B6, K—Q2 49. P—B7, and White wins) 48. P—B6, K—K1, and 49. K—Kt7 escorts the Pawn through.

46. . . .   K—Q2

The King rushes over to hold back the Pawns.

47. P—Kt5

"The passed Pawn's lust to expand," as Nimzovich puts it.

47. . . .   P—K4

Desperation, but there is no promising defense. If 47. . . . K—K1 48. P—Kt6, B—B7 49. P—R5, B—B4 50. K—Kt7 wins for White.

48. P—B5

The simplest. White's three connected passed Pawns should be convincing enough.

48. . . .   B x P

On 48. . . . B—B7 49. K—Kt6, protecting the Bishop Pawn and making way for the Rook Pawn, is the clincher.

49. P—B6

Indicating that it's time to concede. The Pawn cannot be stopped by 49. . . . K—K1 as 50. K—Kt7 sees it through.

49. . . .   Resigns

A beautiful illustration of the technique of exploiting weaknesses on the black squares.

GAME NO. 27

QUEEN'S GAMBIT DECLINED

WHITE   BLACK

Chekhover Rudakowsky

MOSCOW, 1945

1. P—Q4

This move, more than any other, confers an advantage in the opening.

Two pieces are released at once, and a Pawn occupies a center square, as with *1. P—K4*, but extra benefits accrue from *1. P—Q4*:

The Queen's Pawn is protected and safe from immediate attack.

White is not exposed to the threats on his King Bishop Pawn which often arise in King Pawn openings. His control of QB5 makes it impossible for Black to develop his King Bishop at QB4 to attack the vulnerable Bishop Pawn.

1. . . . P—Q4

The simplest way to prevent White from dominating the center with 2. P—K4 next move.

2. P—QB4

The key move in the Queen's Gambit! The versatile Bishop Pawn does many things. Three of these things are concerned with doing away with Black's center:

It offers itself in exchange, so that Black may be lured into accepting a side Pawn in return for his center Pawn.

It threatens, when the right moment comes, to destroy Black's center by capturing the Queen Pawn.

It exerts constant pressure on the Queen Pawn, so that Black is kept occupied with its protection.

Besides all this, the move of the Bishop Pawn assures that the Bishop file is kept free and clear for the convenience of White's major pieces, while a pathway is opened for the Queen, leading to the Queen side.

2. . . . P—K3

Black strengthens the position of his center Pawn. In the event that White plays 3. P x P, he is ready to recapture with a Pawn and thus maintain a Pawn in the center of the board. This is Black's safest defense, even though it does limit the scope of his Queen Bishop.

3. Kt—KB3

This is an excellent move, though not so sharp as 3. Kt—QB3, which adds pressure to the attack on Black's Queen Pawn. Either move complies with an injunction particularly applicable in Queen Pawn openings:

Develop all the pieces as quickly as possible!

"The main principle in the openings," says Capablanca, "is *rapid and efficient development*." (The italics are his.)

3. . . . Kt—KB3

Black's Knight moves in toward the center, attacks the square K5 and adds its weight to the protection of Q4.

It is good policy to mobilize the King-side pieces first, since only two of them need be developed to enable castling.

4. B—Kt5

A powerful move! The Bishop is developed and a restraining hand is put on the adverse Knight. There is no immediate menace in the move. White just "threatens to threaten."

4. . . .   B—K2

The proper way to unpin a Knight. The inexperienced player often grows impatient and drives the Bishop off by 4. . . . P—KR3 5. B—R4, P—KKt4 6. B—Kt3, only to find that he has ruined the Pawn position on the King side as a result of his violent action.

5. P—K3

White strengthens his Pawn center and frees the King Bishop.

5. . . .   O—O

Black gets his King into safety before revealing his plans for the development of the Queen-side pieces. His Queen Knight may go to Q2, or following an attack on White's center, perhaps to B3.

6. Kt—B3

White has no such problems. His Queen Knight can move to B3, since it does not obstruct the Bishop Pawn and the opening of the file. At B3 the Knight takes an active part in the struggle for control of the center.

6. . . .   QKt—Q2

This Knight must never be developed at B3 before the Queen Bishop Pawn is moved. The Pawn must be free, either to advance to B4 and fight for equal rights in the center or to move one square to B3 where it bolsters up Black's own center. But the Pawn must not be obstructed by . . . Kt—B3 !

The development by 6. QKt—Q2 is stronger than appears at first glance. The position is cramped for the moment, but the Knight is ready to support a liberating movement and an attack on White's center by . . . P—B4 or . . . P—K4.

7. Q—B2

A magnificent square for the Queen! From B2, the Queen exerts her powerful influence in several directions: on the partly open Bishop file and on the center, preventing Black from freeing himself by 7. . . . Kt—K5. This attempt to force some exchanges and shake off the pressure is refuted by (after 7. . . . Kt—K5) 8. B x B, Q x B 9. P x P, Kt x Kt (if 9. . . . P x P 10. Kt x P wins on the spot) 10. Q x Kt, P x P 11. Q x P, Q—Kt5ch 12. Q—B3, and White has won a Pawn.

Another feature of the 7. Q—B2 move is that it vacates Q1 for the Rook, whose presence on the same file as Black's Queen will discourage the opponent from making a break in the center. Exchanges of Pawns in the center would clear away some of the obstructions and intensify the Rook's pressure on the file—a pressure reaching all the way up the file to the Queen.

7. . . .   P—B3

This move provides solid support to the center Pawn and gives the Queen access to the Queen side. It looks substantial enough, but the more aggressive 7. . . . P—B4, disputing control of the center by establishing a state of tension there, might be more to the point. The danger in delaying . . . P—QB4 is that Black may never again have a favorable opportunity to get in this thrust.

8. B—Q3

White develops a fifth piece, pointing it at Black's King side, and is ready to castle on either wing.

8. . . .   P x P

Black waited for White to move his King Bishop before making this capture. Otherwise, the Bishop recaptures and develops at the same time. Black's intention, in clearing Q4, is to swing his Knight over to that square, force some exchanges, and free his cramped position.

Nevertheless, Black has surrendered the Pawn center which he so carefully built up.

9. B x BP

White is content with the result of the Pawn exchange. Lines are opened which increase the mobility of his pieces.

9. . . .   Kt—Q4

Obviously to compel White to exchange Bishops.

10. B x B

This is safer than 10. B—B4, Kt x B 11. P x Kt, and White is left with an isolated Queen's Pawn. The Pawn itself is in no great danger, but the square Q5 directly in front of it, is! It is in danger of being occupied indefinitely by one of Black's pieces. *A piece stationed on a square in front of an isolated Pawn can never be driven off by enemy Pawns.*

10. . . .   Q x B

The proper recapture, letting the Queen come into play; taking with the Knight would be developing backwards.

11. O—O

The King finds a safer shelter while the Rooks are enabled to get in touch with each other.

White's position is excellent, the result of simple straightforward development.

11. . . .   P—QKt4

A shot at the Bishop, to force its retreat. Meanwhile, Black gains time for the development of his own Bishop.

12. B—K2

The Bishop withdraws—but not to Q3, where an attack by 12. . . . Kt—Kt5 enables Black to bring about an exchange of Knight for Bishop. White wants to preserve the Bishop, which has excellent prospects for attack when it emerges later at Q3 or KB3.

12. . . .   P—QR3

The usual maneuver of protecting the Knight Pawn, so that the Bishop Pawn is free to attack White's center. If Black can get in 13. . . . . P—QB4 he will still have a respectable game.

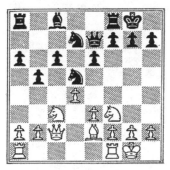

13. Kt—K4 !

Uncovering an attack! The Queen threatens the Bishop Pawn, while the Knight restrains it from advancing to B4. White's idea is to hold the Pawn back forever from B4 (the indispensable freeing move in Queen Pawn openings) and then barricade Black completely by planting a piece at QB5.

13. . . .   B—Kt2

Black protects the Pawn by developing another piece.

14. Kt—K5 !

Very fine strategy! Before settling a piece on QB5, White plays to get rid of one of the guardians of that square, Black's Knight at Q2.

Had he moved 14. Kt—B5 at once, then 14. . . . . Kt x Kt 15. Q x

Kt, Q x Q 16. P x Q leaves him with a Pawn occupying QB5. This would not have the effect of a piece standing on that square. A Pawn is immobile and does little to restrain the opponent. But a piece radiates power in all directions and has a terribly cramping effect on the enemy's movements in the whole surrounding area.

14. . . .   QR—B1

Develops another piece and defends the Pawn which was attacked by two pieces.

Black did not care for the exchange 14. . . . Kt x Kt 15. P x Kt. White could then anchor his remaining Knight at Q6, follow up by planting his Queen at QB5, and throttle Black thoroughly.

15. Kt x Kt

Removes one of the pieces guarding the vital QB5 square . . .

15. . . .   Q x Kt

. . . and lures the other one away!

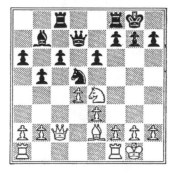

16. Kt—B5 !

With the domination of this square, White's advantage is decisive in the strategical sense. What remains is to exploit the superior position, to translate it into actual victory, and this process of consummating the win is one of the most fascinating features of chess.

16. . . .   Q—B2

Both Queen and Bishop were attacked, so the Queen stays near the Bishop.

17. KR—Q1

The practice of the masters has shown that Rooks are most efficient when they control open files.

Suppose there are no open files? Then the Rooks should be placed on partly open files, or on files likely to be opened.

Suppose none of those seem to exist? Then the Rooks should be brought to the center, to exert pressure on the center files.

But the Rooks must be developed!

17. . . .   R(QB1)—Q1

There are various reasons for this move:

The Rook has no future on the Bishop file while the Pawn at B3 impedes its movements (and there is little prospect of the Pawn's coming to life).

The Rook vacates QB1 for the Bishop. The Bishop cannot stay indefinitely at Kt2, where it is hampered by the Bishop Pawn, and where the Queen is tied down to its defense.

18. R(R1)—B1

White's incidental threat of winning a Pawn by 19. Kt x B, Q x Kt 20. Q x BP is subordinate to the strategical concept of intensifying the pressure on the Bishop file.

18. . . .   B—B1

Black parries the threat of 19. Kt x B and frees his Queen from the job of watching over the Bishop. Now he can speculate on getting some counterplay by the break 19. . . . P—K4.

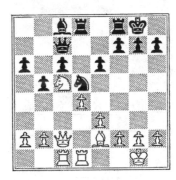

19. Q—K4 !

Magnificent centralization by the Queen, who prevents 19. . . . P—K4 (whereupon the Pawn is simply snapped up) and prepares to switch over to the King side for an attack on that wing.

19. . . .   Kt—B3

The Knight, best defender of the castled position, returns to B3, incidentally with an attack on the Queen.

Against other moves White could play 20. B—Q3, threatening 21. Q x RP mate. This would compel either a retreat by the Knight or a weakening advance of one of Black's Kingside Pawns.

20. Q—R4

The Queen evades the Knight's threat and swings over to the King side to get an attack rolling against the King.

20. . . .   Q—R4

Black tries counterattack on the Queen side—mostly to distract his opponent's attention. There is little he can do to strengthen the defense of his King side. Any move of a Pawn only loosens the position and reduces his chances of resistance. The break in the center by 20. . . . P—K4, which he contemplated making, is risky, to say the least, as 21. Q—Kt3 in reply, pinning the Pawn, is troublesome.

21. P—QR3

The simplest way to save the Rook Pawn and to keep the Queen from moving to Kt5.

21. . . .   P—Kt5

Hoping to continue with 22. . . . P x P, disrupting White's Queen side.

22. P—R4

White avoids any exchanges which let the Queen set foot in his territory.

22. . . .   Kt—Q2

Trying to shake off the grip of the Knight, which, like an Old Man of the Sea, is strangling his Queen side to death. If he waits too long, White pursues the attack with 23. B—Q3, followed by 24. P—Kt4 (to dislodge the Knight which guards

against mate). After the compulsory reply 24. . . . P—R3, White plays 25. P—Kt5, forcing an exchange of Pawns which opens the Knight file. White can then shift his King to R1 and swing a Rook over to attack on the open file. Against this, Black could not hold out very long.

23. P—QKt3

Defends the Rook Pawn, relieving the Knight of that task.

23. . . .   Kt x Kt

There is hardly anything better. The tempting 23. . . . P—K4 succumbs to 24. Kt x Kt, B x Kt 25. R—B5, Q—B2 26. R x KP, and White has won a Pawn.

24. R x Kt

The exchange of Knights results in White's substituting another piece at QB5, and this one maintains the grip on the position.

24. . . .   Q—Kt3

This is preferable to 24. . . . Q—B2, when the attack might proceed thus: 25. R(Q1)—B1, B—Kt2 (to protect both the Bishop Pawn and the Rook Pawn) 26. P—R5 (to isolate the Knight Pawn by preventing 26. . . . P—QR4), and White follows up by 27. R(B1)—B4 and 28. R x KtP, or by 27. B—B3 and 28. P—Q5.

25. R(Q1)—QB1

Doubling Rooks on an open file more than doubles the pressure on the file (and on the opponent). White's immediate threat is 26. R x P.

25. . . .   B—Kt2

The Bishop guards both white-squared Pawns, but its mobility is almost nil.

The subject of mobility is interesting. While it is not always true that the player whose pieces have more room in which to maneuver enjoys an advantage, it works well enough in practice for us to disregard the exceptional cases. It stands to reason that pieces that are free and untrammeled not only have more striking power in the portion of the board they occupy, but they also control and limit the activities of the enemy. Add to this the ease with which they can reach other parts of the board, and you can see the advantages to be derived from the property to move freely about.

Let us compare all the moves the pieces on each side can make. We are not evaluating their worth, whether good, bad or indifferent. What we want to see is the range of their action.

White		Black	
King	2	King	1
Queen	12	Queen	5
Rook(QB1)	8	Rook(KB1)	1
Rook(QB5)	11	Rook(Q1)	8
Bishop	9	Bishop	2
Total	42	Total	17

White's pieces are 250% as efficient as Black's! With so great a disparity in mobility (and consequently in attacking force) how long can Black continue the struggle?

26. P—R5

In order to isolate Black's Knight

Pawn, and incidentally drive the Queen back to the second rank.

26. . . .   Q—R2

On the alternative 26. . . . Q—B2, White can either resume operations on the King side or go after a Pawn on the Queen side by 27. B—B3, R—Q3 28. R(B1)—B4, followed by 29. R x KtP. Winning the Pawn will not diminish the force of White's attack or loosen his grip on the position.

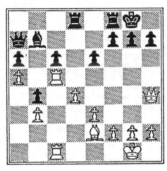

27. B—Q3 !

Now that the Queen side is fixed, White turns his attention to the King side. He threatens mate on the move. Black can easily dispose of this threat, *but only by moving one of the Pawns near his King and thereby creating a weakness which is organic, permanent and irremediable!*

27. . . .   P—Kt3

If 27. . . . P—R3, 28. Q—K4 forces 28. . . . P—Kt3, and two Pawns have been uprooted. White could then continue by 29. R—R5, K—Kt2 (if 29. . . . P x R 30. Q—R7 mate, or if 29. . . . K—R2 30. Q—B4 wins) 30. Q—K5ch, P—B3 (or 30. . . . K—R2, when the neat

double pin 31. Q—KKt5 wins) 31.
Q—Kt3, P—Kt4 (if 31. . . . P—
KB4 32. Q—K5ch, K—R2 33. Q—
B7ch, K—Kt1 34. R x RP wins) 32.
R x RP !, K x R 33. Q—R3ch, K—
Kt2 34. Q—R7 mate.

A simpler way, if White doesn't
want to bother analyzing combinations, is to maintain the pressure
and then apply more! For instance,
after 27. . . . P—R3 28. Q—K4,
P—Kt3, instead of playing 29. R—
R5 White could move 29. P—R4,
threatening to break up the Pawns
by 30. P—R5. If Black replies 29.
. . . P—R4 to stop the advance,
White can either snap the Rook
Pawn off with his Rook or keep
hammering away by 30. P—Kt4, P x
P 31. P—R5.

After the actual move, Black has
weaknesses on the black squares and
holes in his position.

28. Q—B6 !

The Queen plants herself securely
in one of the holes created by Black's
27. . . . P—Kt3 move. A hole is a
square such as KB6 or KR6 brought
into being by the advance of a
near-by Pawn. It is a weak square,
because it is no longer under the
surveillance of a Pawn and is vulnerable to invasion by an enemy piece.
Such a piece can settle itself comfort-
ably in one of these holes, secure in
the knowledge that no enemy Pawn
can disturb it.

White's plan, now that the
Queen has worked her way into a
dominating position on the King
side, is classical in its simplicity: he
will advance the King Rook Pawn to
R4, R5 and R6, and then play Q—

Kt7 mate. If, after the Pawn reaches
R5, it is captured en route, then
mate by the Rook is the instant
penalty.

28. . . .   R—Q3

Black vacates Q1, so that his
Queen can return to that square and
challenge White's. In chess language:
if 29. P—R4, Q—R1 30. P—R5, Q—
Q1, and White's Queen must leave
B6 and forgo the threat of mate.

29. Q—K7

An attack on the exposed Rook,
so that Black will have his hands
full warding off the accumulating
threats. Black has three problems,
each on a different part of the board:

a) On the King side, he must
guard against being mated.

b) On the Queen side, he must
release himself from White's stranglehold.

c) In the middle, he must rescue
any pieces that are loose.

29. . . .   R(B1)—Q1

If instead 29. . . . Q—Kt1 30.
B—K4, R—B1 31. P—R4, Q—B2
32. Q—B6, Q—Q1 33. Q x Q,
R(either one) x Q 34. B x BP or
34. R(B1)—B4, with an easy, routine win.

30. P—R4

Revives the threat of effectuating
mate by bringing the Pawn to R6
and the Queen to B6.

30. . . .   R(Q1)—Q2

The Queen must be evicted from
the premises. Black does not play 30.
. . . R(Q3)—Q2, as he wants the

first rank and the square Q1 available to his own Queen.

31. Q—B6

The menace of mate becomes more acute!

31. . . .   Q—R1

Only by a retreat can Black's Queen rush to the rescue!

If Black tries 31. . . . R—Q4, to stop 32. P—R5, White effects the advance by first dislodging the Rook with 32. B—K4.

32. B—K4 !

Not at once 32. P—R5, on account of 32. . . . Q—Q1 in reply. After the text (which incidentally prevents 32. . . . R—Q4), if Black plays 32. . . . Q—Q1, White exchanges Queens, captures the Bishop Pawn, and wins easily if prosaically.

32. . . .   Q—K1

Hoping to lure White into the premature 33. B x BP when 33. . . . B x B 34. R x B, R x R 35. R x R, R x P regains the Pawn and gives him fighting chances.

33. P—R5 !

Each step the Pawn makes increases the danger to Black's King. The Pawn is headed for R6, where it will settle itself firmly in the other hole in Black's position.

33. . . .   R—Q1

The Rook withdraws, so that the Bishop Pawn may have the added protection of the Queen.

The fact that Black is kept busy warding off threats on both sides of the board is the clue to the next move, which presents Black with an insoluble problem (the hardest kind to face).

34. B x BP !

Removing a Pawn that is apparently adequately protected. As will be seen, though, one of its defenders is overworked. The Queen not only has to guard this point (QB3) and the Rook at Q1, but must keep an eye out for mate threats on the King.

34. . . .   B x B

Black must take the Bishop or lose some material, since two pieces are attacked.

35. P—R6 !

A *Zwischenzug*, an in-between move that threatens instant mate.

35. . . .   K—B1

On the alternative defense by 35. . . . Q—B1, the win is forced, with 36. R x B (threatening 37. R x R, R x R 38. R—B8, Q x R 39. Q—Kt7 mate), Q x P 37. R x R, R x R 38. R—B8ch, and Black must give up his Queen.

36. R x B

White has regained his piece and now threatens 37. R x R, R x R 38. R—B8, Q x R 39. Q—R8ch, winning the Queen.

36. . . .   R x R

There is not much choice: if Black plays 36. . . . Q—Q2 (to reply to 37. R x R with 37. . . . Q x R), then 37. R—B7, Q—K1 38. Q—Kt7 is mate.

37. R x R

White gets his Rook back and prepares to seize the seventh rank by 38. R—B7. This would keep the King from escaping and again threaten him with mate by the Queen.

37. . . .   R—Q2

There is no relief in 37. . . . Q x R, White forcing a winning ending by 38. Q x Rch, Q—K1 39. Q—Q6ch, K—Kt1 40. Q x RP, Q—K2 (otherwise 41. Q—Kt7 wins at once) 41. Q—Kt6, and the passed Pawn cannot be stopped.

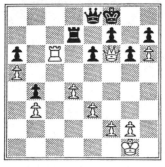

38. R—B8 !

Attacking the Queen with his un-

protected Rook. A pretty enough conclusion, but precisions and pedants may point out that White missed a brilliancy in 38. Q—Kt7ch, K—K2 39. R x KPch !, K x R 40. Q—K5 mate. Many a player has had quicker wins or more artistic ones than actually occurred pointed out to him by lesser lights, who revel in the fact that they found something the master overlooked. The reason the master didn't see the shorter line is that he was not looking for it in the first place! The move with which he wins is the one whose effects he foresaw earlier and analyzed thoroughly *before* starting his final combination. Once the series of forcing moves clicks, there is no reason at all for him to waste time finding other moves that might win. It takes time to analyze combinations, and the shorter way, ventured on hurriedly, might turn out to have a hole in it. The moral is: *Play the move that forces the win in the simplest way. Leave the brilliancies to Alekhine and Keres.*

38. . . .   Q x R

Naturally, 38. . . . R—Q1 39. R x R does not help matters.

39. Q—R8ch

White wins the Queen and the game.

Magnificent play by White, who never once relaxed his iron control of the game. A remarkable feature is the circumstance that none of Black's pieces or Pawns, with the exception of the one brave little Pawn at Kt5, ever crossed the fourth rank—Black's side of the board!

CENTER COUNTER GAME

WHITE	BLACK
Tarrasch	Mieses

GOTHENBERG, 1920

1. P—K4

In his delightful book *Chess for Winter Evenings*, written more than 100 years ago, H. R. Agnel proposed an interesting argument for the superiority of 1. P—K4 to 1. P—Q4. "Moving the Queen Pawn two squares," he said, "gives the Queen a range of two squares and the Queen Bishop a range of five squares. But moving 1. P—K4 gives a range of four squares to the Queen and five squares to the King Bishop. You see therefore that King Pawn two squares is the most desirable move with which to open the game. There is also another reason why this move is desirable—the Pawn occupies a portion of the center of the board. Two Pawns abreast at your King fourth and Queen fourth squares, supported by Pawns and pieces, must be considered as your best military position, and maintained with all the skill in your power."

1. . . . P—Q4

With his very first move, Black tries to uproot White's stake in the center. Black is willing to take some risks for the sake of having the initiative. There is danger though in the fact that his Queen, in recapturing, will come into the game too soon, and there is danger that he will be saddled with an inferior Pawn formation.

2. P x P

Simplest, and keeps Black on his toes. The alternatives 2. P—K5 and 2. Kt—QB3 are tame and occasion Black no trouble at all.

2. . . . Q x P

Black can play 2. . . . Kt—KB3 to avoid taking with the Queen, but the continuation 3. P—Q4, Kt x P 4. P—QB4, Kt—KB3 5. Kt—KB3, B—KKt5 6. B—K2, leaves White with a fine center and much the better prospects.

3. Kt—QB3

The Knight develops and gains a tempo by attacking the Queen.

One of the drawbacks of Black's system of defense is that it subjects his Queen to harassment by the minor pieces without her being able to bother them in return. The Queen, for example, cannot threaten to capture a Knight which is protected as that amounts to giving up the Queen for a Knight. The Knight, though, can attack and threaten to capture the Queen, protected or not.

3. . . . Q—QR4

This move, exerting pressure on the diagonal leading to White's King, is preferable to the shamefaced retreat by 3. . . . Q—Q1. In either case, though, Black has had to make two moves with his Queen, instead of developing another piece.

The beginner likes to give check whenever he can, and here it might lead to something like this: 3. . . .

Q—K4ch 4. B—K2, B—Kt5 5. P—
Q4, Q—K3 6. B—K3, B x B 7.
KKt x B, and White has three pieces
in play to Black's one—and that one
a badly placed Queen.

4. P—Q4

Once again seizing the center.
The Pawn occupies Q4, attacks the
squares K5 and QB5, and does further service in releasing the Queen
Bishop.

4. . . .   P—K4

And once again Black lashes out
at White's center!

5. Kt—B3 !

Far better than 5. P x P, to which
Black's reply is 5. . . . B—QKt5.
White combines a threat (6. Kt x
P) with the development of a piece.

5. . . .   B—QKt5

Black does not defend his Pawn
but intensifies the attack on the
pinned Knight. He does not care for
5. . . . P x P 6. Q x P, which only
speeds White's development.

6. B—Q2

Chess can be so simple! White
brings a third piece into play and at
the same time eases the strain on his
Knight.

Meanwhile he threatens 7. Kt x
P, and to this Black has no defense
in 6. . . . Kt—QB3 as 7. P—Q5,
Kt—Q5 8. Kt x P wins the Pawn.
How does Black meet the threat?

6. . . .   B—Kt5

Answer: by another pin! Apparently Black is not interested in rou-

tine defense, nor for that matter in
normal development. He wants his
pieces to rush out of their corners
fighting. If this strategy is sound,
what is to become of all the principles of development—the precepts
which in the hand of a master are
his greatest weapons?

So far Black has violated the conventions governing proper development, by these acts:

a) He has brought the Queen
into play too early.

b) He has moved the same piece
twice in the opening.

c) He has developed Bishops before Knights.

d) He has launched an attack before completing his development.

The question is: Can he get away
with all this?

7. B—K2

White keeps on developing. He
brings another piece out and unpins
his King Knight. The threat of 8.
Kt x P becomes more acute.

7. . . .   P x P

Black is practically forced to make
this capture which leads to a position in White's favor. But what else
can he do? If he protects the King
Pawn by 7. . . . Kt—QB3, then 8.
P—QR3 can be embarrassing. For
example, if then 8. . . . B—Q3 9.
P—Kt4, Q—Kt3 10. Kt—QR4, and
his Queen is lost, or if 8. . . . KB x
Kt 9. B x B, Q—Q4 10. P x P, and
White has gained a Pawn.

8. Kt x P

The recapture discovers an attack
on Black's Queen Bishop.

8. . . .   Q—K4

Black's response pins the Bishop and attacks the unprotected Knight. Black rejects 8. . . . B x Bch when the recapture by 9. Q x Bch gains another tempo for White.

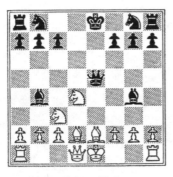

9. Kt(B3)—Kt5 !

Suddenly White turns aggressor! He protects his exposed Knight, attacks Black's King Bishop and threatens by 10. Kt x Pch, Q x Kt 11. B(K2) x B to win a Pawn. All this is directed toward bringing about further exchanges which will speed up his development and gain more and more tempi for him.

9. . . .   B(KKt5) x B

Black is forced into a series of exchanges which remove all the pieces he has developed from the board!

10. Q x B

The recapture pins Black's Queen and leaves him unable to avoid an exchange of Queens.

10. . . .   B x Bch

The Bishops too must come off. Otherwise, after 10. . . . Q x Qch 11. K x Q, B—Q3 (to protect the

Bishop Pawn) 12. Kt x Bch, P x Kt 13. Kt—B5, White wins a Pawn.

11. K x B

The recapture benefits White in that it brings his King toward the center for the endgame and clears away the last obstruction to the development of the Rooks. They can now get to the important open files in the center. As for the King—he is in no danger once the Queens are off the board. And there is no way for Black to prevent their coming off!

11. . . .   Q x Qch

Delaying the exchange is dangerous: White threatens to win a Rook by 12. Kt x Pch.

12. K x Q

White takes with the King naturally, as he does not want to displace the centralized Knight.

Tarrasch himself considered the game to be won at this point: he is five tempi ahead—one move by the King and two by each of the Knights.

12. . . .   Kt—QR3

An awkward move, but it guards the Bishop Pawn and facilitates castling on the Queen side. On 12. . . . K—Q1 instead, Black's Queen Rook will have trouble coming out.

13. KR—K1 !

Very effective in that it prevents Black from developing his King side. If he tries 13. . . . Kt—K2, then 14. K—B3 uncovers a pin on the Knight and ties the King down to its protection, while 13. . . . Kt—B3 is refuted by 14. K—B3 dis. ch, K—

B1, and Black's King Rook is shut in indefinitely.

13. . . .   O—O—O

The King flees (meanwhile mobilizing a Rook) rather than stay in the center and be harassed by White's Rooks. Has Black wriggled out of the coils?

14. Kt x RPch !

A startling combination, but combinations always appear for the player who has established a superior position. They do not emerge by chance but are the logical outcome of orderly, methodical play.

At first glance, White's capture looks unsound, as both his Knights will soon be *en prise*, and one of them apparently is doomed.

14. . . .   K—Kt1

The King attacks one Knight, the Rook the other. How do the Knights escape? If *15. Kt(R7)—Kt5, P—QB3* wins a piece, while if *15. Kt(Q4)—Kt5, P—QB3* again turns the trick. *Two Knights dependent on each other for protection are helpless against a Pawn attack on either of them.*

15. Kt(R7)—B6ch !

The point! White will get a Rook and two Pawns for his Knights. This is not an even exchange, but there are other than material considerations, as we shall see.

15. . . .   P x Kt

Black has no choice, as *15. . . . K—B1* instead loses Rook and Pawn for the Knight.

16. Kt x Pch

Continuing with the combination.

16. . . .   K—B1

Necessary in order to capture the Knight.

17. Kt x R

Removing Black's most dangerous piece. After his Knight is taken, White will be left with two pieces against three, but these two are dynamic Rooks with a whole chessboard to roam around in, while of Black's pieces, two are stuck away in a corner and one stands awkwardly on the sidelines.

17. . . .   K x Kt

Black still has the job of mobilizing his King-side pieces while staving off threats on the Queen side. On that wing, White has three Pawns to one, and this, after an exchange of Pawns, can become two Pawns to none.

Black may have to face an advance of two connected passed Pawns on the Queen side.

18. QR—K1ch

More gain of time! The Rook grabs the open file with check, and Black must lose a move getting his King out of the line of fire.

18. . . .   K—K1

If 18. . . . K—B1 19. K—B3 (threatening 20. R—K8ch, K—Kt2 21. QR—Q8 winning a piece), Kt—B3 20. R—K7, R—B1, and White can either attack on the King side by 21. P—KKt4 or start his Pawn phalanx on the Queen side rolling by 21. P—QR3 followed by 22. P—QKt4.

19. K—Q3 dis. ch

The King moves toward Black's disorganized Queen side, where defense will be difficult.

19. . . .   Kt—K2

Reluctantly, it would seem, Black finally develops his King Knight, but then again, anything else loses! If 19. . . . K—B1 20. K—B4 (threatening instant mate), P—Kt3 21. R—Q8ch, K—Kt2 22. K—Kt5, and White wins the Queen Knight, or if 19. . . . K—Q1 20. K—B4 dis. ch, K—B1 21. R—K8ch, K—Kt2 22. QR—Q8, and the King Knight falls.

20. K—B4

The King gets out of the path of the Rook and prepares to assist his Queen-side Pawns.

20. . . .   P—R4

A peculiar way to develop the Rook, but how else can it come out of the corner?

Black is ready to repel the invasion 21. K—Kt5 by 21. . . . R—R3 followed by 22. . . . R—QKt3ch.

21. R—Q3

So White abandons this tack and indicates that he intends to double Rooks on the King file and win the pinned Knight.

21. . . .   Kt—QKt1

The Knight retreats in order to reach B3 and the aid of his companion.

22. R(Q3)—K3

Doubles the pressure and threatens to capture the Knight.

22. . . .   Kt(Kt1)—B3

The only possible way to save the pinned Knight.

23. P—QKt4

Preparing to stab at the defending Knight, drive it off, and win the other one.

23. . . .   P—B3

Provides a new spot for the Queen Knight. In reply to 24. P—Kt5 he can now play 24. . . . Kt—K4ch, intercepting the attack of the Rooks. If later on the Knight is evicted from

K4, it can retreat to KKt3, where it protects the King Knight.

24. P—B4 !

This keeps the Knight from getting to K4 and renews the threat of 25. P—Kt5.

The position seems lost for Black, but Mieses not only ingeniously slips out of the pin and its terrors but manages to set a subtle trap into which anyone might plunge!

24. . . . K—B2 !

If White now tries to win a piece, this is what he might fall into: 25. P—Kt5, Kt—R4ch 26. K—Kt4, Kt—Q4ch 27. K x Kt, R—R1 checkmate!

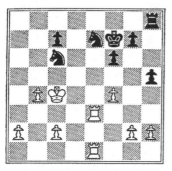

25. P—QR4

White avoids the pitfall and proceeds with the simple strategy governing all endgames:

He pushes the passed Pawn!

25. . . . R—QKt1

Temporarily halting the march of the two Pawns. White cannot play 26. P—R5 as 26. . . . R x Pch wins a couple of Pawns, and if 26. P—Kt5, Kt—R4ch 27. K—B5 (not 27. K—Kt4, Kt—Q4ch, and he's in the mating trap), Kt—Kt2ch 28. K—B4

(moving to Kt4 or Q4 allows a check by the other Knight costing the exchange), Kt—R4ch, and the King makes no progress. Either he retreats or submits to a perpetual check.

26. P—B3

Simple and strong! White guards the Knight Pawn and prepares to advance the Rook Pawn.

26. . . . R—Q1

There is no way to stop 27. P—R5 so Black tries to get counterplay on the open file.

27. R—Q3 !

Brutal but necessary. *White must oppose Rooks on the file.* Black will either have to exchange Rooks or move his Rook away, leaving White in full possession of the file.

One of the points a beginner learns painfully is that he must fight for control of every bit of territory, whether it is a file, a diagonal or a square. It is often necessary to offer an exchange of pieces to secure possession of an important point or area. Such offers must not be avoided for fear of their leading to a dull game, or that such strategy is unsportsmanlike. The player with a material advantage who temporizes because he wants to win brilliantly, and avoids exchanges because they are dull and unsportsmanlike, is torturing his opponent. *A win must be completed in the quickest, most efficient way possible.*

27. . . . R x R

Relinquishing the file offers

Black's Rook no future on any other file—so he exchanges.

28. K x R

White is left with one piece to two. But his lone Rook with its enormous mobility is more than a match for Black's Knights, who must keep in constant touch with each other to assure their mutual safety.

28. ... K—K1

The King rushes to the Queen side to head off the passed Pawn.

29. P—R5

Every move of this Pawn increases Black's danger. Keeping it under surveillance will tie up his pieces so that he will have no time to think of counterattack.

29. ... K—Q2

Black moves closer to the Rook Pawn, meanwhile unpinning his Knight.

30. P—R6

Puts a stop to the King's little trip, as 30. . . . K—B1 is penalized by 31. P—Kt5, and Black must give up one of his Knights. Note again that having the two Knights lean on each other for support is not an ideal arrangement.

30. ... Kt—Q4

The Knight is on its way to the Queen side. Meanwhile it attacks the loose King Bishop Pawn.

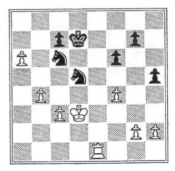

31. R—QR1 !

One way to dispose of a threat is to disregard it and counter with a more urgent one! White's threat is 32. P—R7, which would force Black to sacrifice his Knight for the Pawn.

31. ... Kt—R2

The Pawn must be blockaded! On 31. . . . Kt x KBPch 32. K—K4, Kt x KKtP 33. P—R7, Kt x RP 34. R x Kt, and the win is elementary.

32. P—Kt3

Stabilizes the King-side Pawn position before proceeding with affairs on the Queen side.

32. ... P—B3

With the double object of making it more difficult for White's Knight Pawn to advance, and to vacate B2 for his King.

33. R—R4 !

"Every one of White's moves in this ending deserves an exclamation mark!" enthusiastically cries Mieses, who played the black pieces in this game.

White's idea is to protect the Knight Pawn so that he can then oust Black's Knight from its strong post in the center by 34. P—B4.

33. . . .   Kt—Kt3

The Knight does not wait but turns on the Rook.

34. R—R5

The Rook leaves but loses no time, as it threatens Black's Rook Pawn.

34. . . .   P—Kt3

The only way to save the Pawn. Black can try interposing the Knight at Q4 instead, but after 35. K—B4 and 36. K—Kt3 (to protect the Knight Pawn) White evicts the Knight by 37. P—B4 and wins the unguarded Rook Pawn.

35. P—B4

Keeps the Knight away from Q4 forever!

35. . . .   Kt(Kt3)—B1

Black is running out of good moves: he cannot play 35. . . . K—Q3 on account of 36. P—B5ch, nor can he tighten the King-side position by 35. . . . P—KB4 without letting White break in later by way of K5.

36. R—R1

Rather surprising! White delays any further maneuvers with the Queen-side Pawns and proposes to bring his King and Rook to more aggressive positions. The King will move to Q4 and then B5, the Rook

to the open King file, eventually to penetrate at the sixth or seventh ranks. Black will then have to fight off the Rook's threats on the King-side Pawns as well as to hold back the dangerous Pawns advancing on the Queen side.

36. . . .   Kt—Q3

Black can do nothing but defend patiently.

37. K—Q4

While White proceeds to bring his King to B5.

37. . . .   Kt(Q3)—B1

If Black plays 37. . . . K—B2, ready to reply to 38. K—B5 with 38. . . . Kt—K5ch, White forces an entrance by 38. R—K1 (threatening a deadly check at K7), K—Q2 39. K—B5, Kt(3)—B1 40. P—Kt5.

38. K—B5

The King is now ideally placed, and White is set for a quick finish by 39. P—Kt5 and 40. P—Kt6.

38. . . .   K—B2

Certainly not 38. . . . Kt—Q3 when 39. R—Q1 pins the Knight. A pretty continuation could then be 39. . . . Kt(R2)—B1   40.   R x Ktch !, Kt x R 41. P—R7, and the Pawn cannot be stopped.

39. R—K1

Poised for invasion at K6 or K8 and a raid on the King-side Pawns.

39. . . .   Kt—Kt3

If 39. . . . K—Q2 (to keep the Rook from moving to K6 or K8) 40. P—Kt5, P x P 41. P x P, K—B2 42. R—K6, and White wins as he pleases.

40. R—K7ch

The Rook finally breaks into the enemy camp!

40. . . .   Kt—Q2ch

Of course not 40. . . . K—Kt1 41. R—Kt7ch, and White wins a Knight or two. But this interposition with check looks as though it might still give White some trouble. For instance, if 41. K—Q4, P—B4ch 42. P x P, Kt—B3ch, and Black wins a whole Rook.

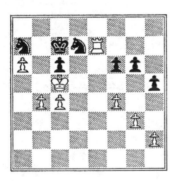

41. R x Ktch !

A brilliant finish! After 41. . . . K x R 42. P—Kt5, P x P 43. P x P, Kt—B1 (or 43. . . . K—B2 44. P—Kt6ch) 44. P—Kt6 followed by 45. P—R7 resolves any lingering doubts.

41. . . .   Resigns

An impressive display in the art of utilizing the advantages accruing from gains of time in the opening.

QUEEN'S GAMBIT DECLINED

WHITE	BLACK
Marshall	Tarrasch

NUREMBERG, 1905

1. P—Q4

Although Queen Pawn openings are played with the idea of obtaining an early positional advantage, Marshall considered the best way to start an attack was to begin the game with 1. P—Q4. One reason for his view might have been that the King Pawn openings no longer could be depended on to lead to wide-open games with opportunities for combination play. In the old days when White began with 1. P—K4, the reply almost automatically was 1. . . . P—K4. White could then offer a Pawn by 2. P—KB4, rely on its being accepted, and joyfully swing into the excitements of a King's Gambit. In taking the Pawn and grimly holding on to it, Black gained material, but the loss of time involved threw him on the defensive. Gradually, after sustaining many defeats, the players of Black tired of being the victims of brilliancies. They took a more rational attitude, and grew cautious. They resorted to 1. . . . P—K3, or 1. . . . P—QB4 or 1. . . . P—QB3, in all cases avoiding direct contact in the early stages. The result was that an aggressive player, starting the game with 1. P—K4, found himself facing "irregular" defenses which forced the game into unfamiliar channels. He found himself involved in tightly knit positions requiring systematic planning, at a time when he was itching to get an attack rolling. He was supposed to have the initiative, but here it was wrested away from him! How could he play a gambit (even at best a risky matter) if his opponent did not oblige him with a forthright 1. . . . P—K4 in answer to his own enterprising 1. P—K4?

In beginning the game with 1. P—Q4, White gets an advantage, slight though it may be, against any system of defense—and with it he retains excellent attacking chances as well!

> 1. . . .   P—Q4

Undoubtedly one of the strongest replies. Black stabilizes the pressure in the center, prevents White from strengthening his hold there by 2. P—K4, and himself opens lines for two of his pieces to get into the game.

> 2. P—QB4

An offer of a Pawn (with strings attached) to induce Black to surrender the center.

> 2. . . .   P—K3

Taking the Pawn is perfectly sound; at least it has not been proven a loss. But why give up the center to win a Pawn—which it turns out you cannot keep? In effect, playing 2. . . . P x P is equivalent to exchanging a center Pawn for a side Pawn—an unprofitable transaction.

After Black's actual move, his Queen Pawn is firmly supported. In the event of 3. P x P, *Black recaptures with a Pawn,* maintaining a Pawn in the center.

It is true that Black's Queen Bishop is shut in by the King Pawn, making its development difficult, and this is a drawback to the defense. But if Black's first two moves are good, and they probably are the best replies to the Queen's gambit, then one can appreciate the terrific strength of this opening, and why so many players move 1. P—Q4 unhesitatingly whenever they have White.

> 3. Kt—QB3

This is somewhat sharper than developing the King Knight first, as additional pressure is immediately put on the central point Q5.

> 3. . . .   Kt—KB3

Tarrasch disapproved of this Knight move, which most of us would make instinctively. It is true that KB3 is the most useful square for the King Knight 99 and 44/100ths of the time, since from there it influences affairs in the center strongly, enjoys great freedom of movement, and is magnificently placed for attack and defense. But Tarrasch feared the strength of the pin which White could clamp on the Knight next move. Instead of 3. . . . Kt—KB3, he therefore recommended that Black challenge White's center at once by 3. . . . P—QB4 (almost a must at some stage in Queen Pawn games), meanwhile opening up the Bishop file for the use of his own heavy pieces.

Why then, you may ask, did Tarrasch play a move which he himself disparaged? His explanation is that this was the first game of a match against one of the World's leading masters (Marshall had recently won the Cambridge Springs tournament without losing a game, ahead of Lasker, Schlechter, Pillsbury and Janowsky) and he did not wish to stray so soon from orthodox paths.

4. B—Kt5!

Naturally! Not only because the Bishop puts uncomfortable pressure on the Knight, but because it is good policy to play moves that the opponent finds disturbing. If Tarrasch thinks that pinning the Knight is troublesome—pin the Knight and make him uneasy!

4. . . . QKt—Q2

This looks clumsy, with the Knight blocking what little view the Bishop had, but pieces can easily step out of each other's way. The Knight belongs at this square and not at B3, where it obstructs the Bishop Pawn. This Pawn must not be hindered from advancing sooner or later to QB4. Little as the Pawn is, it is a major force in disputing possession of the center!

With 4. . . . QKt—Q2 Black sets a little trap for the unwary, invented by Tarrasch. If White, relying on the impotent state of Black's pinned Knight, tries to pick up an extra Pawn by 5. P x P, P x P 6. Kt x P, Black gives up his Queen with 6. . . . Kt x Kt (breaking the pin by force) 7. B x Q, only to regain it with another piece thrown in by 7. . . . B—Kt5ch 8. Q—Q2, B x Qch 9. K x B, K x B.

The moral is: Don't go Pawn-hunting in the opening!

5. P—K3

This sort of Pawn move is not a waste of time. Without a liberating Pawn move the Bishops can never get off the ground, so this is part of the process of developing the pieces.

With the text move White opens two diagonals at once, one for his King Bishop and another one for the Queen. The King Pawn contributes an additional service in bracing up the Pawn center.

5. . . . P—B3

Black too reinforces his Pawn center and gives his Queen an outlet on the Queen side.

6. Q—B2

It is customary to develop the minor pieces first, roughly in this order:

First the Knights, generally to B3, but toward the center in any event,

Then the Bishops (after the necessary Pawn moves), either to control vital diagonals or to pin enemy Knights,

Following this, it is time for the Queen to make her entrance. If the Queen comes into the game too early, she incurs the danger of being harassed—perhaps even surrounded and captured—by adverse minor pieces.

Last come the Rooks, which after castling are brought to K1, Q1 or QB1, to head files in the center which are partly open. These files are likely to become completely open after exchanges of Pawns in the center.

This method of development is not by any means to be considered a fixed course to pursue. Nothing in chess—no convention, principle or recommended procedure—is to be practiced rigidly. The value of any single move or combination of moves can only be regarded with respect to its relationship to a particular position involved. It must fit in with the scheme of the game you are playing and be tempered by the demands of the opponent. A great deal depends on what he does, or lets you do. This is why you may find it expedient to develop the Queen at the sixth move or to castle at the sixtieth move.

In this position Black has indicated that he might counterattack by 6. . . . Q—R4 and 7. . . . B—Kt5, pinning the Queen Knight and then increasing the pressure on it. It might have been more to the point for White to mobilize another minor piece instead by 6. Kt—B3 (like putting money in the bank), with an eye to speedy castling or perhaps to neutralizing the anticipated pressure on the Queen Knight by swinging the King Knight over to Q2.

6. . . .   Q—R4

A many-sided move: The Queen not only unpins the King Knight but starts a counteraction by pinning White's Knight, and threatens to intensify its pressure by bringing the Bishop to Kt5. As an extra, added attraction, Black sets a little trap to catch the careless—and this might even include expert players who at times treat the opening in a perfunctory way. The trap might snap on a player who innocently develops his Bishop at Q3 only to find that 7. . . . P x P in reply threatens both his Bishops at one blow and that after he plays 8. B x Kt, P x B attacking his Queen will cost him a Bishop.

It might be as well to state at this point that Tarrasch did not expect to catch Marshall with a two-by-four trap. Master players do not set them if it involves injuring their own position. A trap which arises in the natural course of development is one thing, but to play for them deliberately at the risk of wasting valuable time is unforgivable.

7. P x P

White neutralizes the Queen's indirect attack on his Bishop and clears away the Queen Bishop file for the benefit of his major pieces.

7. . . .   Kt x P

Tarrasch had planned to recapture by 7. . . . KP x P in order to maintain a Pawn in the center. Now he realizes that danger may be involved in delaying the development of the Queen side pieces any longer.

His Queen Bishop is locked in on one side by the Queen Knight, and this Knight in turn must stay where it is, since it supports the King Knight. If he tries to develop the Bishop on the Queen side, then after . . . P—QKt3 he cuts off the retreat of the Queen.

But the strategy of a master player must be flexible: it must be consistent with the requirements of the particular position at hand. Tarrasch would very much like to have a strong Pawn center but dares not neglect the exigencies of development. So he heeds Nimzovich, who once said, "Giving up the center must not here be regarded as illogical; was happiness no happiness because it endured for but a short time? One cannot always be happy."

Meanwhile the Knight does add to the pressure on White's pinned Knight and renews the threat of winning the exposed Bishop by 8. . . . Kt x Kt 9. P x Kt, Q x B.

8. Kt—B3

"In his anxiety," says Tarrasch, "to guard the threatened Bishop, White makes a decisive mistake."

This is an interesting example of the value of accurate timing in chess. The fact that a normal developing move has intrinsic strength is secondary to the question of its usefulness *in the one position in front of you*, not in vaguely similar positions.

Despite the fact that the Knight occupies a most useful post at KB3, and at the same time protects the Bishop, its development is either too soon or too late. White is doing nothing about the problem of his pinned Knight. This is where pressure is exerted, this is where danger is threatened.

More to the point is 8. P—K4 instead, evicting Black's Knight and forcing it to declare its intentions. If then 8. . . . Kt x Kt 9. B—Q2, Q— R5 10. Q x B resolves an uncomfortable situation.

8. . . .　　　B—Kt5

Tripling the attack on the Knight. Black threatens to win at once by 9. . . . Kt x Kt 10. P x Kt, B x Pch followed by 11. . . . B x R.

How shall White meet the threat? If he plays the natural 9. R— B1, the Knight is adequately guarded: it is attacked three times and defended three times. But Black then capitalizes on a curious fact in connection with the power of a pinned piece: not only is it helpless to make a move but it has also lost its ability to defend! Translated in this position into chess language, if 9. R—B1, Q x P !, a capture startling at first glance but an obvious one if we realize that the Knight's defensive power is illusory—it is nonexistent! I stress this circumstance because it is important. Knowing it, recognizing it and applying it has caused (chess) kingdoms to topple.

All this fuss about winning a miserable Rook Pawn? Let's see what would happen thereafter:

After 9. R—B1, Q x P, Black's method is classical in its simplicity. He follows up by . . . B x Ktch and after the recapture by the Pawn exchanges Queens. He has an extra Pawn, but this is not enough advantage to bring about checkmate. He must increase his material superiority sufficiently to justify him in going after the King, and this can only be done by turning one of his Pawns into a Queen. So he selects the most likely candidate, in this case the passed Rook's Pawn, and pushes it up the board at every opportunity. The Pawn's advance faces the opponent with a problem which becomes more acute with every step taken by the Pawn. He must head off the Pawn or blockade it completely, in either case tieing up one or more of his pieces to do so. The defense is under the strain of keeping the Pawn under constant surveillance, while at the same time having to guard against a sudden switching of the attack toward his King. What often happens is that he either has to give up a piece for the Pawn or allow further exchanges of pieces, a procedure which leads to inevitable loss.

Such long-range plans are not based on exact calculation; they represent a general idea of the method for winning in positions of this nature.

9. K—Q2

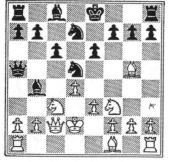

Not an appetizing move, as the King loses the privilege of castling,

but it's the only way to guard against losing some material.

9. . . .   P—QB4 !

"Hits the nail on the head," says Tarrasch. With the subsequent exchange of Pawns, the Bishop file will be pried open, further imperiling the unfortunate Knight.

10. P—QR3

White is anxious to bring matters to a head. The alternative 10. P—K4 yields to 10. . . . P x P 11. P x Kt (or 11. Kt x P, Kt x Kt 12. P x Kt, Q x Bch, and Black wins a piece— the exposed Bishop that seemed doomed from the start), P x Ktch 12. P x P, Q x QPch, and Black is a Pawn up with a winning position.

10. . . .   B x Ktch

Tarrasch simplifies and avoids the difficulties attendant on winning the exchange, such as: 10. . . . P x P 11. P x B, P x Ktch 12. Q x P, Q x R 13. Q x P, R—B1 14. P—K4, Kt x P 15. B—Kt5, Q x R 16. Q—B6, and White forces mate. It is true that Black could save the game at his fifteenth move by playing 15. . . . Q—R4, but why risk all these complications when the advantage can be maintained by less hazardous means?

11. P x B

The only way White may recapture.

11. . . .   P x P

Continuing the good work of opening up the Queen Bishop file.

12. KP x P

Again White has no choice of recapture: the Bishop Pawn is pinned, and 12. Kt x P is refuted by 12. . . . Kt x BP 13. Q x Kt, Q x B, and Black has won a Pawn.

12. . . .   Kt(Q2) — Kt3

White's pinned Knight is gone, but it has been replaced by a Pawn — and this Pawn is pinned! It makes a fine target, so Black directs his fire on it. He threatens to strike at it again by 13. . . . Kt—R5 or by 13. . . . B—Q2 followed by 14. . . . R—QB1.

13. B—Q3

Finally another King-side piece sees daylight!

13. . . .   B—Q2

Black can pounce on the Pawn with 13. . . . Kt—R5. He prefers to complete his development first and then bring all his pieces to bear on it. "Besides," as he says, anticipating Nimzovich, "the Pawn does not run away."

14. KR—QB1

White must develop and defend at the same time. If he gets a moment's respite he will free the pinned Pawn by 15. K—K2, 16. B—Q2 and 17. P—B4.

14. . . .   R—QB1

But Black doesn't let up even for a moment! The Rook seizes control of the beautiful open file and immediately adds its weight to the pressure on the immobilized Bishop Pawn.

15. Q—Kt3

Trying to lure Black into 15. . . . Kt—R5 16. Q x P, R x P 17. R x R, Q x Rch 18. K—K2, when he has counterplay.

15. . . .   O—O

"First," thinks Tarrasch, "let's get the King away from the fighting and bring the other Rook closer."

16. K—K2

Clearly the Bishop Pawn must be lost, as Black can attack it with more pieces than White can summon up for defense, so White saves time by abandoning the Pawn and fleeing with his King.

16. . . .   R x P

The first material gain, and with it entry to the enemy position.

17. R x R

Avoiding the exchange of Rooks by 17. Q—Kt2 lets Black retain his grip on the open file.

17. . . .   Q x R

Much better than taking with the Knight. Black's idea is to occupy a strategically strong outpost on the only open file or bring about an exchange of Queens. The removal of both Queens would simplify matters to his advantage as he is a Pawn ahead.

18. Q—Kt1

Forced into retreat, White manages to incorporate a threat in the Queen's move of 19. B x Pch, regaining his Pawn.

18. . . . P—KR3

The simplest way of saving the Pawn, this provides the King with a useful escape square against a surprise check on the last rank.

19. B—Q2

Driven back, this piece too retires with a threat.

19. . . . Q—B2

The Queen reluctantly leaves the beautiful outpost at B6 but stays on the all-important Bishop file. Note the reason the Queen selects the B2 square: at B3 the action of the Bishop is interfered with, at B1 that of the Rook.

Black threatens 20. . . . Kt—B5ch, forcing an exchange of the Knight for one of White's Bishops.

20. K—B1

Everybody going home?

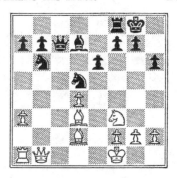

20. . . . Kt—QB5

Begins a new phase. Black drives pieces into the enemy's territory. These will control key squares and cramp White's movements by limiting the mobility of his pieces.

21. B—B1

Just about the only place left, if White wants to keep both his Bishops.

21. . . . B—R5

And this cuts down the activities of White's Queen.

22. Q—R2

Double attack on the Knight! This is less a threat than a convenient means of gaining time to switch the Queen over to the King side. White's only chance, of course, is to dream up some sort of counterattack. Passive play will only lead to his being gradually crushed to death.

22. . . . R—B1

Protects the Knight and simultaneously takes undisputed possession of the Bishop file.

23. Q—K2

White intends to stir up trouble by playing 24. Q–K4 (threatening 25. Q–R7ch, K–B1 26. Q–R8ch, K–K2 27. Q x KtP). Then if 24. . . . Kt–B3 25. Q–R4, threatening 26. B x P, might whip up some sort of attack on the King side.

23. . . .   Kt–B6 !

Not only does this move put a stop to any notions White might have had of starting a counteroffensive, but it restricts his Queen, which is attacked, to one solitary move! Such is the extent of Black's domination of the board!

24. Q–K1

The only refuge left from the terrible Knights who cover seven of the Queen's flight squares!

24. . . .   Kt–R4

With the obvious intention of penetrating deeper into White's position by 25. . . . Kt–Kt6. This would result, as a start, in winning the exchange.

25. B x P

Lashing out with the wildness born of despair!
The game could not have been saved by 25. B–Q2, as after 25. . . . Kt–Kt6 (the Knights now circumscribe the Rook's activities as they did the Queen's) 26. B x Kt, Q x B 27. R–Q1 (or 27. Q x Q, R x Q 28. R–Q1, Kt–B8, and Black wins the exchange or a piece), Kt–B8, and the attack on White's Rook and Bishop will win some material.

25. . . .   Kt–Kt6

Taking the Bishop might lead to a win, but why expose the King needlessly? Black's actual move is simpler and more in keeping with his Queen-side maneuvers up to this point.

26. B–Q2

White could not rescue the helpless Rook, so must content himself with the fact that he has regained the Pawn he lost.

26. . . .   Kt x R

Winning the exchange is the culmination of some clever stepping by the Knights.

27. Q x Kt

White must capture this way, and not 27. B x Kt, which loses a whole Rook after 27. . . . Q x B.

27. . . .   B–Kt4 !

The fine art of simplification! Black exchanges pieces to cut down resistance. With less pieces on the board, fewer complications can be introduced by White, while Black's material advantage becomes proportionally greater. Notice how Black engineers these exchanges without weakening his grip on the position.

28. B x B

As good as there is: if 28. B x Kt, B x Bch followed by 29. . . . Q x B wins a piece, or if 28. Q x Kt, Q x Q 29. B x Q, B x Bch followed by 30. . . . R x B does likewise.

28. . . .   Kt x B

After the recapture, Black threatens 29. . . . Q—B5ch 30. K—K1, Kt—B6, and the threat of mate at K7 forces 31. B x Kt when 31. . . . Q x Bch 32. Q x Q, R x Q leaves an elementary winning position.

29. P—Kt3

White hopes to find shelter for the King at Kt2, where it is less exposed, and also sets up a Pawn support for the Bishop, which might get a new start at B4.

29. . . .　　Q—B3 !

The Queen pounces on the white squares which have been weakened by White's last move. The attack on the Knight gains a tempo for the Queen's further penetration into White's territory.

30. K—Kt2

An advance by the Knight, say to K5, loses the Queen after 30. . . . Q—R8ch, while protecting the Knight with 30. K—K2 runs into 30. . . . Q—K5ch 31. B—K3, R—B7ch 32. Kt—Q2 (or 32. K—Q1, Kt—B6ch winning), Kt—B6ch 33. K—K1, Q—R8ch and mate next move.

30. . . .　　R—Q1

Now onto this file, where the isolated Pawn makes a fine target.

31. B—K3

Guarding the Queen Pawn, as the pinned Knight is no protection.

31. . . .　　Q—K5

The Queen works her way deeper into the heart of the position.

32. Q—Kt2

White tries to get some play for his Queen, while the other pieces huddle around each other for mutual protection.

The Queen does not rush to seize the open file, as after 32. Q—QB1, Kt x QP 33. B x Kt, R x B, the threat of 34. . . . R—Q6 is more than White can stand.

32. . . .　　R—Q4 !

A diabolical move! Not only does Black guard his own Knight, but he threatens to win White's by 33. . . . R—KB4 34. Q—K2, Kt x QP !, an attack on the Queen and a triple attack on the Knight. There is no answer to this as White is pinned all over the place!

33. P—QR4

Driving the Knight off so that it no longer menaces the Queen Pawn.

33. . . .　　Kt—Q3

The Knight leaves, taking care to protect the Queen Knight Pawn.

34. B—B4

Otherwise, Black plays 34. . . .

P—KKt4, threatening 35. . . . P—Kt5 or 35. . . . R—KB4, or both!

34. . . .   Kt—B4

Once more striking at the Queen Pawn.

35. B—K3

White cannot afford 35. Q x P, Kt x QP, and his Queen cannot come back to save the Knight.

35. . . .   Kt x Bch

Simpler than combinations beginning with 35. . . . P—K4. After the text move, two more pieces come off the board, and another Pawn will fall.

36. P x Kt

White must recapture.

36. . . .   Q x KP

This unpins the Knight, but the Knight must stay where it is to protect the Queen Pawn.

37. P—Kt4

White must not play 37. Q x P, as the reply 37. . . . Q—K7ch forces the King away from the Knight and costs a piece. His actual move stops Black from increasing the pressure by 37. . . . R—KB4.

37. . . .   P—B4

Black can afford this opening up of the position. His King suffers less from exposure than does White's. The threat of course is 38. . . . P x P, winning at once.

38. P—Kt5

If 38. P—R3, P x P 39. P x P, Q—B5 40. P—Kt5, Q—Kt5ch 41. K—B2, R—KB4, and the threats of 42. . . . Q x Ktch and 42. . . . Q x KtP cannot both be met.

38. . . .   Q—K5

Once more clamping a pin on the Knight!

39. Q—B3

Carefully avoiding 39. Q x P when 39. . . . P—B5 faces him with loss of the Knight by 40. . . . Q—K7ch, or of the Knight Pawn by 40. . . . R x Pch.

39. . . .   P—B5

Not at once 39. . . . P—K4 as 40. P—Kt6 leaves White threatening sudden mate!

40. Q—B8ch

If White had tried 40. P—Kt6, then 40. . . . R—Kt4ch ends the Knight Pawn's career.

40. . . .   K—R2

To escape any more checks by the Queen.

41. Q—B3

Back to the defense of the Knight and the Queen Pawn.

41. . . .   P—K4 !

Beginning of the last phase: the breakup of White's center.

This is stronger than *41. . . . R x P ch 42. K—B2, R—KR4 43. P —KR4*, and White threatens *44. Kt—Kt5ch.*

The idea of the text is to continue with *42. . . . R x P*, with which Black accomplishes these things:

He has demolished White's center.

He threatens an immediate win by *43. . . . R—Q6.*

He is assured (if the foregoing is not convincing enough) of remaining with two connected passed Pawns in the center.

42. P—KR4

Marshall sees that *42. P x P* loses a piece after *42. . . . R—Q6*, but he still has a few tricks up his sleeve.

42. . . .   R x P

Intending to attack Queen and Knight by *43. . . . R—Q6*, incidentally cutting off the Queen from the Knight's defense.

43. P—Kt6ch

This is one of the traps: if Black plays *43. . . . K x P*, White replies *44. Q—Kt3* (apparently trying to get a perpetual check), *R—Q6*, and now instead of *45. Q—K6ch* White plays *45. Q x R* so that after *45. . . . Q x Q 46. Kt x Pch* followed by *47. Kt x Q* regains the Queen and wins a Rook.

43. . . .   K—R3

Black sidesteps this one.

44. K—R2

So White sets up another: if *44. . . . R—Q6 45. Q x P, Q x Kt 46. Q—Kt5 checkmate!*

44. . . .   Q—K7ch

To this there is no reply: if *45. K—Ktl, R—Q8ch 46. Kt—Kl, R x Ktch* wins, or if *45. K—R3, R—Q6*, pinning the poor Knight for the last time, puts out the last flickers of resistance.

G A M E   N O.   3 0

QUEEN'S GAMBIT DECLINED

WHITE   **BLACK**
Capablanca   Villegas
BUENOS AIRES, 1914

1. P—Q4

In this game, the art of chess is reduced to a simple formula:

Get a passed Pawn, move it up the board, and win!

White begins by getting a foothold in the center, while releasing two of his pieces.

1. . . .   P—Q4

This is probably Black's strongest reply. It equalizes the pressure and prevents White from monopolizing the center with 2. P—K4.

2. Kt—KB3

The Knight leaps in toward the center, intensifying the Pawn's pressure on K5. The Knight does its best work at B3, covering eight squares in the circle of its attack.

2. . . .   Kt—KB3

Black applies the same formula, developing his King Knight to its most effective post. Aside from its admirable potential for attack, the Knight also serves while it stands and waits. In the service of the King, especially after castling, the Knight defends as no other piece can.

3. P—K3

Not the most energetic procedure, but White need not be aggressive from the start. The opening itself is so strong that White can build up a terrific position merely by developing his pieces so that they occupy the most suitable squares without loss of time. The method is simplicity itself:

Put every single piece to work, and move no piece twice until development is complete.

The fact that 3. P—K3 releases one Bishop but shuts in another is of little moment, as the Queen Bishop can get into the game by way of QKt2. White does not indicate his specific intentions: he might play the Colle attack or perhaps simply develop the Bishop at Q3 with a view to early King-side castling.

3. . . .   P—B3

Black supports his Queen Pawn, anticipating an attack on it by 4. P—B4. He prefers this to the alternative Pawn support by 3. . . . P—K3, which confines his Queen Bishop.

But if Black wants to free his Bishop, why not move it at once to B4? There it would stand ready to oppose White's Bishop when it reaches Q3. The almost inevitable exchange ensuing then removes White's attacking Bishop from the board and takes the sting out of the Colle system of attack.

Another possibility was pushing on to B4 at once with his Pawn, striking at White's center, and opening the Bishop file for the use of his own heavy pieces. But why play 3. . . . P—B3, moving a Pawn unnecessarily in the opening? Why waste time defending when nothing is threatened?

4. B—Q3

Quiet, forceful development: the Bishop surveys two fine diagonals and is ready for action in either direction. Meanwhile the King side is cleared for castling.

4. . . .   B—Kt5

As good as there is for this Bishop. The best square the Bishop could occupy is B4, but White's last move made this square unavailable.

5. P—B4 !

Alert play! White strikes at the Black center and opens the Bishop file for the convenience of his major pieces. The diagonal created for his Queen also holds out prospects of a raid by 6. Q—Kt3 on Black's Queen side, weakened by the absence of his Bishop.

5. . . .   P—K3

Black's King Bishop is provided

with an outlet, while the center
Pawn is given further support.

6. QKt—Q2

White defends the King Knight
with a minor piece, relieving the
Queen of a duty. This method of
developing the Knight is preferable
to placing it at QB3, where it might
interfere with the future operations
of the Queen or the Rook on the
Bishop file.

The sortie 6. Q—Kt3 yields no
immediate advantage, Black's reply
6. . . . Q—Kt3 leading either to an
exchange of Queens or a retreat by
White's Queen.

6. . . . QKt—Q2

For Black's Knight too, this is
model development. At Q2 it co-
operates with the King Knight and
supports an eventual attack on
White's center by . . . P—B4 or
. . . P—K4. Either of these freeing
moves is an objective Black must
strive to attain in this opening.

7. O—O

The King rushes off to safer quarters while the Rook comes out of
hiding.

7. . . . B—K2

This develops a piece and enables
Black to castle but is rather unenter-
prising. A more spirited course was
7. . . . P—K4, attempting to have
something to say about affairs in the
center.

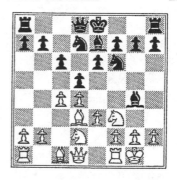

8. Q—B2 !

So White puts a stop to any such
ideas! An advance by 8. . . . P—K4
now costs a Pawn, as White's
Knight, no longer pinned, is free to
pick off the Pawn.

The Queen's development at B2
is modest, but in the early stages of
the game the Queen should rarely
venture beyond the third or fourth
rank. What *is* important, though, is
to move the Queen off the back rank
and into active play.

8. . . . B—R4

Black prepares to swing the
Bishop over to Kt3 to exchange it
for White's aggressive King Bishop.
Had he castled instead, the contin-
uation 9. Kt—K5, B—R4 (if 9. . . .
Kt x Kt 10. P x Kt, Kt—Q2 11. B x
Pch wins a Pawn for White) 10.
P—B4 gives White a powerfully cen-
tralized Knight and excellent attack-
ing prospects.

9. P—QKt3

A Pawn move which provides an
outlet for a piece is always justified.
This one makes room for the Queen
Bishop's development.

9. . . .   B—Kt3

Black continues with the business of forcing an exchange of Bishops.

10. B—Kt2

From a distance the Queen Bishop intensifies White's pressure on the important central square K5. With this square under control, it will be difficult for Black to get in the freeing move . . . P—K4.

10. . . .   B x B

There was no hurry about this exchange. Why not calmly keep on with the job of developing pieces, as White does?

11. Q x B

After this recapture, White has all the play. He can choose from various procedures:
a) A breakup by P—K4, to open lines of attack for his pieces,
b) The establishment of an outpost at K5 by the Knight,
c) A hemming-in process, beginning with P—B5.

11. . . .   O—O

There is no way for Black to meet all these continuations, so he transfers his King to a safe shelter.

12. QR—K1

Before committing himself, White brings another piece into play. The Rook's presence on the King file will add power to the King Pawn's advance.

White does not take action until his development is complete.

12. . . .   Q—B2

Black mobilizes another piece, hoping for some counterplay by 13. . . . P—B4. The development of the Queen also enables the Rooks to establish communication with each other.

13. P—K4 !

Opening up lines of attack, which, says theory, will favor the player whose development is superior.

White rejects 13. P—B5, the reply to which is 13. . . . P—K4 14. P x P, Kt x BP. The line 13. Kt—K5 is no more promising, since 13. . . . Kt x Kt 14. P x Kt, Kt—Q2 15. P—B4, P—B3 lets Black off too easy.

13. . . .   P x KP

Otherwise Black must live in constant dread of P—K5 or KP x P either of which moves White will play at his own convenience.

14. Kt x P

The recapture leaves White with a formidable center.

14. . . .   Kt x Kt

Black exchanges pieces to help free his crowded position.

15. R x Kt !

Anticipating the natural defensive maneuver of 15. . . . Kt—B3, to which White would respond with 16. R—R4. The plan is then to dislodge Black's Knight, which guards against mate. This might be accomplished by 17. P—Q5 followed by 18. B x Kt or by 17. Kt—K5 followed by 18. Kt—Kt4. To prevent capture or uprooting of his Knight and the consequent Q x P mate, Black would be compelled to move . . . P—KKt3 or . . . P—KR3, in either case loosening the Pawn structure and thereby weakening the King's defenses.

15. . . .   B—B3

This prevents 16. R—R4, gives the Bishop more scope and puts pressure on White's center. It also incorporates a pretty threat in 16. . . . Kt—B4 17. P x Kt, B x B, simplifying to Black's advantage.

16. Q—K3

Puts an end to that little scheme!

16. . . .   P—B4

This certainly looks attractive! Black plans 17. . . . P x P, a capture which White cannot avoid, his Queen Pawn being pinned. With the disappearance of White's troublesome center Pawn, the squares K4 and QB4 then become available to Black's Knight, and the Queen Bishop file opens up for counterplay by his Queen and Rook.

17. Kt—K5

The Knight establishes an out-

post. It seems harmless enough: it threatens nothing and does not interfere with whatever ideas Black has in mind.

17. . . .   P x P

Counting on the continuation 18. B x P, B x Kt 19. B x B, Kt x B 20. R x Kt, KR—Q1, and his control of the open Queen's file greatly increases Black's chances.

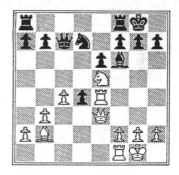

18. Kt x Kt !

A remarkable concept! Not in the fact that White plays a combination which involves a sacrifice of the Queen, but in the circumstance that the offer of the Queen is only a detail! It is subordinate to the over-all strategy of the game. The game is conducted on positional lines, and that's the way it will be won. Any combinations that arise will be incidental to the general plan, which is to create a passed Pawn, move it up at every opportunity and promote it to a Queen.

18. . . .   Q x Kt

If he accepts the offer and plays 18. . . . P x Q, White reveals this combination: 19. Kt x Bch, K—R1 (or 19. . . . . P x Kt 20. R—Kt4ch, K—R1 21. B x P mate) 20. R—R4, (threatening 21. R x P mate) P—KR3 21. R x Pch !, P x R 22. Kt —Q5 dis. ch, K—Kt1 23. Kt x Q, and White with two pieces for a Rook wins easily.

19. B x P

White regains the Pawn, and his Bishop now attacks in two directions. On the one hand it threatens to take the Queen Rook Pawn, on the other it aims at checkmate by 20. B x B, P x B 21. R—Kt4ch, K—R1 22. Q—R6, R—KKt1 23. Q x BPch and mate next move.

19. . . .　　　B x B

The Bishop must be done away with!

20. R x B

White recaptures and gains a tempo by attacking the Queen.

20. . . .　　　Q—B2

The best square of retreat. From here the Queen's mobility is at its maximum.

21. KR—Q1

Now we can appreciate the significance of White's offer of the Queen. It was not an attempt to win the game by surprise tactics. It was the employment of a combination as a device to gain ground positionally!

White's doubling of the Rooks on the Queen file gives him full control of that file, and his Pawn majority of three to two on the Queen

side offers the possibility of creating a passed Pawn on the Bishop file.

21. . . .　　　KR—Q1

He must oppose Rooks before White either establishes a Rook on the seventh rank or triples pieces on the file.

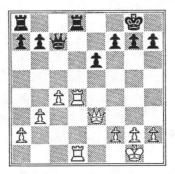

22. P—QKt4 !

This starts the Queen-side Pawns rolling! Capablanca does not even cast a glance at such a transparent trap as 22. R x Rch, R x R 23. R x Rch, Q x R 24. Q x RP, Q—Q8 mate.

22. . . .　　　R x R

The exchange is practically forced. Otherwise the need for protecting the Rook ties down Black's Queen and his other Rook.

23. Q x R

Naturally, White takes with the Queen to keep two major pieces on the open file.

23. . . .　　　P—QKt3

Black must play this or 23. . . . . P—QR3 in order to make use of his Rook. Note that he cannot dispute the open file by 23. . . . R—Q1, as White snaps off the Rook and mates next move.

24. P—Kt3

A safety measure which gives the King a flight square from surprise checks on the first rank. Very often they turn out to be fatal.

24. . . .   R—QB1

Doubling the attack on the Bishop Pawn.

25. R—QB1

In order to save the Pawn, White must shift his Rook from the Queen file. But now the Rook is in back of the Bishop Pawn (the candidate for the coronation) and is in position to keep it under protection, no matter how far up the Pawn moves on the file.

25. . . .   R—Q1

Black's object is to drive the Queen off and command the Queen file himself with his Rook.

26. Q—K3

A shrewd move: the Queen keeps in touch with the Rook, prevents Black's Rook from coming in at Q2, and keeps a weather eye on the strategic square QB5, the Bishop Pawn's next stop.

26. . . .   K—B1

The King approaches the field of action. In the event of a general exchange of pieces, he is prepared to head off the Bishop Pawn.

27. P—B5

The Pawn advances at every available opportunity.

27. . . .   P x P

Expecting White to recapture by 28. P x P, whereupon he blockades the Pawn effectively by 28. . . . Q —B3.

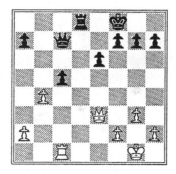

28. Q—K4 !

Very clever! White need not recapture immediately, as Black's Pawn is pinned and cannot escape capture. Meanwhile, the Queen move stops the intended blockade by 28. . . . Q—B3 and prepares for 29. P x P followed by 30. P—B6.

28. . . .   R—Q4

The Rook rushes over to help the Bishop Pawn.

There is a temptation for White to go Pawn-hunting now by 29. Q x RP followed by 30. Q—R8ch and 31. Q x P, picking up a couple of Pawns and creating for himself a passed Rook Pawn. But this sort of random play would not be consistent with White's orderly, economical conduct of the game, and entirely out of character for a Capablanca!

29. P x P

A passed Pawn at last!

29. . . .   P—Kt3

It would not do to recapture by 29. . . . R x P, as White punishes the offending Rook by 30. Q—QKt4, pinning and then winning it.

30. P—B6

Passed Pawns must be pushed! With each step forward of the Pawn, the field of action of White's Rook increases, while the freedom of Black's pieces becomes more limited.

30. . . .   K—Kt2

Black realizes that bringing the King to the center might be suicidal, viz.: 30. . . . K—K2 31. Q—R4ch, K—Q3 32. Q—Kt4ch, K—K4 33. Q—KB4 mate!

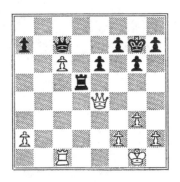

31. P—QR4 !

A beautiful preparatory move! If White were to play 31. Q—QKt4 at once followed by 32. Q—Kt7, (to dispossess the blockader) Black could exchange Queens and then stop the Pawn by 33. . . . R—QKt4, coming in back of it. But with White's Queen Rook Pawn at R4, Black could not bring his Rook to QKt4 !

31. . . .   R—Q3

Puts the Pawn under lock and key. It cannot advance, and White's intended stratagem of maneuvering his Queen over to QKt7 is not feasible, Black's reply to 32. Q—QKt4 being simply 32. . . . R x P. But the very fact that one Pawn can keep Black's Queen and Rook occupied is a tribute to the power of a passed Pawn.

32. Q—K5ch !

In spite of the heavy guard surrounding the Pawn, White with one stroke will lift the blockade!

32. . . .   P—B3

No matter how Black gets out of check, he cannot stop the coming combination.

33. Q x R !

Destroys one of the guards!

33. . . .   Q x Q

And the recapture lures the other one away!

34. P—B7 !

And White wins. The Pawn becomes a Queen next move, leaving White a whole Rook ahead.

GAME NO. 31

QUEEN'S PAWN GAME
(Nimzo-Indian Defense)

WHITE	BLACK
Havasi	Capablanca

BUDAPEST, 1929

1. P—Q4

One way of getting a good share of the center is to take it!

White does so here by planting a Pawn right in the middle of the board. It fills Q4, one square, and secures a grip on two others, K5 and QB5.

1. . . .   Kt—KB3

This is more elastic than 1. . . . P—Q4. Black develops a piece and bears down on the center instead of occupying it with a Pawn. His Knight attacks Q4 and K5, and prevents White from gaining more ground with 2. P—K4.

2. P—QB4

A valuable freeing move in Queen Pawn openings. It attacks the center square Q5, makes the Bishop file a favorable one for the Rook (because of the likelihood of the file being later opened up) and offers the Queen access to the Queen side.

2. . . .   P—K3

Not at once 2. . . . P—Q4, as 3. P x P, Q x P (or 3. . . . Kt x P 4. P—K4, Kt—KB3 5. Kt—QB3, and White has more of the center than he is entitled to) 4. Kt—QB3 gains time for White by the attack on the Queen.

With 2. . . . P—K3, Black prepares a Pawn support for a later occupation of the center by . . . P—Q4. Meanwhile, he releases his King Bishop.

3. Kt—QB3

This is more acute than developing the King Knight. It backs up a threat of 4. P—K4, presenting a formidable array of Pawns in the center.

3. . . .   B—Kt5

The Bishop clamps down on the Knight and by its pin deprives it of the power to attack or defend. Thus, if White carelessly played 4. P—K4, Black could snap up the Pawn at once.

4. Q—B2

With a number of objects in view:

a) The square B2 is generally the Queen's most useful post in this opening.

b) The Queen guards the Knight: in the event Black plays 4. . . . B x Ktch, the Queen may recapture and leave the Pawn position undisturbed.

c) The Queen exerts pressure on the Bishop file, the advantage of which becomes increasingly manifest with the opening of the file.

d) The Queen in commanding K4 renews White's threat of advancing the King Pawn two squares.

4. . . .   P—Q4

Wrests control of K5 from White and restrains his ambitious King

Pawn from taking too long a first step.

5. Kt—B3

Quiet, perhaps too quiet. It gets the King Knight off the ground, but the lull gives Black an opportunity to seize the initiative.

5. . . .   P—B4 !

"Black equalizes in any Queen Pawn opening," says Reuben Fine, "where he can play both . . . P—Q4 and . . . P—QB4 with impunity."

With 5. . . . P—B4 Black aims to destroy White's Pawn center, or at the very least to maintain a state of tension in that important area. As a fringe benefit, his Queen side pieces have a bit more elbowroom.

6. BP x P

White's idea is to clarify the position in the center. The disappearance of his Bishop Pawn also helps increase the pressure of the Queen on the file.

6. . . .   Q x P

Preferable to 6. . . . KP x P, which allows 7. B—Kt5, an annoy-

ing pin of the Knight. The Queen is strongly centralized at Q4, and in no danger of being annoyed by White's minor pieces.

7. P—QR3

Enough of this tiresome Bishop!

7. . . .   B x Ktch

Black must exchange. If instead 7. . . . B—R4 8. P—QKt4 (threatening 9. Kt x Q), P x KtP 9. Kt x Q, P—Kt6 dis. ch 10. B—Q2, P x Q 11. Kt x Ktch, P x Kt 12. B x B, and White has won a piece.

8. P x B

Capturing with the Queen instead lets Black gain a tempo by 8. . . . Kt—K5 attacking the Queen, whereupon the prospect of White's playing P—K4 seems further away than ever.

In compensation for White's theoretical advantage of the two Bishops against Knight and Bishop, Black's Pawn position on the Queen side is distinctly superior.

8. . . .   Kt—B3

The Knight develops with a threat. There is now a triple attack on White's Queen Pawn, and this limits his choice of reply.

9. P—K3

The least of the evils, though it does shut in the Queen Bishop.

If instead 9. P x P, Q x BP saddles White with two weak, isolated Pawns, while if White tries 9. P—B4, Kt x P 10. Q—R4ch (or 10. P x Q, Kt x Qch, and Black wins a

Rook), Q—Q2 leaves Black a Pawn up.

9. . . .   O—O

The King finds a safer shelter, while the King Rook makes its appearance.

10. B—K2

The Bishop develops gingerly. A more energetic procedure was 10. P—B4, to dislodge the Queen from the center, followed by 11. B—Kt2, with fair chances.

10. . . .   P x P

A clever Pawn exchange which keeps the position fluid and gives Black a slight advantage, no matter how White recaptures.

11. BP x P

Understandably, White rejects 11. Kt x P as 11. . . . Q x KtP 12. B—B3, Kt x Kt in reply is ruinous. With his actual move he adheres to the principle of capturing toward the center and increases the Queen's sphere of action by clearing away the Bishop file. Nevertheless it might have been better policy to play 11. KP x P, activating his Queen Bishop.

11. . . .   P—QKt3

Preparing to develop the Bishop at Kt2, where it will command the longest diagonal on the board.

Black's advantage consists mainly in his two Pawns to one on the Queen side, and this, after an exchange of Pawns, turns into one Pawn against none. As for the Bishop file, it can be seized by the Queen Rook. The Rook will drive White's Queen off and remain in control of the file.

12. Kt—Q2

White wants the long diagonal for himself, so he vacates B3 for the Bishop. He hardly hopes to lure Capablanca into a twopenny trap by 12. . . . Q x KtP when 13. B—B3 wins a piece. This sort of thing does not happen in real life.

12. . . .   B—Kt2

The Bishop stands beautifully here, despite the fact that two pieces obstruct its path. Meanwhile, square QB1 is ready for occupancy by another tenant, the Queen Rook.

13. B—B3

The Bishop is well posted here, but at what a cost in time! The Knight has had to retreat, and the development of White's Queen-side pieces has been neglected.

13. . . .   Q—Q2

The Queen keeps in touch with the Knight, which is under attack by two pieces.

14. O—O

Trying to get in the advance of the King Pawn is premature as *14. P—K4, Kt x QP* costs a Pawn, while *14. B x Kt, B x B 15. P—K4, Q x P 16. Q x B, Q x R* loses the exchange.

14. . . .   QR—B1

Threatening *15. . . . Kt x QP*, and thereby suggesting that White's Queen leave the file.

15. Q—Kt1

The aggressive *15. Q—R4* is dangerous as *15. . . . Kt—K4 16. Q x Q* (if *16. Q x P, Kt x Bch 17. Kt x Kt, Q—B3* followed by *18. . . . R —R1* wins the Queen), *Kt x Bch 17. Kt x Kt, Kt x Q* is strong for Black.

15. . . .   Kt—QR4 !

Offering an exchange of Bishops. Refusing it leaves Black in full possession of the long diagonal.

16. B x B

It might have been safer to concede the file by *16. B—K2* and keep more pieces on the board. Exchanging simplifies the position and accentuates Black's superiority.

16. . . .   Q x B

Black is now ready to exploit the circumstance that his opponent's white squares are vulnerable to invasion. These squares have been weakened by the disappearance of the Bishop which operated on the white squares. This advantage, together with that of Black's Pawn majority on the Queen side (a circumstance which generally results in the creation of a passed Pawn)

should be enough to forecast a win for him.

From this point on, we will see a demonstration of the technique of winning a won game.

17. B—Kt2

Finally, White gets his Queen side rolling. Laudable as this object is, it was essential to anticipate Black's next move and play *17. Q— Q3*. This would strengthen White's weak squares and hold off for a time the threatened invasion.

17. . . .   Q—R3 !

A very fine maneuver! The Queen takes leave of the center diagonal to exert great pressure on a more important one.

The Queen threatens to come in strongly at K7 and make co-ordination by White's pieces difficult.

18. R—K1

Parries the threat. On *18. R—B1* instead (to put up a fight for the Queen Bishop file), *Q—K7 19. Kt— B3* (or *19. R—R2, Kt—Kt5 20. R x R, Q x BPch* and Black wins), *Kt— Kt6 20. R x R, R x R 21. R—R2, R —B8ch!*, and White must give up his Queen or be mated.

18. . . .   Kt—Q4

Admirable centralization—but it's only temporary. The Knight is on its way to the Queen side, the theater of action.

19. R—R2

Intending either to oppose Rooks by 20. B—R1 followed by 21. R—B2 or to continue with 20. Q—R1 preventing 20. . . . Kt—B6.

19. . . .   R—B3

Clearly in order to double Rooks on the Bishop file. Black is in no hurry to move his Knight to B6. First he wants to induce White to dislodge the Knight from the center.

20. P—K4

A deceptive move. It looks strong, but the center Pawns are exposed and can easily become targets of an attack.

20. . . .   Kt—B6 !

It may seem strange that Black gives up a healthy Knight for a sickly Bishop, but this precaution is necessary before the Rooks venture into enemy territory. With less ma-

terial on the board, the Rooks will be less exposed to the stings of the minor pieces.

21. B x Kt

The Knight had to be removed, as it was attacking Queen and Rook.

21. . . .   R x B

The recapture enables the Rook to penetrate deeper into White's position.

22. Kt—B3

White makes an effort to regroup his pieces. If he tries to dispute the Bishop file by 22. R—B1, then 22. . . . R x Rch 23. Q x R, Q —Q6 24. Q—Kt2, R—Q1 wins a center Pawn.

22. . . .   KR—B1

The doubled Rooks now dominate the open file.

Theoretically, Black has a won game. His positional superiority is undeniable, and winning, in a favorite phrase of the masters, "is simply a matter of technique." A pleasant state of affairs, but one which involves a psychological danger. There is a tendency to relax and let up on the attack. It is easy to be lulled into a false sense of security, a circumstance which prompted Marshall's observation, "The hardest thing is to win a won game."

23. P—R3

Gives the King an escape square —in lieu of anything better to do.

Black's Rooks cannot be driven off (if 23. R—K3, R—B8ch wins the

Queen) so White temporizes and awaits the turn of events.

23. ...   Kt—B5

The first in a series of skillfully blended moves which speed up the tempo. To begin with, there is a triple attack on the Queen Rook Pawn.

24. P—QR4

No other move saves the Pawn.

24. ...   Kt—R6

Very neat! The Knight attacks the Queen and simultaneously cuts off the Rook Pawn's protection by the Rook.

25. Q—Kt2

Voluntarily giving up a Pawn which he cannot keep. If he tries to hold on to the Pawn by 25. Q—Q1, then 25. ... Q—B5 26. R—Kt2 (the Rook was attacked), Kt—B7 (now the other one is threatened) 27. R—K2, Q x RP 28. Kt—K1 (striking at the pinned Knight), Q x QP ! wins for Black.

25. ...   Q x P

The first tangible gain. Now watch the greatest genius the game of chess ever produced demonstrate the art of transforming a passed Pawn into a Queen. Notice how any combinations, no matter how attractive, which do not relate to that objective, are carefully avoided. Such intensity of purpose is frightening (especially to one who has to face it!).

26. R—K2

White is running out of good moves. He rejects 26. Q—K2, as the reply 26. ... R—B7 leads to further exchanges. An attack on the pinned Knight by 26. KR—R1 is cleverly met by 26. ... Q—Kt4, nimbly extricating the Knight from danger.

26. ...   P—QKt4

Passed Pawns must be pushed! Everything else—combinations to win pieces, gathering up stray Pawns, even attacks on the King—must be relegated to the background as incidental to the main theme of Queening the advanced Pawn.

27. P—Q5

White opens lines for some sort of counterattack, trying to create a diversion.

27. ...   P x P

The simplest response, the recapture will give White an isolated Pawn in the middle of the board.

28. P x P

In return for this, White's King Rook looks out on a completely open file. In fact, White threatens 29. Q x R, R x Q 30. R—K8 mate.

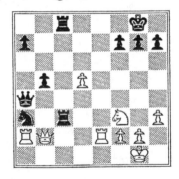

28. ...   P—Kt5 !

An obvious move, but brilliant nevertheless in the number of things it accomplishes:

a) It nullifies White's threat, the square K1 now being covered by the Queen.

b) It threatens the Queen Pawn by 29. ... Q—Q8ch 30. R—K1, Q x P, and White may not respond 31. Q x R, now that the Rook has the Pawn's protection.

c) It protects the Knight, freeing the Queen from that duty.

d) It advances the Pawn one step nearer its goal, the eighth square.

29. Q—Q2

Not only to support his own passed Pawn but to get the Queen into active play.

29. ...   P—Kt6

Complying with the Manhattan Chess Club epigram, "Black passed Pawns travel faster than White."

30. R—Kt2

This holds out longer than 30. R—R1, R—B7 31. Q—K3, P—Kt7, and Black wins.

30. ...   R—B7

Black's play is crystal clear: Since (a) the passed Pawn must be pushed and (b) its path is blocked by a Rook, therefore (c) the blockader must be removed!

31. Q—K3

White hopes to complicate matters, as 31. R x R is not attractive.

31. ...   R x R(Kt7)

The proper Rook to capture, this begins a series of pretty moves that forces the game.

32. R x R

White must recapture.

32. ...   Kt—B5 !

An attack on Queen and Rook which threatens to win the exchange.

33. Q—B1

Rescues the Rook by pinning the Knight. It would not do to play 33. Q x KtP instead as Black simply takes the Rook, and his Knight now protects the Queen.

33. ...   Q—R6 !

The pin of the Knight is met by a counter-pin of the Rook, which Black now threatens to take with his Queen.

34. R—Kt1

But the Rook wriggles out of the pin. Has Black let the win slip?

34. ...   Q x Qch !

Not at all! This compels capitulation: after 35. R x Q, P—Kt7 (the Pawn must move on) 36. R—Kt1, R—Kt1 37. K—B1, Kt—R6 (driving off the last blockader) 38. R—Q1, P—Kt8(Q), and the passed Pawn wins the game for Black.

35. Resigns

QUEEN'S PAWN GAME
(*Queen's Indian Defense*)

WHITE   BLACK
Canal   Capablanca
BUDAPEST, 1929

1. P—Q4

A favorite of modern players, this is the best possible way to begin the struggle for mastery of the center— by occupying it with a Pawn and permitting two pieces to come quickly into play.

1. . . .   Kt—KB3

If unlike *1. . . . P—Q4*, this does not meet the opponent head-on, it does prevent him from continuing with 2. P—K4 and has the added merit of developing a piece at once to its proper square in the opening.

2. P—QB4

There are many good points about this move:

a) It restrains Black from an immediate *2. . . . P—Q4*, as the reply 3. P x P *forcing a recapture with a piece* destroys his short-lived Pawn center.

b) It opens the Bishop file for the use of White's major pieces.

c) It makes a diagonal available to the Queen.

d) It enables the two Pawns standing side by side to get a grip on four squares on the fifth rank.

2. . . .   P—K3

Black's King Bishop is to be de-veloped aggressively, with a view to influencing affairs in the center. If White replies 3. Kt—QB3, for example, in order to follow up with 4. P—K4, Black pins the Knight and makes 4. P—K4 impossible.

3. Kt—KB3

White cannot enforce the advance of the King Pawn, so he makes a normal developing move and awaits events.

3. . . .   P—QKt3

Further restraint on the project! Black intends to place his Bishop at Kt2, where it attacks from a distance. The Bishop will add its strength to that of the Knight in the control of the critical square K5.

4. P—KKt3

White's best course is to oppose Bishops on the long diagonal as one does with Rooks on an open file. In setting up an equal opposing force, he takes the sting out of the adverse Bishop's attack.

4. . . .   B—Kt2

Strictly a modern concept! In olden times they filled up the center with Pawns and then fianchettoed the Bishop, with the result that the Bishop was deprived of any usefulness. Nowadays the Bishop is free to strike all along the diagonal, un-hampered by fixed Pawns cluttering up his path.

5. B—Kt2

With the completion of the fian-chetto, White's King side is cleared, and he is ready to castle.

5. . . .   B—Kt5ch

Before attempting to undermine the center by . . . P—B4, Black develops a piece. Not only does the Bishop's move expedite castling, but it brings about a favorable exchange of Bishops.

6. B—Q2

This is preferable to 6. QKt—Q2, a passive interposition which gives Black time to castle and then attack the center by 7. . . . P—Q4.

6. . . .   B x Bch

Black proceeds with the exchange as the best means of freeing his somewhat cramped position. Withdrawing the Bishop to K2 instead throws him on the defensive and lets White retain the initiative.

7. QKt x B

Theorists and critics of master chess recommend that White capture with the Queen instead. Despite their shrieks that the Knight belongs at B3 in order to help attack the square Q5, the players themselves persist in recapturing with the Knight. They advance as argument that in doing so another minor piece is developed, but the real reason might be sheer stubbornness—rebellion against authority. In any case, if it is less effective than 7. Q x B it is not to be so roundly condemned.

7. . . .   O—O

Before taking any decisive action in the center, Black sees to the welfare of his King and removes him to a safer part of the board.

A strong alternative is 7. . . . P—B4, challenging White's Pawn center. To this White cannot reply 8. P—Q5 as it loses a Pawn.

8. O—O

White makes his King's position more secure and presses the King Rook into service.

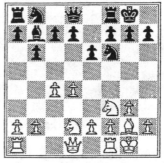

8. . . .   P—B4 !

A strong move, whose object is to undermine White's center.

9. P x P

White has little choice. Moving the Pawn to Q5 loses a Pawn, supporting it with 9. P—K3 (in order to recapture with a Pawn and maintain a Pawn in the center), ties down the King Pawn to the job of defense. The chances then of the King Pawn's ever reaching K4 are rather dubious.

9. . . .   P x P

Black has gained three advantages by a simple exchange of Pawns:

a) He has eliminated a center Pawn in return for a side Pawn.

b) His Bishop Pawn controls Q5, making it impossible for White to settle a piece on that square.

c) His Queen and Queen Rook will be able to operate with good effect on the newly opened Queen Knight file.

10. Q—B2

In most cases the function of the Queen in the opening is not so much to be up and doing as it is to get off the back rank and out of the way, so that the Rooks can get together and work on the center files.

With the departure of the Queen, the King Rook can occupy Q1, exert pressure on the Queen file, and make life uncomfortable for Black's forces on that file.

10. . . .   Kt—B3

The Knight develops toward the center and intensifies the Pawn's grip on Q5.

11. KR—Q1

The attractive 11. P—K4 instead meets its refutation in 11. . . . P—K4 (strengthening the pressure on Q5) followed by 12. . . . Q—K2 and 13. . . . Kt—Q5. White would then face a problem: the pressure of the Knight at Q5 is almost intolerable, but removing it lets Black recapture by 14. . . . BP x Kt, leaving him with a passed Pawn on the Queen file.

11. . . .   Q—Kt3 !

Now there are three pieces bearing down on Q5, while the Queen herself gets a purchase on the open Knight file.

12. P—QR3

White has no wild dream of starting a counterattack with 13. P—QKt4. Mainly he does not want to be surprised by an unexpected . . . Kt—QKt5 move at some later stage.

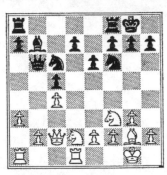

12. . . .   QR—Kt1 !

Fine position play! One is apt to forget that a Rook's first duty to his King is to seize upon any file that is open. Not only because the Rook's attack extends the whole length of the file but that the Rook has a convenient avenue for its progress to other points.

13. QR—Kt1

White's Rook also goes to Kt1, but what a world of difference there is in the two moves! White's Rook has no open file; it has little prospect of increasing its mobility, and its function is purely defensive. In protecting the Knight Pawn though it relieves the Queen of a responsibility.

13. . . .   KR—B1

The Rook was doing nothing at KB1, so it is transferred to a file where it is likely to become useful.

There was no hurry about playing 13. . . . P—QR4, since White is in

no position to try for the break by
14. P—QKt4.

14. P—K4

White's move has a superficial appearance of strength. In reality, the Pawn occupies a square which should be kept clear. White's pieces lose a great deal of mobility in not being able to make use of K4 as a jumping-off point to their various destinations.

14. . . .   P—K4

Stifles 15. P—K5, the lust to expand of White's King Pawn.

Notice how Black has reinforced his hold on Q5. This point now has the power of the Queen, a Knight and a couple of Pawns trained on it.

15. Q—Q3

White hopes for some counterplay along the Queen file, either by continuing with 16. Q—Q6 or in maneuvering his Knight by way of KB1 and K3 to Q5. In the meantime he prevents Black from playing 15. . . . Kt—Q5, the response to which is 16. Kt x P.

15. . . .   P—Q3

A witty, almost impudent, reply. Black guards the King Pawn (so that he can play 16. . . . Kt—Q5) with a Pawn which itself is unprotected!

White, of course, must not touch the Queen Pawn, the penalty for 16. Q x P being 16. . . . R—Q1, winning the Queen.

16. Kt—B1

Indicating that he wants to deploy the Knight to K3 and then Q5.

Excellent strategy, if White can carry it out.

16. . . .   Kt—Q5 !

But Black gets there first! Not only does he establish an outpost at Q5, but he hinders White from doing likewise. If White tries 17. Kt—K3, the continuation 17. . . . B x P 18. Kt—Q5, B x Q 19. Kt x Q, Kt x Ktch 20. B x Kt, R x Kt 21. R x B, P—K5 wins a piece neatly.

17. Kt x Kt

The advanced Knight cramps his style, so White gets rid of it.

17. . . .   KP x Kt

Black is happy to exchange: he has a passed Pawn on the Queen file, which in the course of time might become a Queen. More than that, the Pawn guards the exits. It hinders White's Knight from coming out at K3 and puts an end to its ambition to reach Q5.

The passed Pawn at Q5 is apparently the logical candidate for promotion to Queen, but there are surprises to come—many of them!

18. P—QKt4

Suddenly White bursts forth! His chief threat is 19. P x P, Q x P (Black must recapture with the Queen, which is doubly attacked) 20. R x B, R x R 21. P—K5, and the discovered attack will net White two pieces for a Rook.

How does Black meet this threat? Obviously not with 18. . . . P x P as 19. R x P gives White the best of it. Or if he retreats by 18. . . . Q—B2, then after 19. P x P, P x P (to protect the passed Pawn) 20. P—B4 threatening 21. P—K5 follows, and White's pieces spring to life.

Capablanca's actual reply initiates a remarkable combination. He lets White obtain an advantage in material in return for a position which looks far from promising—except to a Capablanca!

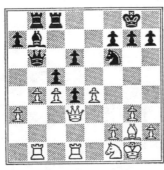

18. . . .   Q—B3 !

Triple attack on the King Pawn! This forces White either tamely to defend the Pawn or to go ahead boldly with the combination he planned.

19. P x P

White plays to win! He takes a Pawn off, opens a file for his Rook, and threatens to remove the passed Queen's Pawn.

19. . . .   P x P

Black must recapture with the Pawn to preserve the precious passed Pawn.

20. R x B

A tempting combination that wins two pieces for a Rook.

Has Capablanca been caught off-guard, or does he see much further into the resources of the position than his opponent?

20. . . .   Q x R

Black captures with the Queen to maintain control of the valuable open file.

21. P—K5

Discovered attack on the Queen, and direct attack on the Knight.

21. . . .   Q—Kt6 !

A remarkable offer to exchange Queens! Usually, the side that is ahead in material tries to clear the board and simplify the ending.

22. P x Kt

White rejects 22. Q x Q as it leads to 22. . . . R x Q 23. P x Kt, R x RP, and Black is left with two passed Pawns.

22. . . .   Q x Q

The idea of this is to force White's Rook in recapturing off the last rank. The rank then becomes available to Black's Rook as a point of entry, enabling it to get behind White's Pawns.

23. R x Q

White has no choice.

23. . . .   R—Kt8 !

The Knight is pinned as a start, and White has to scramble frantically to break the pin.

Against passive play, Black continues with 24. . . . R—K1 followed by 25. . . . R(K1)—K8 and 26. . . . R(K8)—B8. This wins the Bishop Pawn since White cannot protect it by 27. B—Q5 without abandoning the Knight. After capturing the Pawn, Black would have two dangerous connected Pawns rushing to become Queens.

24. B—Q5

White's plan is clear: he protects the precious Bishop Pawn and vacates a square for his King. Following 25. K—Kt2, the Knight, no longer pinned, can come into the game.

24. . . .   R(B1)—Kt1

The doubled Rooks give Black undisputed possession of the all-important Knight file.

White is now faced with two threats:

a) 25. . . . R—B8 followed by 26. . . . R(Kt1)—Kt8. The attack on the Knight would compel the Bishop to return to Kt2, whereupon Black picks up the Bishop Pawn.

b) 25. . . . R(Kt1)—Kt6, forcing an exchange of Rooks, after which one of White's Queen-side Pawns must fall.

25. K—Kt2

Unpins the Knight, which has been a spectator for the last ten moves.

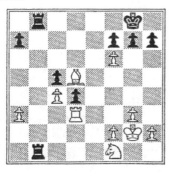

25. . . .   R(Kt1)—Kt6 !

A daring concept! Black offers to exchange Rooks and let White remain with two pieces to his one!

26. R x R

White is happy to oblige!

26. . . .   R x R

Imperils the Rook Pawn next.

27. Kt—Q2

White could not save the Rook Pawn (if 27. P—QR4, R—Kt5 28. P—R5, R—R5), so the Knight counterattacks by going after a Pawn.

27. . . .   R x RP

Winning a Pawn and simultaneously creating a passed Pawn on the Rook file. Will this be the one to become a Queen?

28. Kt—K4

But White's pieces now spring into action! The threat is 29. Kt x P, knocking the support out from under the Queen Pawn and, as further result, giving himself a passed Bishop Pawn.

28. . . .   P—QR4 !

Much better than 28. . . . R—R4, which ties the Rook down to defending a Pawn and makes his role in the ending a subordinate one.

29. Kt x P

After this capture, White's passed Pawn begins to look menacing.

29. . . .   P x P

Not so much to gain a Pawn as

to give the King more freedom. If at once 29. . . . K—B1 30. Kt—Q7ch drives the King back to Kt1, as 30. . . . K—K1 allows 31. P x P winning for White.

Advancing 29. . . . P—Q5 instead allows 30. K—B3 followed by 31. K—K3, and White wins the Queen Pawn.

30. K—B1

The King turns back to head off the passed Pawns.

30. . . .   P—R5

Black does not fear a double attack on this Pawn by 31. B—B6. He would refute this by 31. . . . R—R8ch followed by 32. . . . P—R6, and the Pawn has moved another step forward.

31. K—K2

The King comes closer, definitely putting an end to any danger from the Queen Pawn.

How does Black proceed?

31. . . .   R—R8 !

By scaring White with the threat of Queening the Rook Pawn! Black intends 32. . . . P—R6 next, fol-

lowed by 33. . . . P—R7, 34. . . . R—K8ch (to make way for the Pawn without loss of time) and 35. . . . P—R8(Q).

32. Kt—Q3

Blockades the Queen Pawn and prepares to push his own passed Pawn.

32. . . .   P—R6

Back at the seventeenth move it seemed that the Queen Pawn would reach the eighth rank and become a Queen. The Queen Pawn is blockaded, and it now appears that the Rook Pawn is the one that will be promoted.

But will it be the Rook Pawn?

33. P—B5

White's Pawn can cause trouble, too!

33. . . .   P—R7

Threatening to win on the spot by 34. . . . R—K8ch 35. Kt x R, P—R8(Q).

34. K—B3

The King steps aside to evade the check.

34. . . .   R—Q8

And this move, which attacks the Knight as well as threatens to Queen the Pawn, adds to White's difficulties.

35. B x RP

White must destroy this dangerous creature at all costs!

35. . . .   R x Ktch

With this capture Black nets a piece for his Rook Pawn.

36. K—K4

White does not fall into 36. K—K2, losing his passed Pawn after 36. . . . R—QB6.

36. . . .   R—Q7

More attractive than 36. . . . R—QB6 37. K x P, R x P. The text attacks the Bishop and all the King-side Pawns and revives the Queen Pawn's prospects.

Is this Pawn to be the candidate after all?

37. B—B4 !

An admirable spot for the Bishop. Black can now easily go wrong with 37. . . . R x P 38. P—B6, R—QKt7 (if 38. . . . R—QB7 39. K—Q5 wins for White) 39. P—B7, and White's Pawn crashes through!

37. . . .   K—B1 !

The King takes over the job of restraining the dangerous Pawn.

38. P—B3

Advancing the Queen Bishop Pawn is useless: 38. P—B6, K—K2,

and the Pawn must go no further.

With the text move, White offers his Rook Pawn in return for Black's Queen Pawn.

38. . . .   R x P

Black falls in with the suggestion. Instead of grimly holding on to the passed Pawn, he is willing to simplify, confident that his superiority, however small, is enough to secure the win. This requires a belief in justice on the chessboard, and confidence in one's ability to mete it out properly.

39. K x P

With this capture, White's prospects look brighter. His King and Bishop are in close attendance on the passed Pawn and will bend all their efforts to escort it to the end of the board.

39. . . .   K—K2

Ready to blockade the Pawn.

40. B—Q3

Apparently with the idea of switching the Bishop to K4. From there it guards his King Bishop Pawn, prevents Black's doubled Pawns from advancing, and is prepared to protect his Queen Bishop Pawn when it reaches B6.

40. . . .   P—R4

Threatening 41. . . . R—KKt7 42. P—Kt4, P—R5, and Black wins.

Is the Rook Pawn to be the passed Pawn that becomes a Queen?

41. K—K3

The King comes closer to rescue the Knight Pawn.

41. ...   R—KKt7

In forcing the King to defend the Knight Pawn, Black draws him farther away from his own passed Pawn.

42. K—B4

The only move. Against 42. P—Kt4, the win is easy: 42. ... P—R5 43. B—B1, R—QB7 44. K—Q4, R—B7 45. B—R3, R x P 46. B—Kt2, R—KKt6 47. B—B1, P—R6, etc.

42. ...   R—Kt8

Now to get behind the passed Pawn! In the ending, the Rook does its best work behind the enemy's Pawns. Its power to strike extends all along the line, so that *no matter how far the Pawn advances on the file, it can never escape the Rook's attack.*

43. B—K4

Preparing to protect the Pawn when it reaches B6. If at once 43. P—B6, R—QB8 44. B—K4 (but not 44. B—Kt5, R—B4 45. B—R4, R—B5ch winning the Bishop), and we have the position reached a little later in the game by a transposition of moves.

43. ...   R—QB8

To the uninitiated, this looks strange! Why help the Pawn move farther up the board?

Black's idea is to compel the Pawn to move to a white square. This will tie the Bishop down to its defense and considerably limit the Bishop's sphere of activity.

44. P—B6

The Pawn moves up to come under the Bishop's protection.

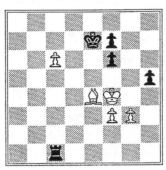

44. ...   R—B6!

A tremendously effective move! It reduces White to a state of *Zugzwang*—move compulsion. What this means is that White might hold the game, except that he must make a move. And any move he makes is fatal because it disturbs the position!

45. P—B7

Voluntarily giving up the Pawn he cannot save! The alternatives are extremely interesting:

a) If 45. K—B5, R—B4ch (to drive the King back) 46. K—B4, K—K3 47. K—K3 (a Bishop move loses the Pawn at once, while 47. P—Kt4 allows 47. ... P—R5, giving Black a passed Pawn), P—B4 48. B—Q3, R x P, and Black wins.

b) If 45. B—Q5, R—B4 46. K—K4 (on 46. B—K4, K—K3 forces the play as in the previous note), P—B4ch 47. K—Q4, R x Bch! 48. K x R, P—B5! 49. K—B5 (or 49. P x P,

P—R5 50. K—B5, K—Q1 51. K—
Kt6, K—B1 wins), P x P 50. K—
Kt6, P—Kt7 51. P—B7, P—
Kt8(Q)ch 52. K—Kt7, Q—Kt8ch
53. K—B8, Q—QKt3 54. P—B4,
Q—R2 55. P—B5, Q—R1 mate.

45. . . .   R x QBP

Removes a potential danger. The
ending still requires winning, and
the manner of its doing is an illustration of smooth, flawless technique.
The demonstration is as lucid and accurate as though it were the solution
of a composed endgame study.

46. B—Q5

To keep Black from moving his
King to the fine square K3.

46. . . .   R—B4

The Rook intends to pursue the
Bishop until it leaves the diagonal
overlooking the K3 square.

47. B—R2

Understandably, the Bishop tries
to stay on the diagonal as long as
possible. If instead 47. B—Kt3, R—
QKt4 forces 48. B—R2 (on 48. B—
B4, R—Kt5 pins the Bishop, or if 48.
B—R4, R—Kt5ch wins the Bishop),
R—Kt7 49. B—Q5, R—Kt5ch ! 50.
K—B5 (if 50. B—K4, K—K3 51.
K—K3, P—B4 wins, or if 50. K—K3,
P—B4 followed by 51. . . . K—B3
wins), R—Kt4 51. K—K4, P—B4ch
52. K—Q4, R x Bch ! 53. K x R, P—
B5 54. P x P, P—R5, and the Pawn
cannot be stopped!

47. . . .   R—QKt4 !

Complete domination! The
Bishop has no moves!

48. K—K3

If 48. K—K4, P—B4ch 49. K—
B4, K—B3 50. K—K3 (the Bishop
cannot move, and 50. P—Kt4 loses
by 50. . . . RP x P 51. P x P, R—
Kt5ch 52. K—B3, P x Pch), R—Kt5
51. B—Q5, P—B5ch 52. P x P, P—
R5 53. K—B2, R—Kt7ch 54. K—
Kt1, K—B4 55. B x P, K x P 56. B—
Q5, K—Kt6 57. B—K4, R—QR7
58. K—B1, P—R6 and Black wins.

48. . . .   R—R4

Allowing the Bishop one square
on the long diagonal.

49. B—B4

The Bishop could not go to Kt3
on account of the ensuing pin, and
if 49. B—Kt1, K—K3 50. K—B4,
R—R5ch 51. K—K3 (on 51. B—K4,
P—B4 wins the Bishop), P—B4
52. B—B2, P—B5ch 53. P x P
(or 53. K—Q2, P x P), R—R6ch
54. K—Q2, R—R7 55. K—B1, R x
Bch, and Black wins.

49. . . .   R—QB4

Dislodging the Bishop from the
diagonal leading to K3.

50. B—R6

On 50. K—Q4, R—KKt4 wins a
Pawn at once, while 50. B—R2 is re-
futed by 50. . . . P—B4, clearing
KB3 for Black's King.

50. . . .   K—K3

Another step nearer the center
and White's remaining Pawns.

51. K—B4

White puts up a hard fight! He is ready to pounce on 51. . . . P—B4 with 52. K—Kt5.

51. . . .   R—B6 !

Again restricting White to a move by the Bishop. Playing 52. K—K4 succumbs to 52. . . . P—B4ch 53. K—B4, K—B3, etc.

52. B—B1

White must keep watch over his QB4 square. Otherwise (if he plays 52. B—Kt7, for example) 52. . . . R—B5ch forces his King to retreat while Black's is enabled to advance.

52. . . .   P—B4

Finally! This Pawn moves up a square and vacates B3 for the King.

53. B—R6

The number of moves White has left is dwindling! If 53. P—Kt4, BP x P 54. P x P, P—R5 55. P—Kt5, P—R6 56. K—Kt4, P—R7 57. B—Kt2, R—B8 wins for Black, or if 53.

K—Kt5, R x P 54. B—B4ch, K—K4 55. K—R4, P—B5, and Black wins easily.

53. . . .   K—B3

Stalemating White's King. What remains now is to force him back to the third rank while Black's King moves up to the fourth.

54. B—Kt7

If the Bishop stays on the longer diagonal, say by 54. B—K2, Black plays 54. . . . R—Kt6 and then drives the King back by 55. . . . R—Kt5ch.

54. . . .   R—B5ch

Compels the King to retreat.

55. K—K3

The only move.

55. . . .   K—Kt4

With the pretty threat 56. . . . P—B5ch 57. K—Q3 (if 57. P x Pch, R x P gives Black a passed Pawn, or if 57. K—B2, R—B7ch 58. K—Kt1, P x P gives him two), P x P 58. K x R, K—B5 !, and Black wins neatly.

56. K—B2

A thrust at the Rook by 56. B—Q5 allows this finish: 56. . . . P—B5ch 57. K—K2, R—B7ch 58. K—Q3, R—B2 (simple but brutal), and Black wins.

With the text, White retreats in order to head off the potential passed Pawn, whichever one that may be!

56. . . .   P—B5 !

This is the specific in all cases! Black threatens to win at once by 57. . . . R—B7ch   58.   K—Kt1, P x P.

57. K—Kt2

Ready to reply to the check with 58. K—R3 saving the Pawn.

57. . . .   P—B4 !

Passed Pawns must be pushed. This Pawn which stood patiently at B2 for 56 moves is, believe it or not, the one that was destined to become the passed Pawn that wins the game!

58. Resigns

White does not wait for the proof: After 58. K—R3, P x P 59. K x P, P—R5ch (a likely-looking candidate, but not the final choice) 60. K—R3, R—B6 61. B—Q5, K—B5 62. K x P, R x P 63. B x R, K x B 64. K—R3, P—B5 65. K—R2, K—K7, and the Pawn marches straight through to be Queened.

The whole game is beautiful, and the ending so fascinating that I could not resist a detailed analysis of its many fine points. A study of it is infinitely more rewarding in entertainment and instruction than the

playing over of a host of "brilliancies" that feature a flinging about of pieces in wanton display.

GAME NO. 33

QUEEN'S GAMBIT DECLINED

WHITE	BLACK
Rubinstein	Maroczy

GOTHENBERG, 1920

1. P—Q4

The opening move, seizing the center with a Pawn and making room for two pieces to come out, is efficient. White intends to develop all his pieces as quickly as possible, posting each of them in one move on its most suitable square. He will make only those Pawn moves which speed his development (releasing pieces or attacking the center) or hinder that of his opponent.

1. . . .   Kt—KB3

Model development in every respect: the Knight leaps in toward the center where it has the greatest potential for attack, exerts immediate pressure on the important squares Q4 and K5, and prevents White from establishing a strong Pawn formation by 2. P—K4.

2. Kt—KB3

White develops the King-side pieces first, to enable early castling on that side. At B3, the Knight stands on its most useful square in the opening. It is beautifully placed for attack—notice how it supplements the Pawn's grip on K5—and is a peerless defender of the King side after castling.

2. . . .   P—Q4

Black cannot wrest the initiative by brute force. He may get it if White plays carelessly (wasting time in the opening or chasing after Pawns) but against normal development Black must content himself with achieving equality.

Black's second move neutralizes White's pressure in the center and opens lines for two of his own pieces.

3. P—QB4

One of the rare occasions when a Pawn move is opportune. This one attacks and threatens to eliminate, by 4. P x P, Black's center. It does additional service in increasing the mobility (actual and potential) of White's pieces. It clears a diagonal for the Queen and assures the Bishop's file being opened for the later use of the Queen or Queen Rook.

3. . . .   P—K3

Black supports the Queen Pawn with another Pawn. If White tries breaking up the center by 4. P x P, he is prepared to recapture with a Pawn, to keep the center intact by maintaining a Pawn at Q4.

Though 3. . . . P—K3 has the drawback of shutting in the Queen Bishop, it is still Black's best move. The difficulty in developing the Bishop effectively may not seem alarming, but if it is not overcome, it will amount to Black's playing a piece short. For the present, in partial compensation, the King Bishop has lots of elbowroom.

4. B—Kt5

This move has a terribly cramping effect on Black's game. It clamps a pin on the Knight which exerts pressure on the Knight and on any pieces behind it. Black cannot move freely about while his King side is gripped by the Bishop.

Years ago, White would have automatically developed the Bishop at KB4, where it commands a useful diagonal. Nowadays we look for sharper, more vigorous moves. If we can mobilize our forces and at the same time restrain the enemy's development, we accomplish more than with routine, often innocuous, measures. The pin of the Knight paralyzes Black's only developed piece.

4. . . .   B—K2

Why all the fuss when the pin is so easily lifted? For one thing, in unpinning the Knight, the Bishop is restricted to a defensive, a passive, role. Its development has been dictated by the fact that White put pressure on the Knight.

Black's play, incidentally, is in no way to be depreciated. The Bishop's move, modest as it is, is a step forward in the process of development. The Bishop has left the last rank, taken up a strong defensive post, and cleared the King side, enabling Black to castle.

5. P—K3

Pawns should be moved sparingly in the opening. But since *some* Pawns must be moved to get the Bishops into play, this must be regarded as a developing move.

5. . . .   QKt—Q2

In Queen Pawn openings, the ideal square for the development of the Queen Knight is not QB3 but Q2. From Q2, the Knight supports an eventual thrust at White's center by the King Pawn or the Queen Bishop Pawn.

The Knight must not develop at QB3, where it blocks the Bishop Pawn. *This Pawn must not be prevented from advancing to B4, where it can dispute control of the center.*

6. Kt—B3

This Knight, contrariwise, is posted excellently at QB3. It does not block the Bishop Pawn and bears down on Q5 and K4, two of the four important squares in the center.

6. . . .   O—O

Black transfers his King to a more secure location and brings his King Rook closer to the center files.

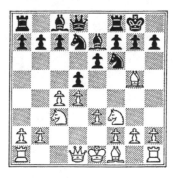

7. R—B1

The Rook develops where it has the most attractive prospects for attack. At B1 it controls and will exert pressure all along the open file. The file is obstructed now by White's own Knight and Pawn, but the Pawn can be disposed of by an exchange and the Knight can take leave and clear the file. Strictly speaking, the file is only partly open, but open or not, the Rook goes to QB1 because:

Control of the Queen Bishop file is absolutely vital in the Queen's Gambit.

7. . . .   R—K1

Black's Rook moves to a center file, where it may play a useful part in any action that takes place in the center. The Rook's presence on the file is of little consequence now, but with every clearance on the file its influence grows stronger and stronger.

Black's game is cramped, but alternatives aimed at freeing it immediately are not convincing:

a) If 7. . . . P x P 8. B x P, and White gains a tempo for this Bishop, which recaptures and develops at the same time.

b) If 7. . . . P—QR3 (in order to continue with 8. . . . P x P 9. B x P, P—QKt4 10. B—Q3, B—Kt2), 8. P—B5 in reply can be very constraining.

c) If 7. . . . P—B4 8. P x BP, Kt x P 9. P x P, P x P (or 9. . . . Kt x P 10. Kt x Kt, P x Kt 11. R x Kt !, B x B 12. R x P, and White wins the Bishop), and Black's center Pawn is weak, while White has the fine square Q4 as a central point for maneuvering his pieces to any part of the board.

8. Q—B2

The best place on the board for

the Queen! From B2 the Queen increases the pressure on the Bishop file and seizes control of the center, making the problem of freeing himself troublesome for Black.

8. . . .   P x P

Black gets impatient and tries to break loose. It would have been better to delay this capture, though, and wait for White to move his King Bishop. Then the recapture costs the Bishop an extra move.

Black might have played instead 8. . . . P—B3, strengthening the position of the center Pawn and offering the Queen an outlet to the Queen side.

9. B x P

Obviously a gain of time for White, whose King Bishop recaptures a Pawn and develops to a good square simultaneously.

9. . . .   P—B4

Black must counterattack or be crushed to death. This offers the most practical chances in that he establishes tension in the center and disputes control in that area. Furthermore, he prepares to oppose Rooks on the Bishop file and fight for equal rights on the file.

10. O—O

The simplest way to keep up the pressure is to continue developing. At one stroke White removes his King to a safer part of the board and brings the King Rook out of the corner and toward the center.

10. . . .   P x P

Black's intention is to force White to a decision regarding the center. If White recaptures with a Pawn, it saddles him with an isolated Pawn in the middle of the board; if with a piece, then his Pawn center is no better than Black's.

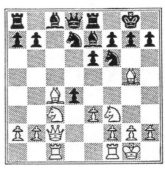

11. Kt x P

Rubinstein prefers this to 11. P x P, which maintains a Pawn, but one that is isolated, in the center.

The weakness of a Pawn separated from its fellows is not so much in the fact that attacks on the isolated Pawn can only be met by pieces, not Pawns, coming to its defense, but by the peculiar circumstance that adverse pieces can settle themselves on the square directly in front of the Pawn (in this case Black's Q4) and stay there indefinitely, secure in the knowledge that no enemy Pawns can drive them away.

The strength of an isolated Pawn in the center (say at Q4, if White recaptured by 11. P x P) consists in its control of the strategic squares K5 and QB5, its ability to spearhead an attack to break up a position, and its value as a support for an outpost—in this case a Knight at K5.

11. . . . P—QR3

Mainly to secure the square Kt4 from invasion by one of White's minor pieces. The objection to this move is that Pawn moves which do not contribute to development are a waste of valuable time in the opening. More to the point was *11. . . . Kt—K4 12. B—Kt3, B—Q2 13. KR—Q1, Q—Kt3*, with a view to getting some action out of his pieces.

Notice that White made only those Pawn moves which were necessary to release pieces, or which added to the mobility of pieces already developed. Every single move, of piece or Pawn, furthered the development of White's position and increased its potential energy.

12. KR—Q1

Now the Rook swings over to the center, placing itself at the head of a file facing the Queen. The Queen is sure to feel uncomfortable, no matter how many pieces separate the two, as threats are constantly in the air. For instance, if Black should play the plausible *12. . . . Kt—Kt3*, attacking the Bishop, the reply *13. Kt x P* wins the Queen by a discovered (and double) attack.

Yates and Winter comment admiringly at this point, "A classical example of correct development. White has brought his Queen, Rooks, Bishops and one Knight to almost ideal squares in one move each."

12. . . . Q—R4

The Queen flees the line of fire, gaining a little time by attacking a Bishop.

13. B—R4

The Bishop retreats but maintains pressure on the Knight.

13. . . . Kt—K4

Now the other Bishop is threatened, apparently with more gain of time for Black.

14. B—K2

Both Bishops have been driven back, but despite this their latent power is enormous. It is an appreciation of the potentialities of two Bishops working in harmony and supplementing each other's efforts on the long diagonals, that precludes from consideration such a move as *14. B—Q3*, which lets Black play *14. . . . Kt x B* and exchange a short-stepping Knight for a long-range Bishop. Condensed, it comes down to this:

It is an advantage to keep both Bishops.

14. . . . Kt—Kt3

Swinging over to the King side, the Knight attacks the black-squared Bishop and forces it still further back. Meanwhile, more and more barriers are being put up about Black's King, who now seems firmly entrenched in a bomb-proof shelter.

Despite all the time Black seems to have gained in his attacks on the adverse Bishops, he should have done something to get his Queen-side pieces off the ground, say by *14. . . . B—Q2* instead. Then the continuation *15. Kt—Kt3, Q—B2 16. Q—Kt1, B—B3* gives him reasonable fighting chances.

15. B—Kt3

The Bishop must step back a square and relax its pressure on the Knight, but now it commands a magnificent diagonal.

Black cannot continue chasing the Bishops in an effort to get rid of one of them: if *15. . . . Kt—R4 16. Kt—Kt3, Q—KKt4* (the Queen must protect the Knight) *17. Kt—K4, Q—R3 18. B—B7*, and White dominates the board.

15. . . .   P—K4

An extremely attractive move! These are all the things the Pawn does:

a) It occupies a square in the center.

b) It opens a path for the Queen Bishop.

c) It cuts down the scope of White's Queen Bishop.

d) It will drive off White's Knight from its centralized position.

Against this, Black's move offers one objection, seemingly a slight one. The square Q4, no longer under the Pawn's control, has been weakened. It offers White the prospect of utilizing this central point for the easy maneuvering of his pieces to any part of the board.

Will this one liability outweigh all the assets? It is this judgment of imponderables, where exact calculation is not possible, that makes chess a fascinating blend of art and science.

16. Kt—Kt3

The Knight must leave but retaliates by getting in a thrust at the Queen.

16. . . .   Q—B2

The Queen evades the attack, and Black prepares to regroup his pieces, perhaps by *17. . . . B—Q2, 18. . . . B—B3* and *19. . . . QR —Q1*.

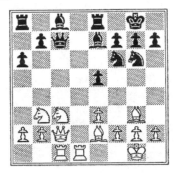

17. Q—Kt1 !

This is White's fifth retreating move in succession, but with every step backward his position improves! Though driven back to the first three ranks, his pieces will gain in dynamic energy. Gradually they will take up stronger positions, dominate the board, and put the enemy to flight.

Black has no time now to develop his Queen Bishop as after *17. . . . B—Q2 18. Kt—Q5, Q—Q1* (if *18. . . . Kt x Kt 19. R x Q, Kt x R 20. R x B* wins) *19. Kt—B7* wins the exchange.

17. . . .   Q—Kt1

Black's Queen was forced to retreat (by the threat of a discovered attack) while White's Queen moved to Kt1 voluntarily.

The difference in the positions is apparent:

a) White's Queen does not obstruct the Rooks, which together control the two open files; Black's Queen and Bishop separate his Rooks, one of which is completely shut in, while the other's action is severely limited.

b) White has two agile, long-range Bishops; Black has one, with the other undeveloped and still at home.

c) White's Queen can leap into the fray quickly; Black's must skulk on the fringes of the board.

18. B—B3

The Bishop seizes the long diagonal and prevents Black from playing 18. . . . P—QKt4 (the penalty being 19. B x R) and then fianchettoing his Bishop.

18. . . .   Q—R2

Black's maneuvering is tortuous, but evidently he wants to bring his Rook to QKt1, then play . . . P—QKt4, and finally develop his Queen Bishop at QKt2.

19. Kt—R5 !

A fine preventive move! It stops 19. . . . R—Kt1 followed by 20. . . . P—QKt4 as then 21. Kt—B6 wins the exchange, while the direct 19. . . . B—Q2 or 19. . . . B—K3 costs Black his Knight Pawn.

Notice how White not only sees to the development of his own pieces but hinders that of his opponent.

19. . . .   B—QKt5

Black tries to chase off the Knight which hampers the free movement of his Queen-side pieces.

20. Kt—B4

The Knight must leave, but in compensation it enjoys the advantage of being nearer the center.

20. . . .   B—Q2

The Bishop moves to the only square available for its development! If Black tries instead 20. . . . B—K3 21. Kt x P wins a Pawn, while on 20. . . . B—Kt5 21. B x B, Kt x B 22. Kt—Q5, and the threats of 23. Kt x B (winning a piece) and 23. Kt—B7 (winning the exchange) cannot both be met.

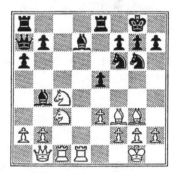

21. Kt—Q5 !

The Knight leaps to Q5 and attacks pieces all over the place! It threatens one Bishop directly (by 22. Kt x B) and the other indirectly, by 22. Kt x Ktch, P x Kt 23. R x B. Added to this, it threatens 22. Kt—B7, an attack on both Rooks which wins the exchange.

21. . . .   Kt x Kt

Obviously, such a dangerous beast must be removed!

22. B x Kt

White recaptures with the threat

of 23. B x Pch, K x B 24. R x Bch, winning a Pawn. White gains a tempo with this, as Black must drop whatever he is doing to parry the threat.

22. . . .   B—K3

Black must rid the board of the terrible Bishop which attacks his King side and restrains his Queen side. It would not do to play 22. . . . B—B3 as 23. B x B, P x B 24. Q—K4 wins the Bishop Pawn or the King Pawn.

23. Q—K4 !

A master move in every respect, and a one-move lesson in position play! Where most of us think of an exchange in terms of what happens after 23. B x B, the great master visualizes an exchange as an opportunity to substitute another piece for one that must come off the board. White is willing to exchange, but only if he can be assured of keeping control of Q5 by replacing the Bishop with another piece.

Let me reword this, so that the message is unmistakable:

Supporting a piece under attack (here the Bishop at Q5) puts more pressure on Black, where a direct exchange or a retreat might relieve it.

Note incidentally the full effect of the Queen's magnificent centralization, and her radiation of power in so many directions:

a) The Queen supports the Bishop at Q5.

b) The Queen adds to the Bishop's attack on the Queen Knight Pawn.

c) The Queen helps in the attack on the King Pawn.

d) The Queen threatens (indirectly) Black's King Bishop.

23. . . .   B x B

Practically forced in view of the many threats. An attempt to drive the Queen off by 23. . . . P—B4 is brusquely refuted by 24. Q x BP, and Black (whose Bishop is pinned) is unable to touch the Queen.

24. R x B

Black rids himself of one troublesome piece only to have another one take its place! For the third time White anchors a piece at Q5, each time intensifying his grip on the position. Now there is a fourfold attack on the King Pawn, by Rook, Knight, Bishop and Queen. While this Pawn is being rescued, White will gain the time needed to double his Rooks on the Queen file, guaranteeing him permanent possession of this vital highway. The effect on Black will be to cut communication between his forces, making an organized resistance difficult.

24. . . .   QR—B1

Protecting the Pawn indirectly by pinning one of it attackers.

White cannot take the Pawn with the Knight on pain of mate, nor with the Rook or the Queen, as that results in loss of material to White. This leaves 25. B x P, and Black is ready to penalize that with 25. . . . P—B3 24. B—Q4, R x Q 25. B x Q, R(K5) x Kt, and Black has gained a piece.

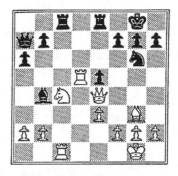

25. R(B1)—Q1

Doubling the Rooks on an open file, an act which more than doubles the strength of the Rooks. White's Knight is now unpinned, and the attack on the King Pawn renewed, with incidentally a threat of discovered attack on the Bishop.

White has a won game theoretically, and Rubinstein wins it in a way that is both efficient and artistic.

25. . . .   B—B1

Black transfers the exposed Bishop (threatened with capture as it was by 26. Kt x P followed by 27. Q x B) to the defense.

Against the immediate counterattack by 25. . . . P—B4, White has a winning line in 26. Q x BP, R x Kt 27. R—Q8 !, R x R 28. R x Rch, Kt—B1 29. Q—K6ch, K—R1 30. Q x R, and he is the exchange ahead.

After Black's actual move, he can answer 26. Kt x P with 26. . . . P—B3, pinning the unfortunate piece. In addition, he contemplates the thrust 26. . . . P—B4, which after 27. Q—Q3 (to protect the Knight), P—B5, occasions some trouble for the Bishop.

26. P—Kt3

Frees the Queen from the duty of guarding the Knight and stops any such move as 26. . . . P—B4, when the Pawn would simply be snapped up.

Against passive play, White continues by 27. R—Q7, invading the seventh rank.

26. . . .   P—Kt4

The object of this is not so much to dislodge the Knight as it is to open a line for the Queen, enabling it to return to the King side and the defense of the King.

27. Kt—Q6 !

A Knight fork which will force an exchange—a simplification to White's advantage. He will maintain the pressure inherent in a superior position without running the risk of being involved in unnecessary complications.

A premature attack, in fact, might even result in a loss for White! Consider this pretty possibility (instead of the actual move): 27. Kt x P, P—B3 28. R—Q7 (apparently a saving move, as White attacks the Queen and threatens to follow with 29. Q—Q5ch unpinning his Knight), Q x R !, and Black wins! The recapture by the Rook allows Black to mate, while 29. Kt x Q, R x Q leaves Black a Rook ahead.

27. . . .   B x Kt

Black had no choice, as the Knight attacked both his Rooks.

28. R x B

The recapture vacates the square Q5 for occupation by the Queen. The tripling of heavy pieces on the Queen file would increase the advantage that White already has. But an even more potent threat is the possibility of establishing a beachhead on the seventh rank by 29. R—Q7.

The posting of a Rook on the seventh rank, in the midgame or the ending, is a tremendous positional advantage.

28. . . .   R—B2

Black does what he can to keep the adverse Rook out and seals up all the entrances.

White has the superior position, but how does he break through?

Let us listen in on what Rubinstein might say to himself in reasoning out a course of action:

My Rooks are as well placed as they can be and doing a good job in controlling the open Queen file. My Queen is strongly centralized and exerts pressure in every direction. My Bishop bears down on his King Pawn and keeps a Rook and Knight chained to its defense. My pieces are all usefully occupied and must stay where they are.

How about my opponent? His defense just about holds together, but his pieces must stay where they are to guard his weak points. If I let him alone, he might consolidate his forces, and even counterattack.

If I let him alone . . .

Say, isn't that the key to the position?

I must not let him alone! I must interfere with the arrangement of his pieces. I must drive them off from their present positions. In fact, I might ruin his game by driving off even one defender!

Since my pieces are all useful where they are, I must not disturb them but look to my Pawns to break up the defense. Which Pawn shall I use, and which of his pieces shall I try to dislodge?

The first thing to do is to find a target. His Queen and Rooks are too far away and too agile to be bothered by Pawns. Any of them can move off to a different square on a file or a rank and still control it. I must aim at a fixed target—some piece which is valuable at the spot where it is stationed and loses its worth as soon as it is displaced. How about the Knight? Suppose I played 29. P—KR4 and gave it a pinch by 30. P—R5? It would have to leave its fine defensive position immediately. Where could it go? If to K2, it blocks the action of the King Rook, and if it retreats to the back rank, it is out of play for a time. Besides, I get another benefit in moving the Rook Pawn. It gives my King a flight square, so that he doesn't fall into a surprise mate on the first rank.

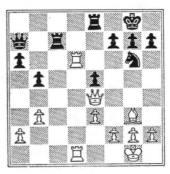

29. P—KR4 !

This is the key to the decisive attack! The obvious threat is 30. P—R5, dislodging the Knight and then capturing the King Pawn. The ulterior purpose is to compel Black to protect the endangered Pawn by 29. . . . B3, weakening the cordon of Pawns near his King. Further weaknesses will then be induced by 30. P—R5 and 31. P—R6, an attack on the Knight Pawn.

29. . . .   P—B3

Clearly, to give the King Pawn the solid support only another Pawn affords.

The alternative 29. . . . R(B2)—K2 succumbs to 30. Q—B6 followed by 31. R—Q8, with an easy win, while 29. . . . P—KR4 (to prevent 30. P—R5) allows 30. Q—B5, winning the Rook Pawn.

30. Q—Q5ch

Simple and strong! The Queen makes a powerful entrance at Q5, seizing control of a diagonal leading to the King and at the same time tripling heavy pieces on the open center file. Notice the admirable use of Q5 as a pivot for the maneuvering of the various pieces. It has been occupied in turn by Knight, Bishop, Rook and Queen—aptly enough, in order of strength!

30. . . .   K—R1

Hoping for safety in the corner. If instead 30. . . . R—B2 31. P—R5, Kt—R1 32. P—R6 leads to a decisive breakup, or if 30. . . . K—B1 31. P—R5, Kt—R1 32. R—Q8, Kt—B2 33. R x Rch, K x R 34. Q—K6ch, K—B1 35. P—R6, R—K2

(nothing else saves the game, 35. . . . Kt x P allowing mate on the move, and 35. . . . P x P 36. Q x BP ending in ruin for Black) 36. Q—B8ch, R—K1 37. P x Pch, and White wins a Rook.

31. P—R5

Not only evicts the Knight from a strong defensive post but drives a wedge into Black's position.

31. . . .   Kt—B1

Against the only other move 31. . . . Kt—K2, White wins easily by 32. Q—B7, with a million threats. Let's take a look at some of the interesting possibilities (after 32. Q—B7):

If 32. . . . R—KKt1 33. R—Q8, R(B2)—B1 34. P—R6 (threatening 35. P x P mate), R(B1) x R 35. R x R (renewing the threat), P x P 36. Q x BP mate.

If 32. . . . R—KKt1 33. R—Q8, R(B2)—B1 34. Q x Rch, Kt x Q 35. R x R, and White follows with 36. R(Q1)—Q8 and wins easily.

If 32. . . . Q—Kt1 33. P—R6, P x P 34. B x P, P x B 35. R x RP, Kt—Kt3 36. R x P mate.

If 32. . . . R(B2)—B1 33. P—R6, P x P 34. B—R4, threatening 35. B x P mate. Black cannot guard against that mate by a Knight move as it leaves his Queen *en prise*.

How many of these variations did White foresee? And how many did Black know he was avoiding when he moved his Knight to B1 instead of to K2?

The answer is—probably none! A good player can sense the effect of a move that is obviously decisive

almost at a glance. He saves himself
a great deal of valuable time when
he does not even bother about analyzing the resources of such a defense as 31. . . . Kt—K2. The fact
that it permits such a paralyzing entrance into the vitals as 32. Q—B7
practically rules it out from more
than fleeting consideration.

32. P—R6

Drives the wedge in still further.
White's object is to break up the
Pawn position around the King. If
Black's Knight Pawn can be up-
rooted, it will make the Bishop
Pawn, the keystone of his game, vul-
nerable to attack. And if that falls,
Black's whole position falls with it.

White's immediate threat is 33.
P x Pch, K x P 34. B—R4, R—B2
35. Q—B6, with an attack on a
Rook and a triple attack on the
Bishop Pawn.

32. . . .   Kt—Kt3

Black gets his Knight back into
active play and prevents White from
striking again at the Bishop Pawn by
33. B—R4. He sidesteps the pretty
loss 32. . . . P x P 33. R x BP, R—
Q2 34. B x P !, R x Q (if 34. . . .
R x B 35. R x Ktch, and mate next)
35. R x Kt double check and mate!

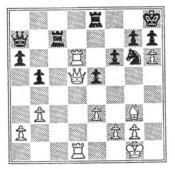

33. Q—K6 !

A spectacular move! White is not
playing to the gallery in offering a
sacrifice of his Queen. All that he
wants is to penetrate still deeper into
the heart of Black's position, and this
is the simplest way to do so. The
move is brilliant nevertheless, and
making a move of this sort (even
vicariously) gives one a thrill.

I must warn the player who likes
the excitement of springing a surprise move on his opponent that it is
a waste of time to look for brilliant
moves in the course of a game unless
the position warrants it. You must
first get an advantage, however
slight. Work on increasing the advantage until you have built up a
position that is definitely superior.
Once you have established your right
to look for combinations, the brilliant moves will come of themselves.

White of course does not expect
Black to take his Queen and allow
34. R—Q8ch and quick mate. What
he has in mind primarily is to secure
complete control of Q7, an important square for his Rooks to exploit.

One of the most interesting
things to me in the position is that
White threatens his opponent with
disaster on three ranks:

a) On the eighth rank by 34.
Q x Rch followed by mate.

b) On the seventh rank by 34.
R—Q7 followed by 35. P x P mate.

c) On the sixth rank by 34. P x
Pch, K x P 35. Q x BPch, winning
easily.

33. . . .   R—KB1

There isn't too much choice, in

view of all the threats. Black's move gives the Bishop Pawn added protection.

34. R—Q7

Threatens 35. P x P—mate on the move!

34. . . .   P x P

No better is 34. . . . R x R when the recapture 35. R x R threatens mate on one side, and the Queen on the other. Or, if 34. . . . R—KKt1 35. P x Pch, R x P 36. R—Q8ch, and White forces mate.

35. B—R4 !

The Bishop which has stood in one spot for twenty-five moves puts on the finishing touch! The threat is 36. B x Pch, R x B 37. Q x Rch, K—Kt1 38. Q—Kt7 mate.

35. . . .   Resigns

If 35. . . . Kt x B 36. Q—K7 threatens 37. Q x R mate or 37. Q—Kt7 mate or 37. Q x RP mate, and no one can survive such a display of feminine power!

An impressive, deeply satisfying game, one of the finest in the literature of chess.

Index to Openings

Printed in the United States
By Bookmasters